The Correspondence of Samuel Butler with His Sister May

The Correspondence of Samuel Butler with His Sister May

EDITED WITH AN INTRODUCTION BY

DANIEL F. HOWARD

University of California Press

Berkeley and Los Angeles

1962

UNIVERSITY OF CALIFORNIA PRESS
BERKELEY AND LOS ANGELES, CALIFORNIA
CAMBRIDGE UNIVERSITY PRESS
LONDON, ENGLAND

PUBLISHED WITH THE ASSISTANCE OF A GRANT
FROM THE FORD FOUNDATION
LIBRARY OF CONGRESS CATALOG CARD NUMBER: 62-13075

DESIGNED BY MARION SKINNER

For M.K.H.

PREFACE

Without trying to reproduce in print the vagaries of manuscript, I have transcribed these letters exactly and made minor corrections only when an overliteral transcription would interfere with the reader's convenience. I have, for example, silently supplied the ends of parentheses and quotation marks, and capitalized the beginnings of sentences, but only when even such minor emendations were necessary to make the sense clear. I have also regularized all headings and paragraph indentations, and consistently run complimentary endings, except the last phrase, into the body of the letters.

I have enclosed in pointed brackets ⟨ ⟩ phrases which in the original letters are overscored but recoverable; frequently such phrases suggest interesting alternative thoughts in the writer's mind.

I have not attempted to indicate the process by which I have identified many of the people whom Butler mentions in the letters, but where a positive identification is made it has been verified. All references to Butler's published works, unless otherwise specified, are to the twenty-volume Shrewsbury Edition edited by Henry Festing Jones and A. T. Bartholomew (London and New York, 1923–1926). In citations where no place of publication is indicated, London is to be understood.

Because there is not yet a definitive edition of Butler's Notebooks, and the text of the published selections is often corrupt, I have cited and occasionally quoted from the manuscript of the Notebooks in the Chapin Library at Williamstown, Massachusetts; but for the convenience of the reader I have also cited published selections from the Notebooks if they contain substantially the same material. (For a discussion of the differences between the manuscript and the printed versions, see Lee Elbert Holt, "The *Note-Books* of Samuel Butler," *PMLA*, 60 [1945], 1165–1179.)

I am particularly grateful to Sir Geoffrey Keynes and Brian Hill for their great personal kindness to me and for permission to publish this correspondence.

Mrs. Donald E. Richmond, formerly Custodian of the Chapin Library, first encouraged my explorations of the Butler manuscripts in her charge, and she has furthered my work at every stage. I am grateful also to H. Richard Archer, the present Custodian of the Library, for his generous assistance.

I am indebted to the following persons for their kind assistance on various problems: Lord Bridges; Professor Geoffrey Tillotson; John McKenzie of the British Museum Manuscript Room; G. J. Merson, Vicar of Granby, Nottinghamshire; Mrs. Henry W. Howell, Jr., Librarian of the Frick Art Reference Library, New York City; Professor Ellis Waterhouse, the Barber Institute of Fine Arts, Birmingham; John E. C. Dakin, Rector of Langar, Nottinghamshire; Dr. Diehl, Stadt-und Universitätsbibliothek, Frankfurt am Main; Heinrich Nidecker, Öffentliche Bibliothek der Universität, Basel; and Margaret Jadot of the British Museum staff.

Without the good taste and keen eyesight of Grace Wilson, my editor at the University of California Press, and of C. F. Main and Paul Fussell, Jr., my colleagues at Rutgers, this book would be faultier than it is. My greatest debt is to Professor Gordon Haight, who generously read the manuscript at a time when he himself was most pressed; without him it could not be.

New Brunswick, N. J. D.F.H.

CONTENTS

LIST OF LETTERS AND POSTCARDS

ABBREVIATIONS

Alumni Cantabrigienses	*Alumni Cantabrigienses,* compiled by John Venn and J. A. Venn (Cambridge: Cambridge Univ. Press, 1922–1954).
Boase	Frederic Boase, *Modern English Biography,* 6 vols. (Truro: Netherton, 1892–1921).
Butler-Savage Letters	*Letters Between Samuel Butler and Miss E. M. A. Savage (1871–1885),* ed. by Geoffrey Keynes and Brian Hill (London: Jonathan Cape, 1935).
Butleriana	*Butleriana,* ed. by A. T. Bartholomew (London: Nonesuch Press, 1932).
Further Extracts	*Further Extracts from the Note-Books of Samuel Butler,* ed. by A. T. Bartholomew (London: Jonathan Cape, 1934).
Garnett	Mrs. R. S. Garnett [Martha (Roscoe) Garnett], *Samuel Butler and His Family Relations* (London: J. M. Dent; New York: E. P. Dutton, 1926).
Hoppé	A. J. Hoppé, A Bibliography of the Writings of Samuel Butler and of the Writings About Him (London: *Bookman's Journal,* 1925).

MS Notebooks	Six volumes, bound by Butler, now in the Chapin Library, Williamstown, Mass.
Memoir	Henry Festing Jones, *Samuel Butler, Author of Erewhon* (1835–1902): *A Memoir*, 2 vols. (London and New York: Macmillan, 1919).
Shrewsbury Edition	*The Collected Works of Samuel Butler*, ed. by Henry Festing Jones and A. T. Bartholomew, 20 vols. (London: Jonathan Cape; New York: E. P. Dutton, 1923–1926).
Shrewsbury *Note-Books*	*The Note-Books of Samuel Butler*, Shrewsbury Edition, Vol. XX.
Times	*The Times*, London.

BIOGRAPHICAL SKETCHES

BUTLER'S FRIENDS

ALFRED EMERY CATHIE (1863–1939?), his manservant whom he engaged in January, 1887. Alfred took it upon himself to shape his employer to his idea of a gentleman, and Butler treated him with affectionate condescension. (See "Alfred" in *Butleriana*, pp. 128–141.)

CHARLES GOGIN (1844–1931), a regular exhibitor at the Royal Academy from 1874 to 1885, and Butler's most trusted authority on matters of art. He drew the human figures in most of Butler's paintings, and his portrait of Butler, painted in 1896, is in the National Portrait Gallery. A collection of unpublished letters from Butler to Gogin is in the Chapin Library, Williamstown, Massachusetts.

HENRY FESTING JONES (1851–1928), his closest friend, later his biographer. Jones took his B.A. at Trinity Hall, Cambridge, in 1873, and was admitted a solicitor in 1876—the same year in which he met Butler. In 1886 Butler gave Jones an allowance of £200 a year so that he could give up the law and become his adviser and companion. They frequently traveled abroad and collaborated on several pieces of Handel-inspired music. (See "Jones and Myself" in *Butleriana*, pp. 101–120; and Jones's *Memoir*.)

CHARLES PAINE PAULI (1838–1897), an intimate friend in the '60's. Butler first met him in New Zealand, urged him to return to London with him, and there granted him an allowance of £200 a year, which he continued to pay till Pauli's death, despite his own straitened circumstances and the increasing coldness of their relationship. Butler idealized Pauli because of his unaffected elegance and suavity (he is the model for Towneley in *The Way of All Flesh*); his first book on evolution, *Life and Habit* (1878), is dedicated to him. (See "Charles Paine Pauli and Butler" in *Butleriana*, pp. 39–96.)

ELIZA MARY ANN SAVAGE (d. 1885), his literary *confidante*, whom he first met about 1868 when they were both art students at Heatherley's School in London. She often discussed literary matters with Butler, and encouraged him to write novels. After she died in 1885, Butler dedicated *Gavottes, Minuets, Fugues* (1885) to her, and then began to reproach himself severely for having been indifferent toward her; in 1901 he wrote a series of embarrassingly personal sonnets in the style of Shakespeare about their relationship. (See *Butler-Savage Letters.*)

BUTLER'S FAMILY

DR. SAMUEL BUTLER (1774–1839), his grandfather, headmaster of Shrewsbury School, 1798–1836, then bishop of Lichfield and Coventry. (See *The Life and Letters of Dr. Samuel Butler*, Shrewsbury Edition, Vols. X–XI.)

THOMAS BUTLER (1806–1886), his father, student of classics at St. John's College, Cambridge (B.A. 1829), then rector of Langar-cum-Barnston, Nottinghamshire; he retired to Shrewsbury in 1876. (See "Father and Son" in *Butleriana*, pp. 25–33.)

FANNY BUTLER (1808–1873), *née* Worsley, his mother, the third daughter of Philip John Worsley, a sugar refiner of Bristol. She married Thomas Butler in 1831.

HARRIET (HARRIE) BRIDGES (1834–1918), *née* Butler, his

older sister. She married George Lovibond Bridges (brother of Robert Bridges, later poet laureate) in 1859, and when he died shortly afterward she went to live with the Bridges family on the Isle of Wight. She joined her father and May in Shrewsbury in 1879 and lived there for the rest of her life.

MARY (MAY) BUTLER (1841–1916), his younger sister, the only one of the Butler children to continue to make her home with their father and mother. After her mother's death in 1873 she assumed the responsibility of her father's household; she stayed on in Shrewsbury with Harrie after his death.

THOMAS BUTLER, II (1837–1884), his brother. Tom attended St. John's College, Cambridge, but left without taking a degree. He married Henrietta Rigby (by whom he had four children), deserted her, disappeared, and was discovered in 1880 to be living with another woman in Brussels. Then he left Brussels, and word of his death on Corsica in November, 1884, reached England early in 1885. Tom and his father disliked each other intensely, and he found little favor with the other members of his family, including Butler.

Butler's Nieces and Nephews (Tom's Children)

CHARLES. Married Alice Leamar, but quickly separated from her; then, restive in several posts as a clerk in London, he joined the Greek army, and to the surprise of his family succeeded as a career officer.

ELIZABETH (ELSIE). Married Richard Burton Phillipson.

HENRY (HAL or HARRY). Married Ada Wheeler, emigrated to Florida. He was the chief beneficiary of Butler's estate, and he returned to live in England after his uncle's death.

MARY (MAYSIE), favorite niece of May and Harriet. She spent considerable time with them at Shrewsbury.

Butler's Maternal Relatives

PHILIP WORSLEY (1802–1893), brother of Butler's mother. He married Annie Taylor (1806–1877), by whom he had five children, of whom the following were particular friends of Butler and May:

RICHARD

REGINALD, a very close friend of Butler's, one of the executors of his will.

ALICE

BESSIE WORSLEY JOHN WORSLEY SARAH WORSLEY	Brother and sisters of Butler's mother. All lived at Clifton, Bristol.

INTRODUCTION

What a lot I have written about my books—but then my books are to me much the most important thing in life. They in fact are "me" much more than anything else is.

—Butler to May, February 1, 1884

After Samuel Butler returned from New Zealand in 1864 and settled in rooms in Clifford's Inn, Fleet Street, he set aside part of each day for writing letters. He maintained his routine for thirty-eight years, till his death in 1902, and toward the end of his life began to collect and arrange what had become an enormous correspondence. After his death, Henry Festing Jones used the collection of letters to compile a massive biography,[1] and afterward bound it into sixteen large volumes, which later were given to the British Museum by Butler's present literary executors, Sir Geoffrey Keynes and Brian Hill.[2] The great bulk of the existing correspondence is now in these volumes in the Museum, but only a small part of it has ever been published, and that mostly in the form of excerpts which Jones used in his biography.

Keynes and Hill published Butler's complete correspondence with Miss Savage in 1936, but public response was slight, and nothing else appeared for twenty-five years. The public had no curiosity about new biographical material because Jones's biography, which had appeared at the height of Butler's reputation in 1919, had seemed so complete. Yet with the best intentions, Jones had selected the facts so that the figure

[1] *Memoir*, 2 vols. (1919).

[2] See "Distribution of Samuel Butler Manuscripts: New Gift to the British Museum," *Times Literary Supplement*, November 23, 1935, p. 764.

which emerged from his pages was the Butler he wanted to remember, an exclusively aggressive, iconoclastic intellectual. It was a portrait that Butler himself encouraged, but it was only a part—albeit an important part—of the whole man.

Because Jones presented a stereotype of Butler and presented it reverentially, the course of Butler criticism after 1919 turned toward partisan quarreling. There were those who believed in the accuracy of Jones's portrait and admired the one-sided figure he presented, and there were those who also believed in its accuracy but reacted strongly against such a figure. The result was that, with the exception of Bernard Shaw, who read Butler carefully and admired him in spite of the deficiencies which he saw very clearly,[3] Butler suffered as much from his friends' uncritical enthusiasm as his enemies' attacks. To both he became a depthless symbol of anti-Victorianism destined to survive no longer than anti-Victorianism itself. By 1936 he seemed a ghost from another age, and Malcolm Muggeridge, examining the spectre with disgust, dispatched it once and for all.[4] In an angry book, the style of which Butler himself would have admired, Muggeridge destroyed the image of the social liberal which Butler's friends had created (ironically, just as the Erewhonians had transformed Higgs into the god Sunchild after he left Erewhon). In place of the fiery iconoclast, Muggeridge revealed a stodgy believer in all the reactionary political and economic institutions of Victorian England; he made clear what an intelligent reader should have admitted at once—that Butler was hardly the same kind of revolutionary as Karl Marx, one of his fellow readers in the Reading Room of the Museum. Indeed, though Butler's life (1835–1902) happened to coincide with one of the greatest eras of social reform in the history of England, he loudly opposed every measure of it. Nevertheless, with the support of Jones's *Memoir*, it had been easy for Butler's friends to misinterpret his lifelong fight against cant and

[3] Shaw's most judicious appraisal is his introduction to the World's Classics edition of *The Way of All Flesh* (1936). See also his preface to *Back to Methuselah*.

[4] *The Earnest Atheist: A Study of Samuel Butler* (Eyre and Spottiswoode, 1936).

hypocrisy as a crusade for liberal modernism, and when Muggeridge shattered this image it was difficult to see that he had not seriously damaged the real Butler at all. After 1936 the task was to recreate a far more complex figure than the one that had been destroyed, and it was begun in two excellent studies, by P. N. Furbank (*Samuel Butler* [Cambridge: Cambridge Univ. Press, 1948]), and Philip Henderson (*Samuel Butler: The Incarnate Bachelor* [Cohen and West, 1953]), who shunned the partisan quarrel based on the old image of Butler and set to work, using all the available manuscript materials, to recover an almost lost Victorian. These letters to May are a further adjustment of the balance.

The fuller picture of Butler contained in the complete May correspondence stands in sharp contrast to the stereotype produced by Jones's selection from the May letters available to him. In using Letter 56 (May 5, 1884), for example, Jones omitted the first paragraph—perhaps out of embarrassment, for Butler says that he hopes May "liked Jones but we are afraid by your going away without wanting to say good bye to him that he had not made so deep an impression as he could have wished." Now Jones does not claim that the letter is complete, and the fact that May seemed unimpressed with him is no doubt irrelevant to his biography of Butler (though his standards of relevancy are not always so strict), but what he conceals—not only here but consistently throughout the *Memoir*—is that Butler was extremely sensitive to his sister's opinions, that he cared very much what she thought of him and his friends. Jones also frequently changed the tone of the May letters by omitting passages that did not fit his conception of his friend. He gladly printed the part of the letter of June 30, 1885, in which Butler reports a belligerent encounter with Grant Allen, a friend of Darwin's and thus a "particular foe," but he left out the first paragraph, in which the dominant tone of the whole letter is set. In it Butler asks May to see if his father "can give me a bed for a few days on Tuesday [July] 14th till the following Saturday. If he can I will come down. Not that I have any thing to say or business of any kind but I shall be going somewhere for my holiday at the end of the month or early in next and unless I go then shall not be able to do so for some time." By omitting this, Jones emphasizes Butler's proud antagonism toward the Darwin group—which fits his conception of him as a crusader—and conceals the fact that at this time in his life Butler was not campaigning against his father but quietly proposing a four-day visit with him for no particular reason at all. The point is not that one regrets that Jones left too much out of the *Memoir*—quite the contrary—but that the pattern of what he chose to leave out gives the reader an elaborately documented view of a trivial man seen always in the posture of a hero.

In their entirety, the May letters present Butler during forty-seven years of his life, from the time he was a Cambridge undergraduate to within a month of his death, and show him in many moods in the midst of an incredible number of interests. Their style is unaffectedly direct, even more informal than that of his books, about which he wanted it clearly understood that he had never taken the smallest pains to make a "style," but "just common straightforwardness." Characteristically he assumed a direct personal relationship with his reader, and this is even more evident in his letters to May. He knew that she wanted to hear what he had to say—whether or not she agreed with it—and he wasted little time in justifying what he had been doing or in laying the groundwork for some elaborate arguments; instead he concentrated on reporting the circumstances in which he developed his ideas, the day-to-day details out of which his books grew. Thus the letters contain a great many biographical details and offer an insight into the way he saw and used the materials around him.

Letter 23 (July 22, 1878), for example, shows him caught up and fascinated by a remarkable variety of things. Just two weeks earlier, tired and discouraged by his inability to finish *The Way of All Flesh,* he had left London and gone to Switzerland to recoup his spirits.[5] Since then, he tells her, he

[5] Letter to Miss Savage, July 2, 1878. *Butler-Savage Letters,* p. 188.

has found the subject of his "magnum opus" of the summer (there is no evidence that he had previously intended a magnum opus); it is to be a series of sketches of the frescoes in a nearby church. Later, his enthusiasm for this project grew, and his conception of the opus developed into the book *Alps and Sanctuaries,* which included not only his sketches of these frescoes but accounts and drawings of other religious folk art of the Alps. In the same letter he tells May that he has been reading Disraeli's novels, has been weighing the lesson that his later novels offer about the sparing use of epigrams. He says that he has been thinking about Ruskin's *Seven Lamps of Architecture,* a book which May is reading and which he remembers liking when he was an undergraduate. He has also returned to look at a clump of woodsia which he had discovered the week before growing vigorously in an unsheltered spot, and, finding them all killed by the heat, he speculates on the limits of freedom within which an organism can choose its environment. In this one letter, then, he is painter, novelist, literary critic, natural scientist—some of the many roles he played in his long career. But at the same time he is not limited to any one of these roles: at no time does he think exclusively as a painter, or as a scientist, but always as the enthusiastic, knowledgeable amateur, delighted as much by the comedy of the pigeons that keep wandering into his room as by the question of natural selection that the woodsia raise.

Sometimes his catholic interests and his insistence upon not limiting his response within any one frame of reference—pictoral, novelistic, scientific—show up less happily. Butler's letters show that in his running feud with Darwin his refusal to confine his involvement to matters of scientific theory leads him to assume that his theory of evolution is inseparable from himself and that anyone who attacks it attacks him. His concern for the scientific issues does not wholly disappear, but the issues become much too emotionally charged to be settled; he comes to argue as much about Darwin's personal honesty and morality as he does about the validity of his theory. By 1885 the quarrel is so much a part of his everyday life that he sees sinister plots all around him. When he tells May about Edward Clodd's invitation to dinner it is "a plant to bring me and one of my particular foes . . . together." [6]

What we see in his letters during the time he was actively working out his theory of evolution is the development of an all-consuming personal involvement from what was initially abstract scientific speculation. Here, his personal intensity was not appropriate to the quarrel about evolutionary theory, and it served only to obscure the valuable contribution he might have made, but when he applied the same intensity to other matters he sometimes fused ideas that are ordinarily discrete into highly imaginative syntheses. In *Erewhon*, for example, he created a fictional world based upon a similarity he saw between the evolution of man and that of the machine. In *The Way of All Flesh* he saw the progress of a young man toward maturity, with varying success, as a horticultural hybridization, as a giant lottery, and as a financial speculation. As long as he was creating an imaginary world, Butler's habit of blending many kinds of experience worked brilliantly; in real life his difficulty was that he could not maintain the necessary distance from his subject matter. The metaphors he proposed grew more and more literal, until as far as he was concerned the two things which he had begun by comparing became identical. When, for example, he first reread the *Odyssey* he saw with his keen common sense that the concept of heroism in the poem and its treatment of the wonders of war were *like* those of a woman who dreamed of adventure but lived in a world of domestic detail. As a critical idea this brought into focus the unique combination in the *Odyssey* of the great and the small, of the distant myth-like descriptions of Odysseus's deeds and the detailed inventory of household utensils, the vaguely seen marvels Odysseus struggles with, and the precise directions for building a raft or slaughtering a bullock. Butler's idea was capable of considerable development, but he could not be satisfied with it merely as a critical idea, as a perceptive analogy; soon he was arguing for it as literal truth. The tone of his reports to May about the theory

[6] June 30, 1885 (Letter 68).

begins to change: a woman actually did write the *Odyssey*, he insists; she disguised herself as Nausicaa in the poem, and in real life she lived in a particular town, which Butler located in Sicily, and at a particular time, which he also determined. In his letters, Butler moves away from an interest in the imaginative truth that his analogy contains to an insistence upon a literal absurdity. When he writes in August, 1891, he has just reread the *Odyssey* and begun to translate it. He tells May how appealing the poem is: "The more I see of the Odyssey the better I like it—it is wonderful, but nothing can well be more *franchement bourgeois* and unheroic." In January, his translation completed, his attention has turned to locating, exactly, the land of the Phaeacians, and his "great triumph" comes in the map room of the British Museum: he finds the place "just nine or ten miles north of Marsala—every condition absolutely fulfilled, and nothing like it anywhere else. So I no longer have any shadow of doubt about my view being correct." [7] At this point Butler has lost his perspective; he is so caught up in his idea that his own world is indistinguishable from that of the *Odyssey*. He reports Alcinous and Arete and Euryclea wherever he turns, and his only interest is in making other people acknowledge the reality of his vision. On February 27 he is surprised that May doesn't already know that Nausicaa was the author of the *Odyssey*. "I beg your pardon," he writes, "I thought I had long ago told you that Nausicaa *did* write the *Odyssey*. I only wish some one would venture to tell me she didn't in a place where I could lay my hands about him."

In his work on the *Odyssey* Butler went through a process much like that of a good satirist: he ran his idea as far as it would go. He turned a comparison into literal fact to test its applicability, just as in *Gulliver's Travels* Swift turned metaphorically petty people into physically little people, and put an abstracted society on a real floating island. Butler himself in *Erewhon* turned the promises of the church into a literal, unspendable currency, and he made the "penalties" of sickness into a real legal code. But the difference between con-

[7] January 18, 1892 (Letter 118).

trolled satirical ideas like these and Butler's theory of the *Odyssey* is that Lilliput, Laputa, the Musical Banks, and the Erewhonian legal system never lose their quality as metaphor. The conscious satirist presents them as *like* the real world but not identical with it, whereas in his own life Butler lost that perspective; he was consumed by the attractiveness of his at first imaginary creation, and though he made use of the techniques of many disciplines—classical scholarship, literary criticism, numismatics, archeology—he refused to subject himself to the orderly procedures of any one. He combined them all in one great personal synthesis, and thus became the unconscious butt of his own ingenious satirical method—an imaginative mind run wild.

A man's work and his personality seemed so inevitably the same to Butler that he made his understanding of a writer's personality one of the key tests of the value of his writing. He read to discover in the work the personal reflection of its author. If, as in the case of Nausicaa and the *Odyssey*, the search at first led him to a fuller understanding of the work, it sometimes led him to trivial judgments of authors who do not readily reveal themselves—Swift, for example, about whom after reading *Gulliver's Travels* Butler could say only that "from all I can make out [he] was a far more human & genuine person than he is generally represented, but I do not think I should have liked him." [8] This emphasis on a writer's personality limited the kind of literature Butler read, because impersonal forms like drama offered little grist for his mill. He loved Shakespeare's sonnets; he committed them all to memory, and he wrote a book about the story and the personality they reveal, but about Shakespeare's plays he complained in all seriousness that Shakespeare should have told us "more about what he himself saw, said, and did, what he thought of the men and things of his day—what people he was fond of, what places he most frequented etc., and less about Hamlet and Othello." [9]

[8] MS Notebooks, I, 122; Shrewsbury *Note-Books*, p. 190.
[9] MS Notebooks, I, 119.

Butler's intensely personal and naïve reaction to the many issues with which he dealt was strongly colored by a sudden, violent awakening at the age of twenty-four to his separateness from his family and his society. The first sign of this awakening that Butler remembered was the night that he boarded ship for New Zealand, when abruptly he stopped saying his prayers. "I had said them the night before and doubted not that I was going to say them as I had always done hitherto. That night, I suppose, the sense of change was so great that it shook them quietly off." [10] Whether or not the date of his conversion to skepticism was quite so definite, it did take place at about the time he went to New Zealand,[11] and, though few personal documents from that time have survived—there is one previously unpublished letter to May from New Zealand—the change that took place in Butler shows up very strongly in the contrast between the letters he wrote to May before he left and those he wrote after he returned. In the earlier letters we see a lively, dutiful young man whom Butler was to draw upon in his portraits of Ernest in *The Way of All Flesh* and John Pickard Owen in *The Fair Haven*. As this young man writes to May there is no doubt that he feels at ease in the Cambridge world. He works diligently for his examinations, involves himself with college gossip, worries lest his aunt and her friend be an embarrassment to him. And he takes his position in the college as a matter of course, without making any judgments on the justice or injustice of the system, but with a keen eye for the foibles around him.[12] But

[10] MS Notebooks, I, 189; Shrewsbury *Note-books*, p. 213.

[11] In *The Way of All Flesh* Ernest discovers the fraudulence of the world at the age of twenty-four, while in jail for his "attack" on Miss Maitland. Overton remarks that "in mind as in body, like most of those who in the end come to think for themselves, he was a slow grower. . . . His education had been an attempt, not so much to keep him in blinkers as to gouge his eyes out altogether" (chap. 61).

[12] Butler's letters to his father at this time are less lively, but they confirm the picture of a dutiful, somewhat anxious undergraduate. On October 3, 1857, he wrote: "No one of you wants a first class half so much as I do: so you need not fear my becoming inflated by any hopes held out but rather rejoice that I am being encouraged which I think a great invigorator when sparingly applied" (British Museum MS.).

by the time he returns from New Zealand, his relationship with the world has changed; he is now judge and jury in a court that is always in session and never fails to grant certiorari. "There are no great musicians now," he writes to May on January 30, 1867, and, that matter settled, he passes on to well-known artists: he has met two—Henry Wallis, whom he liked, "and shall probably meet him again," and Sir Francis Grant, whom he did not like; he "did not seem to approve of my work, but I cared not." Of politicians, he has met Anthony Mundella, but he "did not like [him] at all, and should have no confidence in his judgement." The remarkable change in these post-New Zealand letters is not the primacy of Butler's judgment as much as its exclusiveness; Wallis, Grant, and Mundella have become faceless, phantom figures, not described at all but merely the objects of Butler's opinions. In contrast, we may remember the letters of Thackeray, one of the few contemporary writers whom Butler admired; they fairly burst with detailed, accurate portraits of the people he has seen, so full of life that they will not stay in prose but appear as sketches right on the page. Butler took pride in his skill as an artist, but he never drew even verbal sketches in his letters; in fact, it may be significant that, whenever he wanted figures in the landscapes he painted or in the drawings he made for *Alps and Sanctuaries*, he hired one of his friends to draw them in. His own concern with human beings was not visual or humoristic, but doctrinal. Only if someone was converted to Butler's new realism—or better, if he was willing to be converted, like the priest whom he told May he had met in Italy [13] and who listened intelligently to his view of the late elections in England—only then would Butler respond to him.

In his years of virtual solitude in New Zealand, Butler's reaction against his father's world became a kind of religion and he its prophet. The few friends he had in New Zealand were themselves rebels of one kind or another and did little to temper his zeal or to help him accommodate it to ordinary

[13] July 16, 1880 (Letter 34).

society; instead, they encouraged his burning vision of society's deceptions and afforded him an opportunity to express himself without the customary niceties of argument. Butler described this aspect of his life in New Zealand as "an entire uprooting of all past habits . . . accompanied with a hardly less entire change of opinions upon many subjects. Firstly, I have lost all desire of making other people think the same as myself. If any one wishes to know my opinions upon a subject I can now content myself with stating them as clearly as I can." [14] By the time he returned to England in 1864 he had lost any taste he might have had for the give-and-take of an intellectual community. He did not want a marketplace for competing ideas any more than an evangelist does; he saw people only as friends or enemies, or as subjects for his proselytizing. His analysis of the reasons he was first drawn to Jones illustrates the view he took of people: Jones "was fuel," Butler said. "I saw that a spark from myself had kindled it, and that it began to blaze kindly, as though the wood were dry. Then I liked Jones very much at once, and took all the pains I could to make him become attached to me." [15] Butler responded to the fuel, but, though Jones appears constantly in his letters, in his Notebooks, and in his books, and though Butler lovingly saved Jones's wicked remarks and preserved his opinions, a reader who read everything that Butler ever wrote would not know what Jones looked like, what kind of clothes he wore, how he walked, or what gestures he used. Such objective observations were no part of Butler's emancipating vision of life.

After he returned from New Zealand, Butler approached issues like a man once burned, like his fictional character John Pickard Owen, who as a child watched one of his mother's friends prepare for bed and thereupon made a discovery from which he was never to recover: "The mass of petticoats and clothes which envelop the female form were not . . . 'all

[14] Letter from New Zealand to his cousin Philip Worsley, January 10, 1861, *Memoir*, I, 96.

[15] MS Notebooks, III, 149; *Butleriana*, pp. 105–106.

solid woman.' . . . Women were not in reality more substantially built than men, and had legs much as he had."[16] Butler suffered from the same kind of awakening to the difference between appearance and reality, but he was gently ironic about the results of Owen's formative discovery. Henceforth for Owen

> the world itself was hollow, made up of shams and delusions, full of sound and fury signifying nothing. . . . Truly a prosaic young gentleman enough. Everything with him was to be exactly in all its parts what it appeared on the face of it, and everything was to go on doing exactly what it had been doing hitherto.
>
> Such were the ideal theories of his childhood—unconsciously formed, but very firmly believed in. As he grew up he made such modifications as were forced upon him by enlarged perceptions, but every modification was an effort for him, in spite of a continual and successful resistance to what he recognized as his initial mental defect.[17]

As a reaction to his own vision, Butler vowed to combat hypocrisy with blunt, forthright honesty. This meant that usually he was tactless and almost always unresponsive to his audience. His father was his first opponent, and he set forth to tell him of his doubts about the Church of England—sharply, and with no real consideration for the fact that his father had spent his life as a rural clergyman and was a man of somewhat limited philosophical curiosity. In *The Way of All Flesh* he smiles knowingly at such a trait in Ernest, who dreams of presenting his discovery of contradictions in the Gospels to the Archbishop of Canterbury. "His Grace would have no resource but to admit them," Ernest reasons, and "being an honourable man he would at once resign his Archbishopric, and Christianity would become extinct in England within a few months' time."[18] But in his own life he was unable to smile at his use of such directness. Ordinarily he put his case

[16] *The Fair Haven*, chap. 1 of Owen's Memoir. Shrewsbury Edition, III, 6.
[17] *Ibid.*, p. 7.
[18] Chap. 65.

bluntly, waited eagerly for a reply, and thereupon quarreled openly.

The result of this manner was his almost total isolation from the literary and scientific circles of his time. His letters to May contain few references to famous people, partly because by habit he suspected their reputations much as John Owen suspected women's clothes, and partly because he could anticipate their reaction to his forthright behavior. When he did meet them he was uncomfortable and longed for the homely inelegance of his rooms in Clifford's Inn where he and one or two of his small circle of friends met. His letter to May of December 20, 1884, lets us see him at the home of the William Rossettis; it epitomizes his estrangement from the fashionable literary circles of Victorian London. "I did not know them," he reports,

> but Mrs. Rossetti sent me an invitation and said her father Madox Brown, the painter, would be there and would much like to see me. I used to know the Madox Browns but found that if they gave me a bun at all they wanted me to climb the pole too much and too often to get it so on my return from America I did not call and let the acquaintance drop. In the mean time Oliver Madox Brown had died, and I was supposed not to be as sorry as I ought to have been, the fact being that I hardly knew him at all beyond his calling on me sometimes and reading me his MS. novels which I particularly disliked; I don't mind reading my own MSS. to people, but I don't like being read to, and I did not like either young Brown or his novels—and did not feel his loss so acutely as I ought to have done.

Butler is impossibly self-centered and yet charming in this report. He was annoyed by young Brown's reading him his manuscripts, but he joins his annoyance to an admission that he loves to read his own manuscripts aloud. In his next paragraph he begins to construct the scene in which he at last is face to face with old Madox Brown:

> Two years or so ago old Madox Brown the father wrote me a letter asking if I had any letters of his son's as they wanted them for a biography. I don't believe he ever wrote me a letter; at any rate

I had none, but I took the opportunity to write prettily about the loss literature had sustained etc., and the old man wrote me back an answer saying something about "silent equivoques" (equivokes) which I did not quite understand but it was rather touching, for I knew he had been very proud and hopeful about his son. So when Mrs. Rossetti wrote me thus I thought I ought to go and did and there was old Madox Brown so I went up and said how glad I was to meet him again but he had forgotten all about it and evidently did not know me from Adam, nor care two pence whether he saw me or not—and his being so glad to see me was a *wicked hoax* —I was very much amused and rather comforted.

Butler emphasizes his routine social politeness—his "pretty" reply to Brown's request for any letters of his son, his saying how glad he was to meet old Madox Brown again—but he mutters all the way through this account ("I don't believe he ever wrote me a letter") in a way that foretells the end of such hypocritical etiquette: Madox Brown will not remember him. Hypocrisy is again exposed, and Butler is delighted to draw the moral: "It is perfectly hopeless for me to think I shall get any good [from] the ultra aesthetic cultured and scientific people and I don't mean to follow this up. The Tylors and Mr. Seebohm are their very opposites and I will cultivate them to the best of my power." Tylor and Seebohm were new acquaintances, both of whom had recently praised Butler's work.

In place of the famous, Butler gathered around him a small clique who came to form a kind of family group, the common characteristic of which was reverence for Butler. The tone of the group is very clear in Jones's report of his feelings when he first sought out Butler:

[I] sent Butler a telegram asking whether I might join him. . . . I was a little uneasy at what I had done, for I was not at all sure he would put up with me; and he felt the same as soon as he had sent his reply. He was sixteen years my senior, and we had seen very little of one another. . . . We sat out on the terrace . . . nothing had gone wrong as yet. Presently I pointed out a particular star and asked if he knew its name. Now Butler, though I was unaware of it at the time, considered that he resembled the Emperor

Marcus Aurelius Antoninus in that he was thankful to say he had never troubled himself about the appearance of things in the heavens. He therefore replied with some asperity: "I do not know anything about astronomy" (*Memoir*, I, 281–282).

"I do not know anything about astronomy"—this is the kind of terminal remark which pleased Butler's close friends; it reminded them of Dr. Johnson.

In return for idolatry, Butler offered his friends his own unwavering support for whatever they did or said. He accepted their opinions—Jones on law and music, Gogin on art, Miss Savage on literature—as expert, and he commonly reported to May either that he and Jones or he and Gogin had decided something, or that he had discussed his idea with one of them "and he has no doubt that it is correct."

As readers of *The Way of All Flesh* might suspect, Butler was most comfortable with people when his relationship to them had a clear financial basis. For him the worst relationship was that between a father and son, for there were expectations on both sides, and yet the exact status and amount of the expectation was unclear and at the whimsical disposition of the father. The best relationship, on the other hand, is one such as Ernest establishes with his *de facto* wife and his children. He sends Ellen off to America on a regular pension with the clear understanding that she will make no further demands upon him, and he pays a stipulated amount for his children's board and room—plus a little extra to persuade their guardian to give up smuggling—so that his children, raised without any expectations at all, can only be completely grateful when at the proper time their father gives them the necessary capital for the tools of their trade (steamboats, in this case).[19]

Butler sought some such clarifying arrangement in his own life. First, after he had made a small fortune in sheep ranching

[19] With cats too Butler wanted his responsibilities clear. See his letter to May of October 21, 1885 (Letter 73): "No—I will not have any Persian cat—it is undertaking too much responsibility. I must have a cat whom I find homeless, wandering about the court and to whom therefore I am under no obligation."

in New Zealand he granted his friend Pauli a regular stipend, and he continued to pay it for the rest of his life, despite the obvious deterioration of the friendship, despite his own serious financial losses, and despite Pauli's increasing affluence. He paid because to stop would have been equivalent to admitting that his contract with Pauli was like that between father and son, valid only so long as the donor was pleased to honor it. After he inherited his father's money, Butler also paid Jones a regular salary with the understanding that the payments would cease when Jones came into his own inheritance; and it seems more than coincidental that it was just at the time Jones inherited his money that the first real breach in their friendship occurred. What Butler wanted of his close friends was a more perfect family, a Family Ltd. in which he could be comfortable without the fear of unexpected demands. He was able to create such a family with Pauli, Jones, Alfred, and Hans Faesch; but Miss Savage, who was probably his closest literary adviser, remained troublingly on the outside. Butler's letters to her show him at some moments in affectionate rapport with her and at others brusquely distant. She never became his mistress, but her very existence as a woman contained the threat of a real, unlimited family unit, and one of the best insights into the kind of relationship he sought with others can be found in his rationalization of his behavior toward her. What troubled him most after her death was not grief but the realization of his personal failure. That comes through despite his ponderous logical propositions:

> She haunts me, and always will haunt, because I never felt for her the love that if I had been a better man I should have felt. Granted that I had known her some three years before she (to use her own expression) "found me out. . . ." Granted that I had come to look upon her as an impossible person . . . that she was very lame, was plain. . . . Granted again that she was none of my seeking. . . . Granted that she oppressed me with her very brilliancy—nay bored me, for there is no bore like a brilliant bore. . . . Add to this that if I had . . . married her—nay it was absurd. I should have

married her in cold blood, not because I wanted to marry her, but because she wanted me to marry her.[20]

The life that Butler tried to create for himself was totally unattractive; in deliberately cutting it down to avoid the possibility of pain he excluded a whole range of human experiences. His recurring activities that seem to mark the passing of time in these letters—his regular house cleaning, his double-entry accounting, his regular holidays in the same places on the Continent, his regular hours of work at the Museum—are symptoms of his determination to reduce life to the measurable, and it is sadly ironic that the last words he is reported to have said before he died should so expose the pathos of his love for the settled account. "Have you brought the cheque-book, Alfred?" he said, and slipped quietly into eternity.[21]

The ideal, limited life that Butler tried to lead is not admirable and it is the antithesis of heroism, and yet, encouraged by Butler's own constant assertion that he had found the ideal way of life, Jones tried to make that life seem interesting in itself, whereas the only interesting thing about it is Butler's struggle to make it work. He was never a "natural" man in the sense that he reacted quickly and instinctively; his actions were conscious and had to be painfully thought through, although he admired and envied people who acted with the ease and sureness of an instinctive knowledge of the world. Towneley in *The Way of All Flesh* is the ideal projection of such a man; he knows intuitively that it is Miss Snow, not Miss Maitland, who is a woman of easy virtue, while Ernest, like Butler, has to think the matter through—inevitably to the wrong conclusion. To make matters worse, what small intuitive sense Butler did have was appropriate only to the world in which he had grown up, and since he had rejected that as fraudulent he had no instinctive pattern of be-

[20] Butler wrote this in his Notebooks in March, 1885, shortly after Miss Savage died. He revised it in 1897, and upon reading it in 1902, a few months before his death, he noted: "With most men this [marriage in cold blood] is sufficient" (*Butler-Savage Letters*, pp. 362–364).

[21] *Memoir*, II, 399.

havior at all. What he needed was a bundle of habits to make his day a less frightening and exhausting ordeal, and he set out to make himself a man of habit. We feel as we read his letters that he insists upon his routine as if he were afraid of losing it. After his return from New Zealand he is a man trying with all his rational strength to be habitual, and what interests us is not the tiresome fellow he would have been if he had succeeded—the one Jones admired—but the complex man engaged in a daily and never quite successful struggle to make himself a lesser but more comfortable person.

One of the complications of Butler's life which he tried to simplify was his relationship with his family. The commonsensical view of the matter was that he had found them out, left them, and should deny them any part of his life; his attitude toward them should be as clear as Ernest's after he leaves prison—tinged with a certain cold pity for his aged parents perhaps, contemptuous of his sister Charlotte, and totally aloof from them all. But even in the novel Ernest's new attitude makes him a mere cardboard cutout in the fine clothes of a London gentleman, the manufactured embodiment of a simplified reaction. And in his own life, Butler was simply not able to act commonsensically. This lifelong correspondence with his younger sister (who never left home or questioned the values for which her father stood) suggests as much; for with May, Butler occasionally did manage to strike the pose of iconoclast. He privately added sharp rejoinders to her letters, as when he objected to her reply to his letter in which he described his evening with the Rossettis. May wrote: "I very much sympathize with you in your objection to the ultra-aesthetic Rossetti school. It must have been rather fun to let them see you saw they did not really want you." Her comment seems well-intentioned, but in reading it over later Butler felt obliged to pick at it, to strike the familar pose and comment: "I did not 'let them see etc.,' nor say I had let them see. I did my best to conceal it. This [from May] was meant as a snub for me, it was her way of saying 'you have been to the Rossetti's indeed, but you must not think much of that, they did not really want you at all.' " But at the same time he was exposing his sister's supposedly mean motives and fulfilling his notion of himself as somone not taken in by family hypocrisy, he was selecting and preserving May's letters and continuing to send her warm, full reports of his daily activities.

Another part of his emancipated role was sharing wicked jokes about fathers and sisters with Jones. He made a point of recording them in his Notebooks. " 'Henceforth [said he] let us be to one another as brother and sister.' 'No,' said I, as I thought of my own sisters, 'not so bad as that.' " [22] It required an artificially maintained sense of naughtiness to find any point in this, but Butler kept it up and applauded Jones in his efforts, as when Jones described his thoughts on what he supposed was his deathbed: "[There is] one part of my conduct which I think has been distinctly wrong, and not what it should have been—I refer to my treatment of my mother. I have been much too good to her. If my life is spared I will endeavor to amend this in the future, and treat her more as she deserves." [23]

In the interest of consistency, Butler liked to think that his transparent displays of antipathy toward May established a clear attitude toward her, but there is considerable evidence, even aside from these letters, that he had great affection for the sister whom logically he should have hated. When he was in financial difficulties in the autumn of 1879 and about to begin an acrimonious correspondence with his father about his rights to some family property, he wrote to ask if his father would keep their financial dispute a secret from May.[24] He did not want May to suffer the inevitable arguments about money that were about to begin, and he did not want her to know the long history of his dealings with Pauli that he was about to reveal—"other people's secrets . . . which she ought not to be possessed of." [25] His father refused to keep anything from May, and one suspects that in the ensuing correspondence But-

[22] *Butler-Savage Letters*, p. 308.
[23] MS Notebooks, I, 124.
[24] October 1, 1879 (British Museum MS).
[25] October 4, 1879 (British Museum MS).

ler argued somewhat less acidly that he might have otherwise. The letter in which his father refuses to hide anything from May gives us an excellent idea of how close May was to her father and how much Butler must have realized that close contact with her implied close contact with his father too: "With regard to May," Canon Butler wrote, "she lives with me and is my comfort. There is no one else to whom I can pour out my worries and anxieties; she keeps my household accounts and I cannot consent to any thing that puts a barrier to our free confidence. But I am willing to help you if I can." [26]

May's position in the Butler family was central. She was the youngest child, six years younger than Samuel. Though there were two other children, Harriet (1834–1918), and Thomas (1837–1884), May was the only one to remain at home, and after her mother died in 1873 she assumed the management of her father's household. When he retired to Shrewsbury (where his father had been headmaster of Shrewsbury School), May went with him and turned her energies to charitable affairs. She founded a small home for illegitimate girls and took an active interest in Shrewsbury School. When her father died in 1886, May lived on in Shrewsbury with her sister Harriet and died there in 1916 at the age of 75.

Butler was never as close to Tom or Harrie as he was to May. He and his brother were together at Shrewsbury School and St. John's College, Cambridge, but Butler shared his family's strong disapproval of Tom's early and complete revolt from authority. Tom disappeared from Cambridge under mysterious circumstances, and when he turned up a few years later, he had married Henrietta Rigby, a poor Welsh girl. He drank heavily, disappeared for months at a time, and finally left his wife and four children for his father to support. In 1880 a prostitute with whom he was living in Brussels disclosed his whereabouts by writing to Shrewsbury for money. Tom was summoned home to explain himself—and he came,

[26] October 5, 1879 (British Museum MS).

accompanied by the woman. They both left hurriedly, and Tom was not heard from again until news of his death on Corsica reached the family early in 1885.

Butler never saw in his brother's life the gross projection of his own revolt that an objective observer is likely to see; he disapproved of Tom, from the same point of view as his father, without acknowledging the obvious (even if finally superficial) analogies between their lives. "After all we know [about Tom]," he wrote to his father on November 26, 1881, "we, May least of all of us, shd not recognise Tom, except as a disgrace to us all who is to be put aside once for all, and with whom no words are to be bandied." [27]

About Harriet, Butler's older sister, Mrs. R. S. Garnett (who wrote with the intention of counteracting the poor impression which *The Way of All Flesh* gave of the Butler family) quotes a trusted "informant": She "suffered from a diseased conscience, so over-scrupulous that she feared to do good for fear of doing evil. She was a woman of indomitable will, entirely self-centered and domineering, and she ruled the whole family with a rod of iron." [28] If Mrs. Garnett's informant is correct, Butler's feeling about Harriet (in part expressed in the character of Charlotte in *The Way of All Flesh*) is hardly surprising. "All I know," he wrote about her in his Notebook in February, 1885, "is that I dislike her more than I can properly say." [29] Certainly the letters which passed between him and Harriet are cooler in tone than the May letters, and in general concern only practical matters and financial arrangements, about which he almost never talked to May. In 1859 Harriet married George Lovibond Bridges (a brother of Robert Bridges, the poet laureate), who was seriously ill with tuberculosis. He died some seven months later, but Harriet remained apart from her father and May for twenty years, finally joining them at Wilderhope House, Shrewsbury, in 1879.

[27] British Museum MS.

[28] Garnett, p. 63.

[29] MS Notebooks, III, 179, February, 1885.

The apparent irreconcilability of the lives of Butler and May and the fact that they maintained an affectionate correspondence over a period of forty-seven years suggest the central paradox of Butler's life which no amount of logical, straightforward thinking could solve. When Ernest at last struggles free of the life of Battersby Rectory, he is able to enjoy his freedom only by flaunting it *at Battersby,* by arriving "got up regardless of expense" and slowly breaking the news to his father that he is independently wealthy.[30] In the novel the reader wonders whether independence that must be so insisted upon is real, and in fact in Butler's own life it was not. His rejection of his family always involved a strange acceptance of it. Thus while he was working on *The Way of All Flesh,* satirizing his father and mother in the characters of Theobald and Christina, he was spending even more time and considerable money on preparing two large volumes about his grandfather, *The Life and Letters of Dr. Butler.* In his other books, in his studies of evolutionary theory, and even, incongruously, in his travel books, he was attempting to prove that "the only good influence upon a man's character is to have been begotten of good ancestors for many generations—or at any rate to have reverted to a good ancestor." [31] The effect of his theory was to allow him to relate himself to a long tradition of the Butler family and yet to disassociate himself superficially from his father. The virtues which a man inherits, he maintained, come not from his parents but from some preceding generation; thus in Butler's theory it is the father, not the son, who is disinherited.

Butler then could not, even if he had wanted to, treat May merely as a younger sister for whom he had great affection. She was his contact with his family, and it is in part his respect for the family and his desire to participate in family affairs that lie behind his detailed discussions with May of the world she shared with her father: the coming of snowdrops, their brother Tom's children, the gossip about Mr. Moss's marriage.

[30] Chap. 82.
[31] *Alps and Sanctuaries,* p. 277.

These details never bored him, and in all his letters he set down the daily affairs of Langar and Shrewsbury side by side with the substance of his latest book. Even when he wrote entries in his Notebooks, he put down accounts of his scientific ideas and sketches for his novels next to bits of trivial news from May, for there was in Butler's mind a fusion of many kinds of experience that seem quite separate to most people—and an amazing complexity of values. In his books he struggled to simplify his point of view, to apply a rigorous undergraduate logic to the matter at hand so that with no equivocation he might say what he honestly believed. That is why in his argumentative books he usually seems so arbitrary, so impatient with the subtleties of his subject, while in his novels, particularly in *The Way of All Flesh* (which he allowed to be frankly autobiographical), he allowed himself to present the interplay of contradictory emotions in himself which elsewhere he denied. And his letters, like his best novel, reiterate the complexity of a man who satirized Shrewsbury School in his account of Ernest at Roughborough and yet regularly attended every Shrewsbury School Speech Day.

May was always the most responsive member of the family to Butler's work. She alone read all his books, and it was undoubtedly through her that his father and mother learned enough about the contents of *Erewhon* (which they claimed they did not read) to object violently to their son's having written it. May also understood what he wrote, though she did not always agree with it, and one measure of his respect for her is the answer which he incorporated into *The Fair Haven* to the objections she raised in her letter of July 8, 1872, to his theory of the Gospels. After offering a series of objections to his theory, May concludes: "It is impossible to live in these days, and not be awake to many of the questions and difficulties afloat—and there are few who have any powers of thought at all, who are not led to some extent, at least, to examine the ground on which they stand. I think that we [i.e., May and her father] have perhaps both thought and read more than you think." In Chapter 5 of *The Fair Haven* Butler took up one by one the points which May raised in this letter, and his careful refutation is proof that he was haunted by her statement: "We have perhaps both thought and read more than you think." Butler was determined to over-reply in his rational way to any argument she advanced, perhaps because he could not bear to have his sister play at his game, but also because he respected her opinion.

Butler was aware, however, that May was not a perfect match for him intellectually. She had an irritatingly feminine way of obscuring the real point she was trying to make; and there is a quality in her letters that Butler best defined in his description of Charlotte's letters in *The Way of All Flesh:* "There is a *de haut en bas* tone in all her letters; it is rather hard to lay one's finger upon it but Ernest never gets a letter from her without feeling that he is being written to by one who has had direct communication with an angel." [32] May's reluctance to say anything straight out is her most annoying stylistic habit. In her letter of February 1, 1885, she reports that what few scraps of information she has received indicate that their brother Tom died of dysentery. Then she generalizes:

> How one wishes one could be always gentle. Somehow one begins to see that however much in the wrong people may be, there is always much one wishes one had not done or said or thought when any softening comes, and one is sorry now to think how ready we all were—even I, for I am speaking for myself as much as any of us, to think some evil of this silence [from Tom]—or that if the end had come, it might have come in some far *more* sad way.

Butler was annoyed by this foggy prose in which the subject disappears: the difference between his ideal of straightforward writing and May's writing was never more marked, and he angrily broke in twice, scribbling replies on the letter: after the last sentence, he wrote: "I don't know what she means. I thought Tom's silence meant that he was dead—and

[32] Chap. 86.

he was dead. I did not think anything else." Butler was certainly conscious of May's annoying mannerisms, and yet he constantly encouraged her to develop the talent he saw beneath the manner. As late as 1899 he was urging her to try her hand at writing for publication. May did at one time write a chapter (not one of which Butler could have approved) in a sentimental moral guidebook for young girls entitled *Life's Possibilities.* She did little else, but he believed in her.

The affection between Butler and May is strongest in the letters he wrote at the times of crisis in his life. Just before he sailed to New Zealand he wrote to her, mixing talk about the ordinary details of his preparations for sailing—the furnishing of his cabin, his last-minute appointments in London—with an unstated but ever-present concern with having to leave her. He begins the letter with an attempt to say farewell: "I shall think *very* much indeed of all at Langar, and often I am sure we shall be thinking of one another at the same time and in the same way—." He then writes two more "farewells," also punctuated with long dashes, and each time invents some bit of business—where to forward his mail, what to do with his tailor's bill—to keep the letter open. After his return we can again see his affection in his playful letter of September 24, 1866: "I am sorry your knee is hurt and hope it will soon come right; I don't like people having bad knees: they must get plenty of air in pony carriages at any rate." Butler is aware of May's diminutive world here, but his tenderness with her contrasts sharply with the brashness of his public manner at the time.

Butler's fear that May might have accepted her conventional life too easily, that she was too acquiescent, sometimes manifests itself in what is for him an uncharacteristically involved, nonlogical style. In a few letters it is difficult even to determine exactly what the subject is, but what does emerge powerfully is his strong desire that his sister find some quiet substitute for his own forthright revolt from his father. Thus on October 4, 1866, he writes:

The long and short of it is, I have the utmost confidence in your goodness—but you are dangerously timid—you should never write as though you assumed that your brother had any right to be *angry* with you for doing whatever you think fit to do as regards your own estimate of your own future happiness—therein lies the difference between liberality and illiberality—"if I had been in so and so's place *I* should have done so and so, therefore such and such an other should have done the same."

When, as here, Butler allows himself to respond to his fondness for his sister his prose reflects it immediately. The same concern for May which muddies the surface of the passage above is expressed puckishly in his conclusion: "I wish you were braver: go up and bite the next six people you meet: it would do you a deal of good—and take it quite as a matter of course that you have a right to bite them. I won't come near you till you have bitten six—."

Butler did not collect amusing anecdotes for May as he did for Miss Savage, but his letters to her sometimes have the same easy wit as his best letters to Miss Savage. He could even smile at himself in them, and it was rare that he was able to do that. When he tells May (May 27, 1886) about the first rehearsal of *Narcissus*, a satirical oratorio that he and Jones had written, he seems amused to learn that the violinists they had hired had liked the piece too but had expressed their approval by patting their violins, which he and Jones could not hear amid the "clapping etc.—of our small audience." Thinking of the violinists leads him to think of the cost of the oratorio (which itself is about financial speculation), and he muses, "A tame oratorio is a delightful pet but he is something like a tame elephant and would eat Jones and me out of house and home if we did not keep him in his proper place. As for printing it—we might just as well throw our money into the sea." It was not often that he saw his work as anything but a holy cause, whether it was musical or literary or scientific, and he had to be sure of May's confidence to condescend to it so playfully. We can also sense the half-mocking, half-serious tone of his comments on his nephew Hal in the same letter: "I am very glad to hear he has been so exemplary in putting by money, not only for his own sake but from an avuncular point of view; a pecunious nephew is so far more agreeable in every way than an impecunious one."

Jones tries to show that Butler was driven to write letters to his sisters that were certain to insult them—"there was no stopping him from writing such letters when he was in the mood"—and he uses as an illustration a letter which Butler wrote to Harrie just a fortnight before his letter to May about the rehearsal.[33] It is, like all his letters to Harrie, sharper in tone than any to May; he questions outright what he would have merely noted privately upon a letter from May: "When you say you think Aunt Sarah '*will have* been' glad I called on her, do you mean that, though not glad at present, there will come a time, etc., etc.? I greatly doubt whether she will ever be more glad than she is at present." But in his long report of an interview with his Aunt Sarah it is hard to see how Harrie could take offense. He does compare his aunt to a fluctuating stock whose value fell precipitously in his market when she supported Gladstone's government, and the comparison is perhaps tediously extended, but it has the same lightheartedness as his use of stocks and bonds in *Narcissus*, and while one might agree with the note Butler made on the letter when he read it over ("this stupid letter," he called it), there is no reason to believe anything other than what Jones quotes Butler as having said—that his sisters must see that his letters were written in fun. Jones's attempt to caricature the sisters is revealed in his comment that it was not likely that they "saw anything in them beyond deplorable flippancy and irreverence,"[34] but Butler was always too demanding to have wasted his talents on an unappreciative audience.

Butler was sometimes witty in his letters to May, and he was always honest—at least he was almost always honest, for in one letter (November 12, 1873) he denies that he has ever written or ever will write a book like *The Way of All Flesh.*

[33] *Memoir*, II, 108–109.
[34] *Ibid.*

It is the only direct lie that he tells in the whole correspondence, and it may repay examination:

> I am told there is a report that I have written a book in which I have introduced my father. I fear lest this report should reach you and am anxious to contradict it. I have written no book in which any single character is drawn from life—or to my knowledge hinted at—and shall never do so. All that I have written now bears my name, and it is not my intention to write again anonymously. If you hear of any book's being assigned to me which does not bear my name please to contradict the report. I haven't the faintest conception what the present report can allude to—but contradict it unreservedly.

The awkwardness of the lie gives him away. He protests too much about a report that only might, mysteriously, reach her; he is "anxious to contradict it"; has "written no book," "shall never do so," "not my intention," "please to contradict"; "I . . . contradict it unreservedly"—all the negatives build up to a nervous affirmative. Actually, Butler was hard at work on the early and most satirical parts of the novel, and he was troubled by the fact that for the first time his writing was unambiguously autobiographical. True, he had acknowledged the previously anonymous *Erewhon* and *The Fair Haven*, but he could acknowledge these books, because they made no direct comment upon his family: they were fantasies about an imaginary land and about two imaginary brothers, and that was camouflage enough to allow him to discuss them fully with May, as he does in these letters; but *The Way of All Flesh* or "Ernest Pontifex," as Butler entitled it, was another matter. He denies it here, and never mentions it again throughout the correspondence, though it was probably the book that concerned him more and persisted in his mind over a longer period of time than any other.

In the perspective these letters offer we see that in his many activities Butler shared the basic interests of his age. Like his more fashionable contemporaries he admired the Italian painters before Raphael and the primitive artists of small Italian towns; he admired Handel, and he painted pictures which the Royal Academy hung; he wrote *Erewhon* when scientific utopias were popular; his biographical interpretation of Shakespeare's sonnets followed, and was intended to refute, Sidney Lee's and Oscar Wilde's; and his interest in Homer coincided with a new revival of Greek scholarship. He accepted the interests of his age, but his unique contribution was the great personal force and the commonsensical, amateur point of view which he brought to bear on them. His was a voice much needed in a late Victorian England threatened by narrow, self-regarding professionalism—on one side scientists so cliquish that no outsider could be heard, and on the other *littérateurs* too aesthetic to receive a blunt "styleless" writer. In such a fragmented world Butler maintained his position as an informed nonprofessional and did so with an effective belligerence. His world, as he says explicitly in his most famous sonnet, was a battlefield:

Not on sad Stygian shore, nor in clear sheen
Of far Elysian plain, shall we meet those
Among the dead whose pupils we have been,
Nor those great shades whom we have held as foes;
No meadow asphodel our feet shall tread,
Nor shall we look each other in the face
To love or hate each other being dead,
Hoping some praise, or fearing some disgrace.
We shall not argue saying " 'Twas thus" or "Thus,"
Our argument's whole drift we shall forget;
Who's right, who's wrong, 'twill be all one to us;
We shall not even know that we have met.
Yet meet we shall, and part, and meet again,
Where dead men meet, on lips of living men.

The Butler that this sonnet expresses does appear in his letters to May—the man who defines death as the absence of contention, who says, as if he can hardly believe it, that in death one will not care "who's right, who's wrong." This is the Butler who tells May that he would like to get his hands on anyone who says that Nausicaa did not write the *Odyssey*, and the one who delightedly anticipates a long quarrel with Romanes about the source of the phrase "hereditary memory." Naturally, he was "hoping some praise" (he asks May to seek Arthur Sullivan's reaction to his music), but failing that he wanted blame, for above all he could not stand indifference. When Darwin unfortunately decided to ignore his attacks, he was ready to follow up one book with three and fill the magazines with acrimonious letters till he got the strong response he wanted. But though he plays his role hard, the quarrelsome Butler is only one part of the man we see in the letters. We see, in the round, a man of many moods, not always crusading but at different times playful, affectionate, frivolous, confident, unsure.

He did try to simplify his life by keeping his relationships with his friends precisely defined, by insisting on his hatred for his family because he hated what they stood for; but the result of his attempt was a transparent fiction that only a character like Ernest—or Jones—could believe. His attempt to simplify failed in the sense that nothing actually was simplified: Miss Savage would not be contained within his ideal of friendship, and May, despite all his naughty private comments upon her, was impossibly cast in the role of Cinderella's sister. But in an ironic sense Butler's simplification of life succeeded, by bringing the complex man he was into contrast with the monolith he tried to be. Butler did not have the necessary perspective to see this, though in the best parts of *The Way of All Flesh* he wrote brilliantly about Ernest's self-delusion. His letters to May allow us to gain the perspective on his own life that he himself could not maintain; they help to restore a Victorian more interesting than the stereotype that Butler labored to create.

LETTERS

1. Butler to May

Text: Chapin Library MS.

St. John's. Coll.[1]
Aug. 10 1855

My dear May

I am shocked to find that you already think I have used you ill by not writing; what you will have thought by the time this reaches you I don't know: time flies so quickly that I really did not think more than the usual week had elapsed since I wrote.

I suppose the garden is by this time quite splendid, and hope none of its beauties will be over by the time I return wh: will be on the 15th of September if all is well, as on that day the coaches go down and we are all turned out to admit of the college being cleaned, a very awful process that of taking up the carpet, scouring the floors and thoroughly cleansing some 300 sitting rooms as many bed rooms and no few stairs and staircases. At present the college is being painted, I mean the outside of it. I shall have them very soon; more's the pity for they are a great nuisance and the paint, (on the *outside* of the windows and the outer door) smells most unpleasantly, especially as the window must [be] kept open all the while notwithstanding that it is the outside.

How I should like to be in Harrie's[2] plan about the musical festival; you may tell her that I have copied from a friend the most beautiful bit of quaint old music by a man of the name of Couperin,[3] organist to the royal chapel of Louis the XIVth. Such an odd bit: yet so very pretty. I cannot play it, but will learn it when I come down, and send it to Carrie;[4] I would do so earlier, but really I know I shall never find the

Letter 1:

[1] Like his father and grandfather, Butler matriculated at St. John's College, Cambridge. He went up from Shrewsbury School in 1854.

[2] Harriet, Butler's older sister. (See Biographical Sketches.)

[3] François Couperin, "le Grand" (1668–1733).

[4] Frances Caroline Bridges (1834–1929), sister of Harrie's future husband. As children she and Butler had a strong common interest in music. (See Garnett, p. 53.)

time. We have had a great deal of wet lately, but yesterday a complete change seems to have set in, and the heat was tremendous. I am very glad of it, for our early bathing had dwindled to a very few (I have been a most unflinching adherent) owing to the daily encreasing chilliness of the water: and as I consider it a grand institution I don't like seeing it decay.

Aunt Susan[5] comes back on Tuesday. So the tea drinking must soon come off. I don't mind being seen anywhere with Aunt Susan, but I shall certanily [*sic*] not like smuggling Mrs. Parry[6] into college at all: especially as I am sure she will sit at the window all the time to watch the gownsmen.

How vexatious about that abominable girl Marion Cowes! I am most inquisitive to know all about her but suppose I must wait.

With best love to all I remain

Your affectionate brother
S Butler.

2. *Butler to May*

Text: Chapin Library MS.

Febry. 5. 1857
St. John's. Coll:

Dear May

I write to wish you many happy returns of your birthday[1] and to beg your acceptance of the accompanying small work, which if not very entertaining is first rate in kind and which you will someday I think like.

I don't know what Harrie will say to me when she receives my enclosed note to her—

[5] Susannah Apthorp (1782–1863), sister of Butler's paternal grandmother. She lived in Cambridge.

[6] Elizabeth Barwick Parry, widow of the rector of North Muskam-cum-Holme, a neighboring parish in Nottinghamshire.

Letter 2:

[1] February 7.

I am in for the Craven [2] and have done pretty well resisting the great temptation of bolting and cutting the whole concern for skaiting, no slight one I can assure you. The examination has been so far exceedingly hard, and I don't fancy that any freshman will carry off the Craven this year.[3] Mrs. Parry is still Mrs. Parry though I fancy matters are getting more like the real thing; more's the pity for the agreeable and ladylike Miss Marshall whom I met at an entertainment at Aunt S[usan]'s a week ago. Papa's and Mamma's health was drunk by Aunt S after dinner which was chiefly formed out of our hamper; everything was exceedingly nice and the ham much admired.

I thought of you on the ball night and fancy that you were all more comfortable where you were than at Clumber; [4] at least I know one who would be. I hope that he continues mending—I have the gout in two fingers and am very tired as we have had a hard day in the senatehouse with long papers and, comparatively for the length, short time which makes the work much harder. I must do better than this in the tripos—but as I have another year we must hope for the best. Bateson [5] is Master—France [6] at present declines the public oratorship which I am sorry for as I should have liked to have had an examiner in the college; one would stand a better chance of being blown up for putting this that or the other. Tom [7] is well, but his room smokes so fearfully that he is not happy today. I went in and found such a state of soot as I never could have conceived. Tell Mamma that she will think me base for not having written but will perhaps pardon me as just at present I have an extra press of work on hand. With best love

[2] A scholarship of particular interest to the Butler family. Butler's grandfather successfully competed for it against Coleridge in 1793.

[3] The Craven was won the year before by a freshman (from Shrewsbury School).

[4] Apparently Clumber Park, seat of the Duke of Newcastle, in Nottinghamshire near the Butlers' home.

[5] William Henry Bateson (1812–1881), an alumnus of Shrewsbury School, who had recently been elected master of St. John's.

[6] Francis France (1816–1864), pupil of Butler's grandfather at Shrewsbury School, at this time fellow of St. John's, and later president.

[7] Butler's brother. (See Biographical Sketches.)

to her and you all and many happy returns of the day I remain

Your affectionate brother
S Butler

3. *Butler to May*

Text: Chapin Library MS.

4. Taviton Street—
Gordon Square, London. W.[1]
Sep. 27. 1859

Dear May,

Many thanks for the prayer book which I left behind quite accidentally: I am very glad to have it indeed, and thank you for sending it. I trust you will not think *too* much of me, but am sure that I shall think *very* much indeed of all at Langar,[2] and often I am sure we shall be thinking of one another at the same time and in the same way—

I could not write yesterday—or I would have done so: perhaps now I had better detail my adventures from the date of my arrival in London to the present time. I got here without adventure, and after lunching here drove for Messr. Jas. Morrison and Co. There they told me that the ship will not leave dock till Thursday, & Gravesend on Friday morning.[3] However I shall not have any too much time & am fully occupied till the time of sailing which I am very glad of. Thence we went and chose fittings for cabin⟨s⟩—a little table, chair, (both to stand in the recess) a piece of carpet 6 feet square—a looking glass—lamp (screwed to the wall) filtre, washing stand &[c.] . . . and thence drove straight to Mr. FitzGerald [4]—who was all kindness and cordiality—and will

Letter 3:

[1] The home of Philip Worsley (1802–1893), brother of Butler's mother.

[2] Butler's father was rector of Langar-cum-Barnston, near Bingham, Nottinghamshire.

[3] Butler was about to leave for New Zealand to take up sheep ranching. His ship, the *Roman Emperor*, cleared Gravesend on Saturday, October 1, and arrived in Lyttelton, N. Z., on January 27, 1860.

[4] James Edward Fitzgerald (1818–1896), first superintendent of Canterbury Province, New Zealand, who was in London at this time as agent of the province.

bring me my letters of introduction on board with him at Gravesend. By the way he advised me quietly, sub rosa, so mind not a word goes further—to fight shy of Mr. Dampier [5] who was not considered an *over* reputable character. He approved of all my other introductions. Thence I went to Chappell's to see about Harrie's piano forte. I like it much. It is *very* plain, but in their case I should take it myself. And thence after a short call on Perring [6] I returned home. Two Mr. Needhams, father and son,[7] came to dinner. The elder was a very jolly old fellow and had written the brewery lot of introductions for me.

This morning I went to the East India Docks the first thing after breakfast—saw the ship and liked her much—and am very well pleased with the cabin and general accomodation—thence returned to the fitting of the cabin, and called on Maull & Polyblank.[8] They said the day was so *very* gloomy (which it is) that I have appointed 10 tomorrow as the time at which I will call on them. Thence returned in time for lunch home.

By the way a letter from my friend Biron [9] told me that I might fall in with a farmer's daughter of the name of Buss (what a name!); he describes her as "of pleasant exterior." And sure enough, she has taken the next cabin to my own: she lives near Biron's people. How I trust she is engaged and going out to be married—*if not* I mean to offer her any reasonable compromise to make love to Mr. Newton (a young man who called with introductions to Mr. Fitz.G. but whom Mr. F. G. did not particularly fancy. Mr. Inman is the nice young fellow whom he liked) and not to me. Will you offer anything more on your own account?

Mr. FitzGerald hopes Papa will call on him next time he

[5] Probably Christopher Edward Dampier, solicitor to the Canterbury Association.

[6] Philip Perring (1828–1920), curate of St. James, Westminster, with whom Butler lived in 1859 while he considered taking orders.

[7] John Manning Needham (1807–1876) and Frederick Needham (d. 1875). The elder Needham and Philip Worsley were partners in the Whitbread & Co. brewery, a fact that Butler puns upon in the next sentence.

[8] Photographers.

[9] Henry Brydges Biron (1835–1915), a friend of Butler's at Cambridge, who had recently been ordained.

comes to town. Please forward letters to Taviton street if any arrive either on Wednesday or Thursday—as I shall not leave Taviton street, till Friday after post time.

Tomorrow I go first to Maull & P's, thence to the East India Docks—thence to Perring's. As these places lie hugely apart it will be one or two o'clock 'ere I reach Perring's; then I send Harrie's box, and my own table to Highmoor House—and stay with Perring till 4. Then go and dine with my friend Fisher [10] and bid him good bye. (By the way I am going to Mayer's as soon as I have done writing this.) And on Thursday I hope to find all my cabin complete—call on Mr. Mackenzie & do whatever final jobs remain.

I had a letter from Mr. Moorhouse yesterday enclosing introductions to his son.[11] *Entre nous* I don't incline to *old Mr. Moorhouse*. I will write again on Thursday, as I don't think I shall be able to do so ⟨on⟩ tomorrow—and drop one line from Gravesend. And now dear May, I must conclude. Papa and Mamma will consider this letter equally their's and with my very best love to you all I remain ever

Your affectionate brother
S— Butler—

P. S. If any letters come after I am gone either send them to N.Z. or else to Paley [12] at St. John's College, who will read and answer them—unless they are evidently from people known to all of us. If Redfarn & Banham [13] send in a bill I don't owe them a penny—& mind no tailor's bill comes in in my college account—

I don't suppose any more letters will come for me—

[10] George William Fisher (1835–1898), another Cambridge friend, later mathematics master at Shrewsbury School.

[11] The son, William Sefton Moorhouse (1825–1881), was the second superintendent Canterbury Province. He became a close friend of Butler's in New Zealand.

[12] George Alfred Paley (1838–1866). He took his degree at St. John's two years after Butler.

[13] Tailors at Cambridge.

4. Butler to May

Text: Chapin Library MS.

[New Zealand]
[*ca.* March 21, 1861]

My dear May

I send you two musical notes. [In] one, that in Alexander's Feast,[1] (which may be purchased for 2s) you will find some splendid music. "War he sang is toil & trouble" is the perfection of ennui, the song being to all appearance taken from the natural tones of the human voice in which a man would exclaim that war & every thing else and every body else were toil & trouble, but the chorus "So love was crowned but music won the cause" is amusing, and gives evidence of the way in which Handel evidently sided with Music versus love. He repeats the "But music won the cause" three or four times at the end of the piece & winds up with a pretty little sly chuckle of triumph in the word[s] "won the cause," which complete the ⟨movement⟩ piece and give music the last word. These three words coming in after a pause are quite ludicrous. The next note is that the first three notes in the chorus "He trusted in God" are the natural intonation of a shout of derision—HA! HA! HA! I am confident that this is what Handel meant, though I consider the taste of meaning it to be questionable.

P. S. Mar. 22. Pattisson [2] has come, but the box will not be opened till it gets home; it is now on its way. I like the looks of Patisson well: please give Harrie my best thanks for so kindly sending me dear George's handkerchiefs—they will be very acceptable. I have not had time to write a note to Whatton,[3] but will make the opening of the box an excuse for

Letter 4:

[1] Handel's setting to music of Dryden's "Alexander's Feast, or, the Power of Music; an Ode in Honour of St. Cecilia's Day."

[2] John Coleridge Patteson (1827–1911), first missionary bishop of the Melanesian Islands. Butler's cousin, Thomas Lloyd, joined him as a missionary two years later. Butler misspells Patteson's name here, and misspells it differently in the next sentence.

[3] The home of Thomas Dickinson Hall (1808–1879), near Langar. It was through Edward Algernon Hall (1853–1933), the sixth son, that Butler met Jones in 1876. May was a close friend of Alice Elizabeth Hall, the eldest daughter.

doing so, and for not having done so previously. I have examined the college,[4] but it was almost a farce—the boys knew next to nothing and the little they did know was very superficial. I have expressed my opinion in the report, I hope politely, but at the same time unmistakeably. I showed the Bishop some of the papers and he quite coincided in my opinion that they wanted a good rubbing up. The last mail (i. e. the February mail) has not yet arrived, and this is overdue now, but I shall not wait as I have had a promise that my letters shall reach Rowley's[5] as soon as possible after the mail comes in. Best love to you all.

Your affectionate brother,
S. Butler—

5. *Butler to May*

Text: Chapin Library MS.

15. Clifford's Inn
Fleet Street E. C.
Sep. 24. 1866—

Dear May

Many thanks for your's which reached me on Thursday just as I was starting by the boat for Newhaven: [1] the sea was treacherous—leaden and smooth to look at from the shore, but oh! far from smooth to ride upon and rough with half a gale of wind before we got to New Haven. I was not ill—really perfectly unscathed but poor old Pauli was an awful sufferer. One poor little boy told the steward to take away the basin—saying very piteously "I have not *got* any more." I am very

[4] Patteson and George Augustus Selwyn (1809–1878), bishop of New Zealand, maintained St. John's College, a boys' school near Auckland. It was partly for native and partly for English boys and also contained a training school for missionaries. Selwyn was a friend of the Butler family.

[5] A station between Butler's sheep ranch and the harbor at Lyttelton.

Letter 5:

[1] Butler had returned to London from New Zealand in August, 1864, and begun to study painting. At this time he was returning from a month's stay in Dieppe with Charles Paine Pauli (see Biographical Sketches).

glad to be back, and having tidied up my rooms to the remotest corner ⟨and⟩ am at peace and hope to begin regular work again tomorrow, of which I must really have a fair spell before I come home. I am in a state of profound dejection about art—having done very badly at Dieppe. A little time will I know from past experience set me as sanguine as ever again, but I must get well straight again before I can leave off for a day. I am very sorry to have missed Cousin Mary [2] and Miss Sherington; the Talbot Bakers [3] I don't think I *am* sorry to miss. Emma I shall hope to see at Langar. What is this talk, just rumoured of which I hear at Taviton St. about Mentone? I heard nothing save that someone had said that some one else had said that there was some talk about it. Are you going? I am sorry your knee is hurt and hope it will soon come right. I don't like people having bad knees: they must get plenty of air in pony carriages at any rate.

I have just written to Etta,[4] and promised to go there for a few days at Xmas. I shall begin sending the Times to Harrie again—but no—after sending the one which I have folded up I shall drop it till I hear of her return. I hope you are all pretty well and with best love

Your affectionate brother
S. Butler

6. *Butler to May*

Text: Chapin Library MS.

[15 Clifford's Inn]
Oct. 4, 1866—

Dear May—

I was very sorry for your last—but angry! The idea is preposterous—no one has any right to be angry with any one—

[2] Mary Lloyd, daughter of Butler's paternal aunt Harriet.

[3] Talbot Hastings Bendall Baker (1820–1900) was at this time vicar of Preston-cum-Sutton-Poyntz, near Weymouth.

[4] Henrietta Butler, *née* Rigby, Tom's wife. Butler did visit her at Maes-y-Porth, her home in Wales, on December 22 (MS Notebooks, III, 100).

on such matters—this is about the sixth letter I have tried to write you & shall make as much a mess of this as any of the others. The long & short of it is, I have the utmost confidence in your goodness—but you are dangerously timid—you shd never write as though you assumed that your brother had any right to be *angry* with you for doing whatever you think fit to do as regards your own estimate of your own future happiness—therein lies the difference between liberality & illiberality—"if I had been in so & so's place *I* shd have done so & so, therefore such & such an other shd have done the same": this is pure bigotry & you need never fear *me:* you thought—and did what you thought right because you thought it right. Who has any right to think a syllable against it qua you?—though he might have been fairly glad to have heard a different termination. However I fear I am trenching on forbidden ground, you must pardon me. I shall say no more except that you must not be so afraid of me, & that I shall forget all about it, I mean appear to forget. I wish you were braver: go up & bite the next six people you meet: it wd do you a deal of good—& take it quite as a matter of course that you have a right to bite them. I won't come near you till you have bitten six—and then there won't be any occasion for you to bite more.

Please give my love to my mother: I am *very* sorry that she has been poorly—she will indeed have her hands full with so many visitors: I shall delay ⟨g⟩ coming home till the 22d. Have finished my portrait of myself sucessfully [*sic*]—I think the best I have done: am at work on poor old Paley for Mrs. Hoare,[1] also sucessful. Am not earning nor like to earn a farthing yet—all in good time—"Wait"—as Tennyson says—"My faith is large in Time / "And that which shapes it to some perfect end."[2] It is nonsense but sounds pretty. Time

Letter 6:

[1] Beatrice Ann Hoare, *née* Paley, wife of Butler's close friend at Cambridge, Henry Hoare. Her brother, George Alfred Paley, also a friend of Butler's at Cambridge (see note 12 for Letter 3), was at this time seriously ill; he died in the following February.

[2] "Love and Duty," ll. 25–26.

cannot come to a perfect end or any end at all qua man, as long as he is alive. I should be *very* glad to meet Emma at Langar & shd like to time my visit to meet her.

With my very best love to you I am your affectionate brother

S. Butler—

7. *Butler to May*

Text: Garnett, pp. 198–200.

15 Clifford's Inn,
Jan. 30, 1867.

Dear May,

Thank you very much for yours received this morning. I am very sorry that Etta has lost her father, and hope that whatever decision be arrived at nothing will go wrong; I have no doubt that Dr. Roberts will decide rightly one way or the other: also I am very sorry to hear of my father's having so much cough, and trust that it is nothing serious. I shall call at Taviton Street to-morrow morning and shall probably catch him before he goes to see Dr. Burrough.

I am very much pleased that you are translating Miss Koch's work—ought I to call her Fräulein Koch? or what? I hope it may be a prelude to your doing more with your pen: what say you to going to old Mother Barratt [1] and making her tell you how she and her brother walked down into Northamptonshire to see an uncle and enquire whether he meant to leave them any money, and writing it all down as nearly as you can remember it? I think it would make a charming little sketch and might be tried at *All the Year Round* or *Once a Week*. She tells it very naïvely, and indeed it wants no touches: if it could only be taken down verbatim it would be perfect. It was very snowy weather too—and when she says, "Oh dear, oh dear, how it did snow," she seems to feel the

Letter 7:

[1] In *Alps and Sanctuaries* (p. 175) Butler identifies Mother Barratt as a resident of Langar. Parish records show that a Sarah Barrett, aged 78, died there in 1876.

cold to this day.—However—enough of that—think it over. I went to *Judas Maccabaeus* the other night, and liked it very much indeed; it is the only thing I have been to; I am glad you went to the *Elijah;* but I like Mendelssohn less and less, and Handel, Bach and Beethoven more and more: there are no great musicians now. I was going to say no great musicians and no great painters now, but I suppose there are some very good painters—though no giants: no, I don't think there are any great painters either—not in England, at any rate. I met the Mr. Wallis who painted the "Death of Chatterton,"[2] the other night, and liked him, and shall probably meet him again. Sir Francis Grant[3] also spoke to me the other day in the National Gallery, where I was copying, and asked me what I thought of the new Rembrandt which was close by where I was working; I didn't know who he was, but answered with decorum. He did not seem to approve of my work, but I cared not. I had only just begun and there was nothing to say. I think I am going on pretty well. I am very glad that Gertrude mends, and shall be much pleased to see the illustrations. With my best love to my mother and to you all, I am

Your affectionate brother
S. Butler.

8. *Butler to May*

Text: Chapin Library MS.

15. Clifford's Inn E. C.
Aug. 30, 1868

Dear May

I am afraid I have left your pleasant little note some days without an answer, (nay—I see it was only written on the 26th) but by day I have no time for writing, and at night am generally pretty well tired so that I fear I am but a poor correspondent to any one. I am very sorry that you continue

[2] Henry Wallis (1830–1916).

[3] Francis Grant (1803–1878), at this time president of the Royal Academy.

so evidently below par. Do you think you eat too much salt? Our homeopathists say that people take a great deal too much of it, and that what the cook puts into the food is quite enough: they say that it is one great cause of a predisposition to take cold: and I mean to try what hardly using it at all will do this winter, and see whether I take cold less: certainly my mother takes a good deal and catches cold very easily, but that is too small an experience on which to form a conclusion. My eye certainly continues to improve but has its ups and downs: [1] on the whole the ups preponderate, and I make no doubt of ultimately getting quite rid of it: at present it hardly interferes with my work at all, but I ease it in every way I can: of my work I can give good accounts: I have had a comfortable time of it every since my return and am making rapid progress: the study just finished is one of an ugly old man dressed in a huge wig with a violent scarlet & no less violent lilac cotton satin costume of the time of Charles the Second: as hideous a conception as ever entered into Mr. Heatherley's [2] brain: but I got a very good likeness out of it: he is such a good fellow that we don't complain no matter what monstrosities he inflicts upon us, and of course as far as the exercise goes it is the same thing, but it is vexing to have one's best work (and this is out & out my best) expended on a subject which can gratify no one and could never sell: Mr. Heatherley admired the study so much that I have given it him: and very glad I was to be able to gratify him with a study which I really cannot see could have given pleasure to any one else. Will you give all kind messages from me to Aunt Lloyd, to Tom & William [3] and the Bathers.[4] I have seen

Letter 8:

[1] Never strong, Butler's eyes were particularly troublesome to him at this time and he was seeing an oculist (MS Notebooks, III, 100).

[2] Thomas Heatherley (d. 1914), proprietor of a school of art at 79 Newman Street at which Butler studied.

[3] Sons of "Aunt Lloyd," Harriet Lloyd.

[4] Butler's paternal aunt, Mary, was the wife of Edward Bather (1779–1847). Their nephew, Henry Francis Bather (1832–1905), vicar of Meole Brace, near Shrewsbury, was a good friend of Butler's. The manuscript of *The Way of All Flesh* shows that Butler first thought of calling Theobald's parish "Bather's Bridge."

Robert Bridges[5] two or three times lately: he has called on me: but I cannot say that I much *liked* him though I am sure he is an excellent fellow. I shall probably be down at Langar in about a month and shall no doubt then see you, for present I will add no more but remain

Your affectionate brother
S. Butler.

9. *Butler to May*

Text: Chapin Library MS.

15. Clifford's Inn E. C.
Sunday July 4. [1869]

My dear May

I hope that long ere this reaches you my mother will have quite regained her tone & be none the worse for the really, as it sounds, serious check she has received. I hope the chemist has been threatened with an action for it is an abominable thing to have done. I have no doubt I shall have a line in a day or two to say how she is getting on, and in the mean time have taken for granted as I have not heard that all was going nicely. Do you have East wind there? We do every day: it looks nice as the sky is bright & there is no rain, but it is nasty as it has no ozone in it. Now I want ozone. I can't do without ozone. I see by the Illustrated that ozone is brought from the sea by the West & S. West winds and that it doesn't come with an East Wind[1]—why I cannot tell, but I am very sensitive of its presence and should like some more of it. They say sunflowers exhale it—but they won't grow in Clifford's Inn or I would get some. In other respects I am very well and quite satisfied with my work, i.e. that it is all I cd wish it. I went to the Royal

[5] Brother of Harriet's husband; he became poet laureate in 1913.

Letter 9:

[1] "The sea is the great reservoir of ozone . . . ocean phosphorescence is the chief source of its production. . . . The sea wind or equatorial is that of phosphorescence and ozone . . . the polar or land wind is that of non-luminosity and no ozone" (*Illustrated London News*, May 22, 1869, p. 531c).

Academy Soirée which was a brilliant affair. I liked it very much—went early and stayed late. Prince Teck [2] was the only one of the Royal Family there as the others were with the Viceroy of Ægypt at Windsor.[3] But I saw lots of notables—Millais—Leighton & many artists. Lord Cairns, Lord Lytton & several political swells, and there were plenty of people I knew. I hope I may get there again next year. I have painted a girl in a red figured satin dress in a pensive attitude looking down, with one hand to her head and another to her heart: I am going to paint a fireplace and a burning correspondence behind her: this is one of Heatherley's greatest conceptions. This fortnight we have a man in Greek costume in an awkward meaningless attitude, & I don't quite see what I can do with him: the word Missolonghi haunts me vaguely as though it had some connection with the matter but what it will come to I don't know. I asked one of the men where & what Missolonghi was. He said his sister was in a class when none of the girls knew where Missolonghi was—nor what. The governess said "Why my dears when I was your age I never could hear the name mentioned without bursting into tears." [4] Sic transit &c. I have heard nothing of Tom lately. Have the Woods & Forests people [5] put him out of his misery, & done what he wanted: I hope the straits softened the explosion; [6] what an awful thing it must have been, and one doesn't know how much they mayn't have in London (Nit. Glyc. I mean) & when it mayn't go off. Please give my best love to my mother & believe me your affectionate ⟨sister⟩ brother—

S. Butler—

[2] Francis Paul Charles Louis Alexander (1837–1900), created Prince of Teck by the King of Wurtemberg.

[3] On the same evening as the Royal Academy soirée, there was a royal dinner party at Windsor in honor of the visit of the Viceroy of Egypt.

[4] Byron died at Missolonghi. Christina is given the same sensitivity in *The Way of All Flesh*, chap. 11.

[5] The Commissioners of Her Majesty's Woods, Forests, and Land Revenues. Tom Butler's connection with them is obscure.

[6] A few days before, two carts of nitroglycerin exploded in a deep valley in Wales.

10. Butler to May

Text: Chapin Library MS.

Hotel de la Lune
Venice. Mar 20, 1870

My dear May

I got your pleasant note two or three or [more] days ago and am under a certain conviction of sin in not having answered it before I left Florence. I wrote last from Turin: I thence made for Modena, dropping a train at Parma and seeing the gallery chiefly famous for Correggio who is not one of my friends: the cathedral however is magnificent: at Modena there was a most interesting and really very fine collection: I went on thence in the afternoon to Florence where I spent exactly a week the greater part of wh: time I was in the Uffizi & Pitti galleries. I have had to alter and modify a good many opinions on this second visit to Florentine Galleries: you may perhaps remember that I went there 4½ years ago: my first impression was that some one had gone round and spoiled almost all the pictures in the interim, but after a while this wore off and though I see that the old masters are not everybody but that in some respects the moderns really are ahead of them, still I can retain my affection & admiration for them undiminished. One or two pictures however exploded once & for ever: notably the 3 Fates by Michael Angelo: it is impossible that he can have ever had any hand in them: [1] they are so *very* bad: I cannot comprehend how they can ever have obtained their reputation: the engravings [2] are worth 10 of the original picture. Guido Guercino & the Bolognese school I hated pretty heartily already; but I hate them worse now: on the other hand Titian, Raphael, Bellini and the early painters seem to go up & up & up: also Rembrandt,

Letter 10:

[1] Butler's view that the "Three Fates" was not by Michelangelo—as catalogued in the nineteenth century—is confirmed by recent scholarship. See Adolpho Venturi, *Storia dell'Arte Italiana*, IX, Part 6 (Milan: V. Hoepli, 1933), p. 165*n*., and Bernard Berenson, *Pitture Italiane del Rinascimento*, tr. by Emilio Cecchi (Milan: V. Hoepli, 1936), p. 169.

[2] Two studies of the heads of the Fates are in the Uffizi Gallery.

Rubens & Vandyke: the weather was bitterly cold: snow fell a little one day, & I saw ice in the shade of the Pitti Palace: I walked over to Fiesole one afternoon & saw the walls: they really *are* fine. I left Florence yesterday morning & slept at Padua last night: this morning I saw Giotto's chapel: [3] this was a great treat & surprise: I knew he was a swell: but I had no idea what a tremendous swell he was: it is impossible to form any idea of his genius until one has seen this series of frescoes: there was no one fit to hold a candle to him for the next hundred years, and even now his manner of telling a story and his incidents—his ornamentation, & his colour will hold their own with any one.

The town of Padua is one of the most delightful imaginable, and I would gladly stay & work there but that the cold winds are so intolerable: sitting in any shady place is not to be thought of: and the N. wind is as cold as England: only in the sun is it warm: & even there the wind is fierce: I came on here this afternoon and have been prowling about the town ever since: the gallery was closed before I arrived: but I went through St. Mark's & the Ducal Palace: it's absurd writing about such places, I can only say that I know none like them: I wish I could give you any clue as to my movements: I shan't stay here longer than I can help: I can't get exercise enough: I shd think it will be about 3 or 4 days—not more: and shall come home sooner than I intended: now that I have left Mentone & find myself all alone & unsettled I begin to get very sick of it and to want to [get] back at my work again: or at any rate to be working at something [4] wh: I really cannot do here: my hands are now as cold as ice & I am wrapped up in my gt. coat & comforter: I expect this is

[3] The Madonna dell'Arena Chapel. Ruskin had praised it highly. See *The Works of John Ruskin*, ed. by Cook and Wedderburn, XXIV (London: G. Allen; New York: Longmans, Green, 1906), 13–123.

[4] Though unaware of it at the time, Butler later came to feel that this trip to Venice marked a turning point in his career. Discouraged by his painting, he "went home resolved to do at any rate something, in literature, if not in painting—so I began tinkering up the old magazine articles I had written in New Zealand, & they strung themselves together into 'Erewhon'" (MS Notebooks, IV, 105–106; *Memoir*, I, 132–133).

the last of it, but it shows no sign of changing: I have had that abominable song com'e gentil la notte al mezzo d'Avril [5] in my head for the last two months, & been hating the winter because I suspect that he would have put warm evenings earlier had they existed: as it is there are 11 days of Mar. & 15 of April before they can become warm; still al commincio d'Avril wdn't have come into the metre so he may be lying, & the end of March wouldn't have rhymed so there is a bare possibility that he may have driven them off to the middle of April on the score of his confounded poetry—I don't know—all I do know is that it is very cold. Still it is a great pleasure & profit to me to have seen so many pictures again. I *won't* go to Munich: if it gets warm very soon I will do a little out door work & then come home: if it doesn't then I'll come home at once—or before very long. I sent my pictures by grande vitesse from Florence: but don't expect they'll be hung.[6] I shall send in 5 in all. Mr. Heatherley will see to them for me. Miss Moberley was wrong in thinking I ran away from her: I tried the Splendide, and shd have gone there but they were full: I also tried the Mediteranée but saw it was full of foreigners: I only went to the Grand Hotel because the Moggridges [7] told me they gave tea in the salon: I ran after the tea and not away from Miss Moberley: if Miss Moberley had been tea I would have followed her any where: staying at the Londres was purgatory: I never slept a single night comfortable, & one or two nights hardly a wink: they had not a single newspaper, & except the Hallens who were good souls enough there was no one in the inn: I was wretched: I shd be wretched in this inn also: it is all French & German: if I stay longer in Venice than 3 or 4 days I will shift to some other: there isn't an English person in the hotel: I travelled yesterday with a very nice gentlemanly fellow who turned out to be son

[5] From the serenade in Donizetti's *Don Pasquale*, Act III, scene vi.

[6] These paintings, submitted for the Royal Academy Exhibition which opened on April 30, were not accepted, but six of Butler's paintings were hung in the Academy's exhibitions from 1869–1876.

[7] John Traherne Moggridge (b. 1842) was a friend of the Butler family who shared Canon Butler's interest in botany and his love of the French Riviera.

of Rimmel the gt. perfumer: [8] but he was going to Ferrara to shoot snipes: I will leave this open till tomorrow & revolve upon my future movements so that I may tell you where to write.

11. *Butler to May*

Text: Garnett, pp. 200–201.

15 Clifford's Inn,
Sunday night. [July, 1870]

Dear May,

I got yours two or three mornings ago, and gather that you are at Maes-y-Porth; indeed, my conscience smites me that I have been a vile, bad correspondent to Etta: please let this be considered a joint epistle: if I am in Etta's black books (which I feel that I deserve to be) open them when she is not looking —scratch out my name—and write it in the white ones. I am so glad to hear good accounts of the children: I *must* come and see them as soon as ever I can: but won't trespass upon Tom and Etta's hospitality. I have been in a muddle about my paintings for some time past; that is at Heatherley's. I saved my last study; yet as by fire: I shall come out of this fit greatly strengthened: at least I hope so: I have had many such before, and I always gain after them, but this is a long one and a bad one, longer and worse than I have had for some time. I am very well, but very hot. I hope Tom will mend. I have taken to drinking a little wine and water and think it does me good. I like it awfully. With kind remembrances to Rachel and best love to the rest of you.

Believe me your affectionate brother,
S. Butler.

[8] The great perfumer was Eugene Rimmel (1820–1887). He was particularly well known in London, where he maintained three shops; he had one in Paris.

12. May to Butler

Text: British Museum MS.

[Langar]
July 8, 1872

My dearest Sam

The difficulty which you set before me is no new one.[1] But I find it very hard myself to see how any clear unprejudiced mind can think the 2 accounts *so* irreconcileable as to effect [*sic*] belief in the story told in either Gospel. I do not however wish to send you any harmony of them, for two reasons—1. That you would probably find flaws in my harmony, knowing so much better the little differences of the Greek &c. 2. That my views are not my own—(except in so far as all that thoroughly commends itself to one's common sense becomes one's own) but are gathered from such writers as Trench, Ellicott, Westcott [2] &c—whose books (or similar ones) you have probably read long ago if you have studied the subject from both sides at all. If not, I refer you to them, for they would speak for me far better than I should speak for myself. Even were it found *impossible* to harmonize the two accounts exactly—as perhaps in some minor sense it may be—I can see no difficulty in believing that both would prove true if one knew *all* the facts. It is constantly happening in daily life that two almost opposite statements both prove true. I remember such an instance striking us much lately when Papa & Tom were abroad—when two accounts might have reached us of their movements apparently quite contradictory, yet both would have been true, & would have wanted only a connecting

Letter 12:

[1] Butler studied closely the differences between the accounts of Christ's life given by Mark and Matthew. In chap. 5 of *The Fair Haven* (which he was writing at this time), he disposes of the argument for their harmony which May advances in this letter. In this chapter he says: "Those who say that we should find no difficulty if we knew *all* the facts are still careful to abstain from any example (so far as I know) of the sort of additional facts which would serve their purpose."

[2] Writers on the harmony of the Gospels, all particularly well known at this time because they were serving on the Committee for the Revision of the New Testament.

link out of our power to supply to make them both intelligible.

There are, no doubt, numberless difficulties in the Bible history—but the difficulties of *unbelief* in the great Bible facts, such as the Resurrection, are beyond question greater, even historically, than those of belief—& we acknowledge a higher evidence (their truth in their present potent *power*) than even historical evidence can give.

It is impossible to live in these days, & not be awake to many of the questions & difficulties afloat—& there are few who have any powers of thought at all, who are not led to some extent, at least, to examine the ground on which they stand. I think that we have perhaps both thought and read more than you think.

If you still have my letter, & will look at it again, you will see that what I represented as unfair was not that you did not tell us your views, but that you wrote about them ⟨before⟩ you had done so.[3] Mere curiosity is a thing which can have no place in such a ⟨question⟩ if there is any heart in the matter.

I would most gladly have believed that [there] were points in common between us, & tried thro' them to understand your position. If, however, you do not wish to reply to my questions on any terms but those of following your difficulties step by step, I can but say that I am scarcely strong enough for such a strain, either physically or intellectually.

Yet (without despising intellect a *bit*) it must be *spirituality*, not *intellect* which is the guide to spiritual truth. I do not mean to set myself up as having attained this, but I think it is the *way* by which such truth has & will widen out and become clearer & clearer. When we come to know perfectly, we believe that spiritual truth & intellectual truth will never be found to have been at cross purposes.

It has been terribly hot here, & I hope you are not still

[3] Butler had recently told his family that he was the author of an anonymous pamphlet "The Evidence for the Resurrection of Jesus Christ as Given by the Four Evangelists, Critically Examined," published in 1865.

overworking. Papa & Mamma & I are hoping to go abroad in August, if a curate can be got by that time, & think of Chateau d'Oex or Les Plans.[4] We do not want to go too far away, or into uncivilized regions, on Mamma's account.

She is now at Kenilworth,[5] & seems enjoying the change. Harrie is here—looking very well—a bright letter from Etta—seems to like Bangor thoroughly, & she sounds very well there.

Goodbye, dear Sam, I am glad you are still practising.

Yr. very affectionate sister

May—[6]

13. *Butler to May*

Text: Garnett, pp. 202–204.

[15 Clifford's Inn]
Feb. 23, 1873.

Dear May,

Thank you for yours received a few days ago, whereby I learnt, and was glad to learn, your change of abode.[1] I always fancy that Mentone is the nicest of all those places except perhaps Bordighera and San Remo. I hope my mother has been able to get out and gain ground, and that with spring she may do so still more, but it is hard to imagine spring anywhere just now, for we are having a thoroughly heavy day's snow, with all its attendant dreariness, and for the last month the wind has always been North and North-East. I have been confined to my rooms this last three weeks, though not seri-

[4] Les Planches—like Chateau d'Oex a Swiss resort.

[5] At the Stone House, Kenilworth, Warwickshire, birthplace of Butler's grandfather, and at this time the home of Butler's cousins.

[6] Butler later wrote on this letter: "There had been an earlier letter from her, which I am sorry to say I cannot find. It was much worse than this."

Letter 13:

[1] Canon and Mrs. Butler and May spent most of the winter of 1872–1873 at Mentone in an effort to improve Mrs. Butler's health. She died there on April 9.

ously amiss. I was getting on to the top of a 'bus and the driver began to go on without warning, and I fell, fortunately not far, and on my feet, but not rightly on my feet, and have sprained myself—but I am nearly well now, and can walk half a mile or so. In health I never was better, in spite of confinement almost to an armchair for a fortnight, but not in any pain worth mentioning. It has thrown me out a good deal and I have done no painting, or music.

I read Traherne Moggridge's book [2] and liked it immensely. It is excellently written, and very interesting. I am very sorry to hear of his being so ill, pray remember me to him very kindly.

When do you think of returning? I presume not before the middle of April.—Since my last I have dined nowhere, seen no one, but Hoare [3] and Pauli and a few others, and heard nothing, having indeed been laid up almost the whole time; but I have read a good many books, a duty which I have too greatly neglected lately. I have not seen them at Taviton Street since Xmas, but shall hope now to call there very shortly; and what is worse, I have only once been to the Old Masters,[4] where I positively must go again before it closes. It is a lovely exhibition. I don't suppose you much care about politics, but I am getting deeply disgusted with the present condition of affairs, and Pauli and I have both resolved to vote for the Conservatives next time [5]—not, I fear, that they will be much better, but because nothing can be worse than these people now in power.

I wish I could tell you more that would be likely to interest you, but for the last three or four weeks I have been neither interested nor interesting—yes, I have been interested in a good deal that I have read; in one novel—the only one I have

[2] *Contributions to the Flora of Mentone, and to a Winter Flora of the Riviera* (1867). (See note 7 for Letter 10 [March 20, 1870].)

[3] Henry Hoare. (See note 1 for Letter 6.)

[4] The Royal Academy exhibit of old masters; it opened on January 4 and closed on March 8.

[5] General reaction against Gladstone's domestic reforms—in the ballot, the civil service, the army, and the courts—and his liberal attitude toward Irish Catholics led to his defeat in the election of 1874.

read—especially. It is called *Ready Money Mortiboy*,[6] and is very powerful and clever, but I don't think you would much like it. There are few good novels written now.

I trust you are well and cheerful yourself and that you have found friends who are a pleasure to you, and I need not say how sincerely I trust that my mother is going on comfortably. You need not be in the least uneasy about me. I am only a little lame, and another week or ten days will set me quite right.

Your affectionate brother,
S. Butler.

14. *May to Butler*

Text: British Museum MS.
[*The following letter from Butler's father contains a postscript by May.*]

Hotel d'Italie Mentone [France]
Alpes Maritimes, Mar. 2., 1873

Dear Sam

You will I know be sorry to hear that I can give but a sad account of your Mother. She has for some time suffered a great deal of pain & it is only kept under by Morphia injected under the skin, but the saddest sympton is her almost constant sickness.

Of course she takes little food & has become thin. She constantly mentions you. If I say with anxiety & distress I must also say with the deepest affection & love. May is an unspeakable comfort to us.

I am most anxious to be able to bring her home. And the doctors give me hope that this paroxysm may pass & that I may yet be able to do so. I trust they may be right. They say

[6] The first (1872) of the popular novels on which Walter Besant and James Rice collaborated. Butler had begun *The Way of All Flesh* at this time and was no doubt attracted by the way Besant and Rice twisted the prodigal-son-returned plot so that a most unrepentant son returns in order to victimize his miserly father.

there is no appearance of any immediate sinking but she is sadly weak.

I think she would like you to know that she finds prayer an inexpressible comfort & that her faith is able to support her in the suffering which she endures.

If she should rally I should move as soon as she was able to bear it. If otherwise, God's will be done. She has been a blessing & a comfort unspeakable to me for 42 years.[1]

Yr. affectionate father
T. Butler

I must add a line of my own to Papa's letter, dearest Sam. I am afraid it will make you very uneasy. We cannot help being so sometimes, for this sickness tells so very much upon her strength. Yet I quite hope & think it will pass away again. We had thought of sending for Harrie if it were likely that we should be here quite indefinitely, but the doctors give us every hope that this will not be the case, & if so, it is better for us all to be spared the excitement of a fresh home face, & for Mama to be kept from the feeling that she was so much worse as Harrie's coming out so late in the season would imply. I am quite well—& don't get knocked up—people are so wonderfully kind all round us. If Mama knew we were writing she would send you her warmest love. She says sometimes that she hopes you all know how much she thinks of you tho' she cannot write.

Yr. loving sister
May.

Letter 14:

[1] "'She has been the comfort and mainstay of my life for more than thirty years,' said Theobald as soon as all was over, 'but one could not wish it prolonged,' and he buried his face in his handkerchief to conceal his want of emotion" (*The Way of All Flesh*, chap. 83).

15. Butler to May

Text: Garnett, pp. 204–206.

15 Clifford's Inn,
Mar. 12, 1873.

Dear May,

I have to thank you for a little box of pretty flowers which arrived quite safely last night, and the flowers look as if they had been only gathered yesterday. Thank you very much for sending them. By your silence I gather that my mother is going on well, and I most heartily trust that I may be right in so conjecturing. No meals but a little light food every hour is really alarming to me, and I shall be very thankful to hear any better account. What is it that the doctors say is the matter with her? I never rightly understand; and do they hold out hopes that she will ere long return to her former state of health? I presume and conclude that they do by your saying that they take a bright view of the case, but so much and such long-continued sickness and pain is most distressing to hear of, and must I fear, be hardly less wearing to you than to herself. Pray let me have another line or two in a day or two, and give my mother all kind messages from myself.

I am very sorry to say that I am laid up again. Having been allowed to walk, I fear I overdid it, though I am not aware that I exceeded permission; the consequence is that I am compelled to keep perfectly quiet again, though I trust for no considerable period. My health is excellent. I sit in an armchair, with my leg up, and paint from my own head. I believe I am doing a far better one than any I have done yet, and shall send it in to the Academy.[1] I should have gone to Heatherley's on Monday, but it was plainly out of the question, for any position save a semi-recumbent one causes a return of swelling and tendency to inflamation; I suspect the trio Samsons [2] which I went to last week had as much to do with it

Letter 15:

[1] It was not accepted.

[2] The full three-part version of Handel's oratorio "Samson" was given by different companies on March 6 and 7.

as overwalking. Fortunately, as long as I keep quiet I am in no pain, and am well and interested in what I am doing. I am also reading *Middlemarch;* it is very clever, but that is a matter of course; nevertheless her characters are not lovable, and there is something hard about the book, which makes it grate upon one, though I do not exactly know what it is.[3]

I forget where the Hotel d'Italie is, but fancy that it is in the East Bay, not far from the Gran Bretagne.[4] Did I tell you that I had been one evening to the home of the two old Smiths, daughters of one of the authors of *Rejected Addresses?*[5] I met some distinguished literary people there. I think I must have done so. Other news I have none.

Your affectionate brother,
S. Butler.

16. *Butler to May*

Text: Garnett, pp. 207–209. *Extracts published:* Malcolm Muggeridge, *The Earnest Atheist* (Eyre and Spottiswoode, 1936), pp. 192–193.

15 Clifford's Inn, E. C.
Mar. 24, Monday afternoon. [1873]

My dear May,

My father's and your joint letter reached me this morning, and I am deeply grieved at the desponding tone of my father's half. In spite of the more cheerful tone of your portion of the letter, and of the report of the medical men, I cannot help being thoroughly anxious and alarmed. I rack my brains in vain to think of anything which I could do toward alleviating

[3] Butler states his opinion of *Middlemarch* more forcefully to Miss Savage: "I call it bad . . . a long-winded piece of studied brag, clever enough I dare say, but to me at any rate singularly unattractive" (letter of *ca.* March 18, 1873, *Butler-Savage Letters,* p. 40). Jones (*Memoir,* I, 184) suggests that Miss Savage had recommended the book to Butler.

[4] Butler is referring to hotels in Venice. They are on the East Bay.

[5] Butler must have seen Eliza, known as "Miss Horace Smith," and Rosalind, two daughters of Horatio (Horace) Smith (1779–1849), collaborator with James Smith (1775–1839) on *Rejected Addresses, or, the New Theatrum Poetarum* (1812), a parody of the Romantic poets.

pain, the account of which is most distressing to me. Alas! I can do nothing. I can understand your wishing to remain alone together as long as it is possible to do so, but I trust that you will not allow any immediate danger to arise without sending for me at once. I could not think of myself as going about my daily affairs and my mother lying perhaps at the point of death, without a sight of the one whom I am very sure that she loves not the least of her children. It would be intolerable to me to think of this, yet I know and deeply regret that my presence could not be without its embarrassments.[1] However, you must judge for yourselves, and I trust that the necessity may not arise. I am still a close prisoner, closer than ever; fortunately still well, and still painless, and not threatened with any serious complications, nevertheless a troublesome and unpleasant complication has arisen, which I cannot enter into more than to say that it is utterly unimportant except in so far as it keeps me a prisoner. But what is this in comparison with what you must yourselves be witnessing! I find nothing so depressing to myself as the sight of suffering in others; but how much more so when the sufferer is the one whom one would naturally most desire to save from suffering. You will say then why have written *Erewhon?* The mistake was in not keeping it more quiet, and then in thinking that the very great success which the book has met with would make my father and mother proud of my having written it. I suppose you know that *The Coming Race*—the book which *Erewhon* was allowed to have equalled, if not more, was by Lord Lytton? [2] I thought my father and mother

Letter 16:

[1] In the spring of 1873 Butler asked his parents' approval of his plan to acknowledge his authorship of *Erewhon* in the second edition. His father replied that he might do as he pleased but because he had written *Erewhon* could never visit Langar again. Butler's next interview was at Mentone, shortly after he wrote this letter, when his mother was dying. At his mother's funeral his father told him that the publication of *Erewhon* had killed her. (Correspondence in the British Museum.)

[2] Like *Erewhon, The Coming Race* was an anonymously published satire on scientific utopias. It appeared in 1871, and it soon became known that Bulwer-Lytton (Edward George Earle Lytton, first baron) had written it. *Erewhon* appeared in 1872 and was at first thought to be a sequel by Bulwer-Lytton; sales were brisk until Butler announced that he was the author.

would be proud of my having met with the approbation of the most intelligent classes of my countrymen, and that not in half measure, but in whole measure. I am sorry I was mistaken. But had I known that my mother's health was failing at the time, I would have kept it back. Whatever else I do, I will do my utmost to do without it reaching the ears of those whom it will pain; but I cannot hold my tongue.

Pray thank my father for his letter, and assure him that I will endeavour to cause no anxiety which I can avoid, either to him or to any of you. Give my very best love to my mother, and believe me

Your affectionate brother,
S. Butler.[3]

17. *Butler to May*

Text: Garnett, pp. 209–212.

15 Clifford's Inn, Fleet St.,
Aug. 5, 1873

Dear May,

I am afraid it is a long time since I wrote to you, and now I have to thank you for a pleasant letter from which I am truly glad to find that you are better and stronger; still I fear that you are far from being so strong and well as we could all wish you to be. I am glad you like the children,[1] and hope you are not too much fatigued with them. As you know, Charlie and Elsie are my two favourites, though I have no sort of quarrel with the other two. But it is now some time since I saw them.

By the way, can you find out for me the address of my father's brokers. It used, I think, to be 29 Threadneedle Street,[2] but I could not find it there the other day. I am

[3] Butler's mother died in April, 1873.

Letter 17:

[1] Tom and Etta's children.

[2] Henry Tudor & Son, a firm founded by Henry Tudor of Shrewsbury; their address was still 29 Threadneedle Street, London.

expecting a considerable sum of money,[3] and should wish to know their address. Hitherto I have always used Hoare's brokers, and shall continue to do so if Hoare wishes it, but should myself prefer to go to someone else if I could find someone on whom I could depend. I see they have had a meeting against moving Shrewsbury School.[4] Mr. Tudor wrote to me, and I answered that though I am a consenting party to the sale of one of the possible sites, I have never made any secret of my thinking that any change of site is inexpedient—as indeed I most decidedly do. I am glad to see that my father seems not unwilling to afford any facility for the retaining [of] the present site. I cannot see that there is sufficient ground for a change; but I expect that the opposition has come too late. I see they read a letter from me at the meeting, of which the above is the substance. I was at school with Tudor, and have seen him occasionally since.

I have been to Dieppe for a week since I wrote and painted a little picture of the cliffs. I should have stopped there longer but I had not a soul to speak to, and feeling really very well, I came back and am now working regularly at Heatherley's, not uncomfortably. Harrie wants me to come down to Ventnor.[5] I will go later on, but have only just come back from an outing.

There is nothing going on in town just now and everyone is gone or going away. For my own part, I like this time well enough. The extreme heat is over, and as soon as this is the case London becomes very pleasant. I am sorry to hear of

[3] Butler was expecting £8000, which he had recalled from New Zealand; on the advice of Henry Hoare, he was about to invest most of it in the ill-fated Canada Tanning Extract Company.

[4] Land in which Butler had a contingent interest, Whitehall, was considered as a possible new site for Shrewsbury School. John Tudor, who was at Shrewsbury School with Butler in 1854, organized a committee in opposition to any move (see his letter to the *Times*, August 25, 1873, p. 4e). This committee's proposal that the school be expanded in its present location was supported by Butler's father, who offered to sell the school his property contiguous to it (*Times*, August 27, 1873, p. 4f). It was finally decided to move the school to the suburbs, but not to the site in which the Butlers had interests.

[5] At this time Harrie maintained a home at Ventnor on the Isle of Wight.

Gretton's[6] mishap. An artist friend of mine has been nearly killed in the Wigan accident[7] and, I fear, is much hurt. With kind love to Etta and the children, believe me your affectionate brother,

S. Butler.

18. *Butler to May*

Text: Chapin Library MS.
[*Written on black-bordered paper*[1]]

15, Clifford's Inn E. C.
Nov. 12. 1873.

My dear May

I am told there is a report that I have written a book in which I have introduced my father.[2] I fear lest this report should reach you and am anxious to contradict it. I have written no book in which any single character is drawn from life —or to my knowledge hinted at—and shall never do so. All that I have written now bears my name,[3] and it is not my intention to write again anonymously. If you hear of any book's being assigned to me which does not bear my name please to contradict the report. I haven't the faintest concep-

[6] Frederick Edward Gretton (1803–1890), a friend of Butler's father, at this time rector of Oddington, Gloucestershire.

[7] The night express to Scotland was derailed at Wigan on August 2, 1873. Butler's friend, John Fraser (1839–1898), an artist known for his water landscapes of Scotland, suffered a fractured collarbone and bruises about the head (*Times*, August 4, 1873, p. 12a).

Letter 18:

[1] Because of the death of his mother.

[2] Butler was perhaps incautiously open about his work on *The Way of All Flesh* in his correspondence with his friends. See, for example, his letter to Frederick Gard Fleay in August, 1873 (Hoppé, pp. 172–173). He was, however, anxious to keep the novel secret from his family—and partly for that reason it was never published during his lifetime.

[3] Butler's anonymous pamphlet "The Evidence for the Resurrection" was not reissued and thus did not bear his name, though much of it was used in *The Fair Haven*, the second edition of which was signed. He did not publish anonymously again.

tion what the present report can allude to—but contradict it unreservedly.

Of course I expect to be vilified for what I have written and shall probably write: but I write on public grounds, for the public—introducing public and common types of character, and looking solely to the verdict of the public, who I imagine would severely blame me for personalities even if I were inclined to indulge in them, which I certainly am not. With all good wishes both to Harrie & yourself. Believe me

Your affectionate brother
S— Butler.

19. *Butler to May*

Text: Chapin Library MS.

[En route to Montreal [1]]
Sat. June 20. (?) [2] [1874]

Dear May

We are now well in the St. Lawrence only about 300 miles from Quebec—and expect to be there by this time tomorrow. I hope to send this off by the pilot boat. We have had a delightful passage—no rough weather, no fog, pleasant fellow passengers and no misadventures of any kind. I was not sea sick for a moment, and in fact have enjoyed the voyage extremely. It has already done me infinite good, far more than a trip to Switzerland or Italy wd have done in the same time, and I look forward to returning as well as ever I was in my life or better, for I have still six clear weeks of holiday or what is just as good, and am already in very good condition. We saw some fine ice bergs: they are quite equal to their reputation for beauty: we are now passing close to the coast—

Letter 19:

[1] Butler was on the first of three unsuccessful trips to Canada as representative of the English stockholders in the Canada Tanning Extract Company. The extract tanned leather cheaply, but to such a nauseous color that it could not be sold.

[2] Butler's question mark. The date is correct.

a lovely cloudless day and I grudge every minute that I am not on deck. Every bit of land that could be seen we saw as there was no fog—the South Coast of New Foundland is very bleak: mountains ranging up to I shd think 1800 or 2000 feet, but with large fields of snow, and sometimes gullies with snow filling them not more than 200 or 300 ft. above the sea. I hope that Harrie is quite well by this time.

Yr. affte. brother
S. Butler—

Sunday. No letter went off with the pilot boat, so I post this at Quebec which we reach in 3 or 4 hours: all well.

20. *Butler to May*

Text: Chapin Library MS.

Frid. Augt. 13, 1875
In the St. Lawrence—[1]
address: "Cana. Tang. Ext. Co. Ld, Montreal"—

Dear May

I did not get yours of the 4th till some time after we had started, people not knowing my name, and I not expecting a letter. The screw shakes the ship so that I can hardly write but I send a few lines which I can drop at Father Point where we take in the pilot.

We have made an unprecendently [*sic*] quick passage, but the icebergs in the straits were many and dangerous; we passed near some very large ones. Lord Houghton [2] and other notables are on board and have shewn me much civility—Lord Houghton giving me a letter of introduction to Lord Dufferin [3] which I may or may not present. On the whole it

Letter 20:

[1] Butler was on his second trip to Canada.

[2] Butler does not tell May—as he does Miss Savage—that he won 26*s*. from Lord Houghton (Richard Monckton Milnes [1809–1885]) at whist.

[3] Frederick Temple Hamilton-Temple-Blackwood, first Marquis of Dufferin and Ava (1826–1902), at this time Governor-General of Canada.

has been an agreable[4] passage—but I shall be glad to be getting on in my absence—

Please excuse more, the saloon is full of people and the screw makes writing a slow process. With all kind love believe me

Your affectionate brother

S. Butler—

21. *Butler to May*

Text: Chapin Library MS.

Hotel del Angelo, Faido—June 2, 1876.
Address: Poste Restante
Como, Italy.

Dear May

I have not heard from Langar since a few days before I left home and think it not impossible that a letter to me may have miscarried, so write this line to say that I am well, or at any rate a good deal better than when I left—but I believe I had gone to the extreme length of my tether before I did leave. I am getting a lot of material together which will I think be useful to me, but have not yet hit upon a *system* which quite satisfies me—tho' going round it in gradually narrowing circles—at least I hope so. However in one shape or another I believe I have all that is necessary for 5 pictures and I need not say hope to get enough for many more before I return. I think a fairly large extremely careful outline—as a companion to it a smaller study in oil without any slavish adherence to form but aiming chiefly at effect and colour. These two things shd be enough. This at least is the system towards which I seem to be gravitating.

I have had no events and made no acquaintances—I may mention one incident. The church porch at Prato[1] pleased me

[4] Miss Savage chided Butler about his spelling of "agreeable": "[It] is spelt with two e's. I mention this because you never will put more than one" (November 10, 1873, *Butler-Savage Letters*, p. 75).

Letter 21:

[1] For Butler's sketches and description of this church and the town of Prato, Switzerland, see *Alps and Sanctuaries*, pp. 25, 28, 30.

exceedingly and I had made a study of it—doubting how far it was the correct thing to eat my lunch in the porch I had gone round to the back of the church to eat my lunch in a field where a poor woman was weeding corn: we talked for some time and I, meaning to be amiable shewed her my study of the porch—she examined it for some little time and then extending her hands in an imploring manner she exclaimed "Signore mio, son pratica far la contadina, ma per la geographia non son capace." [2]

Hoping that you are all well I am

Yr. affte. brother
S. Butler.

I shall leave here the day after tomorrow—I think.

Perhaps better in each letter say where you addressed to—so that if I have not had it I may write. I wrote from here a week ago—and I think from Wassen also.

S. B.

22. *Butler to May*

Text: British Museum MS. *Extracts published: Memoir,* I, 274–275.

15. Clifford's Inn
Fleet Street E. C.
Mar. 27. 1878

Dear May

Thank you for your's of the eighteenth in answer to which I have very little of importance, but have an evening unoccupied which as I have for some time been painting at night, does not too often happen. I believe the most interesting piece of intelligence I can send is that I saw an open cowslip in a boy's hand—root, flower and all, on Sunday last. I had my self seen some buds very nearly open, and last Sunday fortnight found some buds just beginning to show. I am not

[2] "Dear sir, I am a good peasant woman, but I'm no good at geography." Butler spells the Italian word *geografia* as if it were English. He repeats the story to Miss Savage in his letter of June 4 (*Butler-Savage Letters,* p. 130).

however fortunate enough to find a head actually in flower. The same afternoon however it came on to snow—the same squall that *must* have wrecked the Eurydice [1]—and in an hour the ground was fairly white: since then the weather has been bitter.

I send in four things to the Academy [2]—two portraits, an oil landscape, and a watercolour landscape—but I am not very sanguine; indeed, I am distinctly depressed about my work at present, and wonder whether I ever *shall* paint; on the other hand, I have had these depressions very often, and know that they come more from being able to see what I could not see before than anything else. . . .

I dined out the other day and took in a very pretty young lady to dinner, and sat opposite a very nice, quiet gentlemanly man to whom I vented now and again Conservative opinions which I imagined were well received. When the others were gone, I asked my hostess who it was I had taken in to dinner, and was told it was Miss Cobden (Cobden's daughter). I then asked who had sat opposite me. "Mr. Chamberlain, M.P. for Birmingham," was the reply.[3] Really people should not introduce one in a perfectly inaudible voice.

I am sorry you should think my sending those reviews to my father was "forcing differences upon him." [4] That was not my intention, but rather to show him that disinterested third parties considered me as in more substantial agreement [with him] than he was perhaps aware of. And this I believe to be true; indeed I am more and more sure of it every year.

Letter 22:

[1] On the afternoon of March 24, 1878, 300 lives were lost when an extraordinarily violent and sudden squall captized the naval training ship *Eurydice* off Ventnor. Snow fell heavily for a short time after the squall passed.

[2] They were not accepted.

[3] The hostess was Mary Beale, *née* Thompson, wife of William Phipson Beale (1839–1922), a barrister; she was a close friend of Butler and Jones. Richard Cobden (1804–1865)—he had five daughters—and Joseph Chamberlain (1836–1914) represented two generations of Liberal politics, which Butler abhorred.

[4] Butler sent his father two reviews of *Life and Habit*, which was published in December, 1877: one from *Truth* (January 31, 1878, p. 155), and one from the *Standard* (February 28, 1878, p. 2). The reviews are short and only cautiously approve the book, but they do state its thesis that evolution is controlled by design, and not, as Darwin believed, by chance.

However, I sincerely hope this bitter weather is doing no harm either to him or you.

Yr. affte. brother
S. Butler.

23. *Butler to May*

Text: Chapin Library MS.

Hotel del Angelo, Faido—
Canton Tessin, Switzerland
Mond. July 22, 1878

Dear May

Thank you for yours of the 17th from which I was glad to gather that you were enjoying yourself. I am doing the same, and am rapidly getting set up again [1]—or—to speak more accurately—am getting set up again steadily, and in such a way as makes me perfectly easy that there is nothing really wrong with me.

So you are reading the Seven Lamps.[2] It is so long since I did so that I have quite forgotten them, but I remember being very enthusiastic about them when I was at Cambridge—and I have no doubt ⟨that⟩ there is a great deal that is very true in them. I will look at them again when I get home, and see whether I still like them. The general impression however on my mind concerning Ruskin is one of decided dislike. I am myself occupied with Lord Beaconsfield's novels. Admiring him very heartily I wanted to read his younger work with considerable care, and have taken with me the worst as well as the best that he has done. I have just finished The Young

Letter 23:

[1] Late in 1877 Butler abandoned his attempt to make painting his career, though he remained a devoted amateur. At that time he returned to the writing of *The Way of All Flesh,* but by July 8, 1878, he was too tired and too dissatisfied with what he had written to go on; depressed, he left for a holiday on the Continent (*Butler-Savage Letters,* pp. 158, 188).

[2] Ruskin's *Seven Lamps of Architecture* was published in 1849, seven years before Butler went up to St. John's.

Duke,[3] and must own to having found it rather laborious reading in spite of many brilliant sayings wh: it contains, but as we all well know ⟨epigrammatic⟩ (I have scratched out this word because I don't know whether epigrammatic shd or shd not have two m's) epigrams and smart sayings are a delusion and a snare unless used sparingly—the greater part of a book, like the greater part of a life, or a building, shd be plain straightforward, and business like. No one I am sure knows this now better than Lord Beaconsfield, but one sees he had to learn it by experience, and this is pleasant and enhances the pleasure & interest of Lothair which is certainly a most delightful book.

Yesterday afternoon I went to look at the Woodsias of wh: I had found some magnificent specimens. Imagine my disgust at finding them—or most of them—*quite dead*—withered by the intense heat of the last week. I had thought they were growing in a place ⟨in⟩ which sensible Woodsias wd not have chosen, but they were so magnificently grown that I concluded they knew their own business.

I have found a subject for my "magnum opus" of this summer. It is the interior of a church at Giornico 6 miles off [4] —and I think it will come well, but it will take me some time to do. It is a very early and remarkable building now disused or nearly so.

The pigeons here come into my room while I am writing, and I have to keep chasing them out. Of course *I* like them, but the housemaid doesn't.

Yr. affte. brother
S. Butler—

[3] Disraeli published *The Young Duke*, a political novel, in 1831 when he was 27. *Lothair*, written after his first ministry, appeared 39 years later.

[4] Giornico is south of Faido on the Ticino river. The projected "magnum opus," Butler's sketch of the Romanesque church of San Niccolo da Mira, is on pp. 54–55 of *Alps and Sanctuaries*.

24. Butler to May

Text: Garnett, pp. 212–213.

15 Clifford's Inn, E. C.,
Oct. 21, 1878.

Dear May,

Thank you for yours of the 15th. What a journey you must have had. I was much pleased to hear of Maggie Goodwin's engagement, as I have the greatest respect for comic talent, and if young Mr. Brown has an engagement in London I will make a point of going to hear him.

I am decidedly better, and have enjoyed a short outing to the Isle of Wight. Harrie had often asked me, and as I had not seen her for over two years, I determined to run down. She gave me a hearty welcome, made me exceedingly comfortable, and I enjoyed my visit very much; but I only stayed one day as I am anxious to send in two things for the Dudley,[1] on the 4th prox. I saw Carisbrooke Castle, which I had never seen, and which is very good. Also, I saw Chichester on my return, which was quite a surprise—it is so fine: the Norman nave is magnificent. I hear C—— G——[2] is going to live there, but did not succeed in seeing the house she is to occupy, which Harrie rather wished me to do. . . . Very sorry to hear of Mr. W. Lloyd's [3] return of illness. I hope you will use your influence with my father to prevent his doing more preaching than is good for him. Three Sundays running, or nearly so (as by your last letter), would seem as though he were more in demand than I could wish. Pray give him my love and believe me

Your affectionate brother,
S. Butler.

Letter 24:

[1] The Twelfth Annual Exhibition of Cabinet Pictures in Oil opened at the Dudley Gallery on November 23, 1878—without a contribution from Butler.

[2] Carrie Glover (Frances Caroline Glover, *née* Bridges), Harrie's sister-in-law. (See note 4 for Letter 1.) Her house, "The Treasury," was in the cloisters of Chichester Cathedral.

[3] William Valentine Lloyd (1825–1896), vicar of Marton, Shropshire, in 1857–1858, but at this time chaplain in the Royal Navy.

25. Butler to May

Text: Chapin Library MS.
[*Written on black-bordered paper*[1]]

15, Clifford's Inn
E. C.
Jany. 18, 1879

Dear May

Thank you for your's of the sixteenth. I hope that you are really none of you much the worse for this weather—but *I* shall I am sure be a great deal better when it ⟨was⟩ is over. Yesterday *black fog—dense midnight* for more than an hour about noon, and candles necessary all day. Today a heavy wet slushy snow storm from 8 o'clock till now (4.30) and looks like going to take up and freeze again. Have you yet seen an aconite? or a snowdrop? I have not even seen a sign of either above ground, nothing but a few crocus tops.

By the way I am sorry I forgot to thank you for the House that Jack Built. I had seen it, as also John Gilpin,[2] which is no less amusing—quite as good I think but not better. I am beginning to think that that kind of art is the only kind worth living for, except portraiture and landscape, and the dreams of such men as Bellini, Botticelli, & Mantegna. However thank you very much for sending it. I was painting *out of doors* yesterday for more than [an] hour, and very glad I was to have been out when I returned and found the fog in full possession of London. Today I have been at the Museum. I was compelled sorely against my will to begin looking through Buffon—44 quarto volumes.[3] I had never heard anything of

Letter 25:

[1] "I fancy I must have found some old mourning paper, and used it having none other handy"—Butler's note on his letter to Miss Savage dated February 3, 1879 (*Butler-Savage Letters*, p. 197).

[2] Shilling children's books which appeared in 1878. "John Gilpin" is Cowper's poem, reprinted with illustrations by Randolph Caldecott.

[3] There are 44 quarto volumes in the Museum's set of *Histoire naturelle, général et particulière, avec la description du cabinet du roi* (Paris, 1749–1804) by Buffon and his collaborators. Butler was trying to demonstrate that Darwin's

him except that he was a beautiful writer, but very superficial and inaccurate. Every one in fact thinks it right to throw a stone at him: however in the course of my work it became necessary that I shd go through a good deal that he has done, and I can hardly express the surprise and pleasure which I have derived from doing so, tho' I am not yet a quarter through him. I shall certainly, as the Americans say "run him." He is so broad, simple, and full of common sense that I feel when reading him almost as tho' I were listening to an air of Handel.

By the way Harrie writes me she is going to read Professor Mivart's Lessons from Nature—the Professor Mivart she adds, whom *I* met. Harrie is taking advantage here of the privilege of her sex. I only said I was asked to meet to [*sic*] Prof. Mivart [4]—and so I was—but Prof. Mivart never came—so I did not meet him.

What a scandalous estimate about the schools! *I am so glad.* I regard the whole thing as a dirty piece of intrigue, and like all other really charitable people take pleasure in any disfavour which may attach to those who differ from me. I have not yet seen them at Chester Terrace.[5] I hope my father still adheres to his idea of going abroad in the spring; I cd have wished he had done so earlier.

With all best wishes to you both I am Yr affte brother

S. Butler—

---

theory of evolution not only was derived from older theorists but was also in many respects not as valid. (See Butler's *Evolution, Old and New,* chaps. 6, 8–9, and 10–11.)

[4] St. George Jackson Mivart (1827–1900), a zoölogist interested in evolution, who, in opposition to Darwin, maintained that evolution proceeded according to teleological principles. *Lessons from Nature as Manifested in Mind and Matter* (1876) is a collection of his essays. Butler discusses Mivart's position in *Life and Habit,* chap. 14.

[5] Philip Worsley had moved from Taviton Street to 26 Chester Terrace.

26. *Butler to May*

Text: Chapin Library MS.
[*Written on black-bordered paper*]

15. Clifford's Inn
E. C.
Feb. 11, 1879

Dear May,

Thank you for your last—of course if my father does not want to go abroad I have not another word to say, except that I am rather sorry to hear it, though I shd be even more sorry if his going were to lead to your doing so when you think you ought not.

Well—at last spring seems to have set in and I never was more glad to welcome it—I see a few snowdrops being sold about the streets for the first time today, and on Sunday saw a few nearly out in a cottage garden, but I also saw some great drifts of snow still unmelted on the lee side of hedges some of them still three or four feet deep.

Very sorry to hear of May's [1] eyes—but we most of us had bad eyes about her age—mine I remember were very bad for a couple of years or more than that but I got over it. I found nothing so good for them as bathing them with *very* weak brandy and water.

The thaw gave me a heavy cold but I am shaking it off. On the whole I have had less cold than usual this winter in spite of its severity and am not much amiss.

What a horrible disaster at the Cape.[2] I see a son of my old friend Mr. Anstey [3] (whom I have not seen for years) is among the missing or killed. It is the greatest misfortune we have had since the Indian Mutiny and will I fear do us a great deal of indirect mischief—still one is thankful that it is not in Afghanistan where those odious liberals wd have been able to

Letter 26:

[1] "Maysie," one of Tom and Etta's daughters, twelve years old at this time.

[2] News of a Zulu massacre of Lord Chelmsford's camp at Isandhlwana, Zululand, reached London on February 11, 1879.

[3] Edgar Oliphant Anstey, 24th Regiment, 2nd Warwickshire, was killed in the massacre.

make more capital out of it.[4] I wish there were no black people: I feel towards them much as Montesquieu did who wrote "these people are all over black, and have such flat noses that they are scarcely to be pitied" [5]—A very shocking sentiment, but I have more sympathy with it than I quite approve of myself for having.

The Museum is open again,[6] and I have been there all day; my new book is nearly done,[7] and I believe is a very good one, but the Darwins will be very angry with it as I stand up for Dr. Erasmus Darwin's view of evolution as more right than that of his grandson—but the book which I have been much delighted with is Paley's Natural Theology [8]—which I have used largely and wd have used much more if space permitted. If you do not know it you shd read it at once. In Life and Habit I supported the "purposive" view of organisms, that is to say insisted on the evidence for design which they exhibited, but have done so much more strongly in this present book.[9]

With all best wishes to you both I am

Yr. affte. brother
S. Butler—

[4] British troops marched into Afghanistan in the autumn of 1878 to strengthen Disraeli's program for greater British influence in Central Asia. Never wholeheartedly supported even by Disraeli's own Cabinet, this action was loudly denounced by the Liberals, who made it an issue in the spring, 1880, elections in which they were returned to power.

[5] Montesquieu is mocking the attitude he expresses ("De l'esprit des lois," Book XV, chap. 5), though he was often taken seriously. In an entry in his Notebooks in September, 1883, Butler shows that at least at that time he was aware of Montesquieu's irony (MS Notebooks, I, 214).

[6] The British Museum had been closed for alterations. At about this time Butler began to work at the Museum regularly, every Monday, Wednesday, and Friday from ten to one (*Butler-Savage Letters*, p. 150).

[7] *Evolution, Old and New*, which appeared May 1, 1879.

[8] In chaps. 2 and 5 Butler quotes extensively from William Paley's *Natural Theology* (1802). Of Paley (1743–1805), he says: "I know few writers whom I would willingly quote more largely, or from whom I find it harder to leave off quoting when I have once begun" (pp. 13–14).

[9] The "purposive view of organisms" is put forth implicitly in *Life and Habit*, but on p. 1 of *Evolution, Old and New* Butler proposes the question directly: "Can we not see signs in the structure of animals and plants, of something which carries with it the idea of contrivance so strongly that it is impossible for us to think of the structure, without at the same time thinking of contrivance, or design, in connection with it?"

27. Butler to May

Text: Chapin Library MS. *Extracts Published: Memoir,* I, 294–295.

Frid. Mar. 14, 1879
15. Clifford's Inn
E. C.

Dear May

Thank you for your's of Mar. 1, which I wd have answered sooner if I were not in the very thick of putting my new book through the press. It will be out in about three weeks or even less, now, I hope, and should do me good. I am less fagged with it too than I generally am when I come to the end of a book—though this is nearly 400 pp. so near as I can measure it. In fact I am very well in spite of the last two or three days bitter East Wind.

I went the other night to see the British Museum lit with the electric light [1]—the superintendent of the reading room having offered me a ticket; it looked very well; and I also went last night to the Albert Hall to hear the Dettigen Te Deum [2]—(which is magnificent—) and there found more electric light, but not so good as at the British Museum. The chorus "To thee Cherubin and Seraphin continually do cry" was wonderful. I have counted the "continually's" and find the word repeated exactly 50 times. If you will ⟨try and⟩ say the word "continually" ten times on each of your five fingers you will find it give[s] you an idea of the fine effect produced.[3] I heard it some years ago, and for some reason or other

Letter 27:

[1] Several trials of electric light in the Reading Room were held throughout the month of February, 1879. They were deemed successful, and permanent electric lighting was installed.

[2] Handel's *Dettigen Te Deum* was given on March 13 in honor of the marriage of the Duke of Connaught to Princess Louise of Prussia.

[3] Butler was so fond of this effect that he made use of it in *Narcissus,* a comic cantata which he and Jones wrote. In the lyric,

> How blest the prudent man, the maiden pure,
> Whose income is both ample and secure,
> Arising from consolidated Three
> Per Cent Annuities, paid quarterly,

Jones says that they "remembered Handel's treatment of 'continually,' and thought we could not do better than imitate it for our words 'paid quarterly' " (*Memoir,* I, 295).

liked it less than most of Handel's works, but last night quite changed me. Did I tell you that some time ago I went to Elijah,[4] determined to like it, and with another man [5] too—we having both resolved to keep our minds open, and to look out for the good & not the bad. Well—of course we saw *some* good, but on the whole we hated it. I never mean to go and hear it again if I can help doing so. I don't know anything about Sydney Dobell [6]—but will look him up on your recommendation. As a general rule I distrust "energetic joyous temperaments," and as you know I am no lover of poetry, however, I will have a look at him.

I hope my father is well, with all best wishes to him and to yourself. Believe me

Yr. affte. brother
S. Butler—

28. *May to Butler*

Text: British Museum MS.

Nottingham.
July 31. 1879

My dearest Sam

I have got this far on my travels you see, & go on to the Garrisons tomorrow. I enjoyed my visit at Fulham [1] very much, and managed to see both the Academy and the Grosvenor. There were not a *great many* pictures which I cared for in either, but some very much, & as a whole I liked it better than the last time I saw the Academy about 3 years ago. I liked 'Evangeline'—& 'Esther',[2] & one—*only* one—of Leighton's 'Amarilla' [3]—the colouring was so soft and rich,

[4] Mendelssohn's *Elijah* reminded Butler of Handel's *Jephtha*, but he disliked everything in the piece that did *not* remind him of Handel (MS Notebooks, II, 96).

[5] The other man was Jones (*Memoir*, I, 294).

[6] Sydney Dobell (1824–1874), a member of the Spasmodic School of poets.

Letter 28:

[1] A suburb of London.

[2] A painting by Edwin Long (1829–1891) favorably received by the reviewers of the Royal Academy Exhibition.

[3] There were seven other paintings by Frederick Leighton on display at the Academy.

& Millais' Gladstone—and—don't be horrified—Burne Jones's Annunciation [4]—at least the Virgin's figure—I did not care about the Angel—

Also, today I have been seeing the Museum of Art here, and was surprised to find that I really *did* like Frank Miles's 'Salmon Leap' [5]—It is such a daring picture—but surely it *is* clever, though I dislike him so much that one doesn't want to think so!

It has been a pouring wet morning, and it is only now that the distance is clear enough for one to look over the old country [6] from this high ground, & think how very pretty it is after all!—[7]

29. *Butler to May*

Text: Chapin Library MS.

Mesocco.
Grisons, Suisse
Thursd. Augt. 21. 1879

Dear May—

Thank you for yours of the 14th from Whatton,[1] Harrie will have already sent you my congratulations but pray accept them again. I suppose you and my father will by this time be back at Wilderhope and I dare say you will neither of you be sorry; I do not intend returning before the 21st. having deferred it a fortnight or three weeks. I stay here till the 3d. or 4th. prox. and am then joined by my friend Jones,

[4] In the Grosvenor Gallery Exhibition.

[5] Frank (George Francis) Miles (1852–1891) was the son of the rector of Bingham, Nottinghamshire. Canon Butler had been Rural Dean of Bingham. Some of Miles's paintings were part of the permanent collection of the Castle Museum and Art Gallery, Nottingham.

[6] May and her father had left Nottinghamshire after his retirement from Langar in 1876 and were at this time living in Wilderhope House, Shrewsbury.

[7] The rest of this letter has not been preserved.

Letter 29:

[1] May had been staying with the Thomas Dickinson Halls. (See note 3 for Letter 4.)

and also by a bride groom and bride [2] of all people ⟨and⟩ in the world; the husband wrote to me on the eve of his marriage *begging* to be let to come and I was nothing loth as I have known both husband & wife since they were boys & girls, a matter of ten years now, intimately, having worked long with them at Heatherley's. The husband is one of our most promising young painters and has a very good picture on the line.[3] I shall be very glad to show him my work here, and shall, I doubt not, profit by his coming. I like this place better and better. In the church I have found some very fine old frescoes of the 15th Century—the upper subjects sacred, the lower secular, & with no religious motive except their beauty.[4] I have made a drawing of one, and must do some others. The one I have taken is a young man *crowned with white roses,* going out hawking with his hawk on his fore finger and his dog following beside the horse. On a pil[l]ion behind him sits his bride and behind both rides an esquire who holds a flower in his hand,[5] all done with the most delightful freshness and naiveté. I hear there are more frescoes by the same man a little lower down the valley & must go and see them. The priest and the monk here are both very good to me: the first is a good fellow, the second a wretch judging by his appearance, but he is exceedingly civil.

Glad to hear good accounts of Anne.[6] I must call on Mrs. Wade on my return; or rather call to enquire how she is. No more reviews since the Athenaeum,[7] but an allusion in the Pall Mall Gazette to "unconscious humour" in inverted commas 'as

[2] Jones identifies the bridegroom (*Memoir,* I, 307) as Henry Marriott Paget (1856–1936). His bride was the daughter of Dr. William Farr.

[3] Paget's picture at the Royal Academy exhibition of 1879 was "Enid and Geraint."

[4] Butler describes this church, St. Cristoforo, at great length in *Alps and Sanctuaries* (pp. 183–195).

[5] Butler's description here telescopes two frescoes into one: April (the "esquire who holds a flower in his hand") and May (the young man going hawking with his bride behind). In *Alps and Sanctuaries,* however, he treats them as two of twelve separate scenes representing the months of the year.

[6] Anne Wade, nurse to the Butler family at Wilderhope.

[7] The reviewer in the *Athenaeum* (July 26, 1879, pp. 115–117) praised *Evolution, Old and New,* though he regretted the dull earnestness of the book in contrast to the lively humor of *Erewhon.*

tho' every one wd know where the words were taken from: such things show that the book is being read and talked about. I shall have a small one out at the beginning of the winter [8] and then no more for twelvemonths. I am painting a lovely charnel house. Also you know the aesthetic school have run sunflowers lately: [9] for the last few years they have been all the rage, and I have been trying to think of something to cut them out. In the monk's garden I have found I think a combination that will do. It consists of chickory, French marigolds and seed onions. I am persuaded that as fine a melancholy may be seen among these as any other vegetables ⟨and⟩ in the world; no one hitherto has *felt* the poetry of seed onions.

With all best wishes to you both I am Yr. affte. brother

S— Butler—

30. *May to Butler*

Text: British Museum MS.

Wilderhope.
March. 12. 1880.

Dearest Sam

We have just heard from the Whitehall [1] of Aunt Lloyd's death. She had another stroke in the night & passed away in her sleep. The day before yesterday we met her at Preston Montford,[2] quite bright. She had driven over in an open carriage.

[8] Butler had begun to think about *Unconscious Memory* at this time, but he found it necessary to read extensively in evolutionary theory and was not able to publish it until the beginning of the following winter, November, 1880.

[9] The sunflowers that William Morris painted in the Oxford Debating Room in 1857 became a symbol of the Aesthetes. Oscar Wilde, lecturing in New York on January 9, 1882, said: "Let me tell you that the reason we love the lily and the sunflower, in spite of what Mr. Gilbert [in *Patience*] may tell you, is not for any vegetable fashion at all. It is because these two lovely flowers are in England the two most perfect models of design . . . , the gaudy leonine beauty of the one and the precious loveliness of the other."

Letter 30:

[1] A sixteenth-century Tudor mansion, the home of "Aunt Lloyd," Harriet Lloyd, near Shrewsbury. Under the terms of his grandfather's will it was eventually to revert to Butler.

[2] The home of Harriet Lloyd's son in Bicton, Shropshire. Her grandson was vicar of Holy Trinity Church there.

The shock is a sudden one to Papa, but he is well and bright, & takes it very quietly and simply—they will all feel a terrible blow at the Whitehall

Your very affectionate sister
May.

31. *Butler to May*

Text: Chapin Library MS.
[*Written on black-bordered paper*[1]]

15. Clifford's Inn E. C.
May 3, 1880—

Dear May

Thank you for your last from which I was glad to hear good accounts of you both & that my father had enjoyed his trip in Wales; I am afraid he must have found it cold, for I have been hindered from doing any outdoor work these three weeks by the East Winds. I hope however that the weather is now going to take up. I am rather overdone, & pumping for breath more than I like—a sure sign that I am fatigued, but the Museum is closed this week & [I] shall take advantage of it to do as little as I can. I hear very bad accounts of the Academy & am pained at finding many of my friends turned out—men to whom the being rejected is a matter of serious importance—I am told nearly 8000 pictures were sent in & not more than 1000 hung, excluding of course sculpture. It is really very sad—

I have finished my translation of Von Hartmann on Instinct.[2] It is odious, but I am very glad to have done it & can now read German tolerably easily.[3] You mention cuckoos in

Letter 31:

[1] Because of the death of Harriet Lloyd.

[2] This translation constitutes chaps. 7–9 of *Unconscious Memory.*

[3] In 1874 Butler read *Wilhelm Meister* in translation, disliked it, and told Miss Savage that he was glad he had never taken the trouble to learn German (*Butler-Savage Letters*, p. 98). Early in 1880, however, Butler taught himself German in order to attack Darwin's use of German sources.

your letter: in the course of what I am doing I have had occasion to investigate a fact about about [*sic*] them, & was introduced by Mr. Garnett [4] to the gentleman who attends to birds in the British Museum and who I understand is the best authority we have on ornithological subjects.[5] He assures me that he entertins no doubt that the cuckoo actually does imitate the eggs of the birds in whose nest she lays, & that so closely, that they are indistinguishable from the genuine eggs except by being a trifle larger, tho' much smaller than the cuckoo ought to lay according to her size. Is not this forgery with a vengeance? And yet there is no bird of whom we are fonder. His father's gardener told him there was a cuckoo's egg in a certain water wagtail's nest. He examined the eggs carefully, and refused to believe the fact—but sure enough a few days later a cuckoo was hatched, & a similar case was reported to him in respect of a hedge sparrow whose eggs differ widely from the water wagtail's. I also find that the cuckoo invariably lays her eggs on the ground, & *carries* them to the nest she has chosen.

I will write to Miss Brooke, & am sorry I have not done so sooner—glad to hear that Mr. Bradshaw [6] has got rid of How [7] without loss of income. I think before so many years are over we shall have things cheaper now that the importation of meat from Australia has proved a success [8]—unless Mr. Gladstone gets us into some horrid mess, as, I for my part think only too likely. I feel as though nothing short of some serious national disaster could awaken the minds of most people to the dangers we run at the hands of the so called liberal party. The only two of the ministers whom I have ever met are Mr.

[4] Richard Garnett (1835–1906), at this time Assistant Keeper of Books and Superintendent of the Reading Room.

[5] Richard Bowdler Sharpe (1847–1900), curator of the Museum's bird collection. Butler refers to his observations in *Unconscious Memory* (pp. 50–54, 188, 214–215). Sharpe later made the same points himself in *A Hand-Book to the Birds of Great Britain* (1896–1897), II, 25–30.

[6] John Bradshaw (1812–1880), vicar of Granby, Bottesford, Nottinghamshire, a great favorite of the Butler children (MS Notebooks, V, 48).

[7] Thomas Maynard How, a solicitor in Shrewsbury.

[8] The first mechanically refrigerated cargo of meat from Australia arrived in London on February 3, 1880.

Chamberlain[9] & Mr. Mundella:[10] the first I liked, but shd not have liked if I had known who he was, the second, whom I have met more than once, I did not like at all, and shd have no confidence in his judgement. I am afraid it will not be long before we have cause to regret what has been done at these elections.[11] As for the doctrinaires & men of science now most prominent,[12] the more profoundly do I distrust them, with very few exceptions—finding them wherever I am able to test them to the full as given to jobbery & disregard of their own first principles as ever were the Roman priesthood in less tolerant times, and with much less excuse.

I am sorry to hear of John Bather's son's[13] having broken a blood vessel—I have never seen him—is he the eldest son? He may do worse than emigrate still, if he goes to a warm climate. Sorry also to hear of Dr. Burd's[14] accident.

Yr. affte. brother
S— Butler—

32. *Butler to May*

Text: Chapin Library MS.
[*Written on black-bordered paper*]

15. Clifford's Inn E. C.
June 10, 1880.

Dear May—

Thank you for sending me Elsie's photograph—it is a nice good face, and I am glad to have seen it. If you have any

[9] For Butler's account of his meeting with Joseph Chamberlain, at this time president of the Board of Trade, see Letter 22.

[10] Anthony Mundella (1825–1897), Privy Councillor.

[11] Gladstone was returned to power in the spring of 1880 after six years of Tory rule.

[12] Butler means Darwin, Huxley, Tyndall, Grant Allen, Ray Lankester "*et hoc genus omne;* [they] would soon repeat all the trickery of the Roman Catholic pseudo-miracles. They would cook their experiments just as the priests made their Madonnas wink" (MS Notebook, II, 13; November, 1883).

[13] John Bather (1819–1886), nephew of Butler's paternal aunt Mary (see note 4 for Letter 8). He had five sons, all living at this time.

[14] Henry Edward Burd (1826–1917), the Butler family's physician in Shrewsbury.

photos of the boys please send them & I will return them. How old is Hal now & what is he doing? I shall write to Harrie & get her to give me a full account of the young people.

I was laughing when I said George Eliot had paid me a compliment in Theophrastus Such. The compliment consisted in a certain chapter on machines which she introduced into that book, & which so closely resembled a certain other chapter on machines [1] that I had the satisfaction of feeling that great minds had thought alike—that was all; but the resemblance is so close that there can be no doubt where she drew from. It is quite legitimate, still it *is* a compliment. You ask me do I ever still think of writing a life of Handel—of course I do, & continually accumulate notes but I do not see my way to it at present; I never meant that I was going to cram up for a life of Handel, & I have a lot on hand.

I am *very* tired. I went yesterday somewhat unwillingly, but I think it was as well on the whole—to the Shrewsbury dinner,[2] & every one said how well & strong I looked in comparison with what I used to do. So I am in a way, but I am *fagged* for all that, & my present book is present with me continually & I cannot shake it off. It is very nearly done, and I am always like this at the end of a book. I saw Carlyle said some years ago that he never wrote one of his books without being made seriously ill by it.[3] I cannot say as much as this, but a book does take it out of one for all that. Professor Hering of Prague has my translation of his lecture.[4] He asked me to send it him that he might look it over, & I have this

Letter 32:

[1] There is some similarity between chap. 17, "Shadows of the Coming Race," in George Eliot's *Impressions of Theophrastus Such* (1879) and chap. 24, "The Book of the Machines—*continued*," in *Erewhon* (1872). Miss Savage may have called the resemblance to Butler's attention. On September 24, 1879, she wrote: "The only bit in the least bit readable [in *Theophrastus Such*] is a crib from *Erewhon*—a most bare-faced crib" (*Butler-Savage Letters*, p. 210).

[2] The first of an intended annual series of Old Salopian dinners, held in London on June 9, 1880.

[3] "Inaugural Address at Edinburgh, 21 April 1866, on Being Installed Rector There."

[4] "Uber das Gedachtnis als eine allgemeine Funktion der organisierten Materie" (1870), by Karl Ewald Konstantin Hering (1834–1918). The lecture was brought to Butler's attention by an article by Edwin Ray Lankester (1847–1929) in *Nature*, 14 (July 13, 1876), 235–237, which found Hering's lecture an ad-

morning received from him without a letter, so that I do not know yet what he says to my translation, a copy of another of his lectures which seems exceedingly interesting. I can make out a thing in German now roughly even without a dictionary, but I must translate a good bit yet before I can get that facility in reading which is necessary before It can be of the use to me which I hope it will be. Still less than six months ago I could not read a word of it.

The weather is awful, & I get no sketching done—this increases my fatigue for by taking one or even two days sketching [*A page or more is missing at this point.*] it over with him. Please thank my father for his letter which I was very glad to get—

Yr. affte. brother
S— Butler—

33. *Butler to May*

Text: Chapin Library MS.
[*Written on black-bordered paper*]

15. Clifford's Inn E. C.
June 29, 1880—

Dear May

I am very sorry I said nothing about the Botticelli picture. I feel sure that there is no photograph of it unless a small one, and I know there is no engraving of it—for I looked at the British Museum Print Room & could find nothing but an unsatisfactory reproduction of a part of it, done some years ago, before the picture was appreciated. I have it on my agenda to make enquiry tomorrow & will inform you if there is one, but unless you hear please conclude that I am right—I feel sure I shd have known of it if there was one—I will see that you have it if there is one.

---

mirable attempt to substitute something better for Darwin's provisional hypothesis of pangenesis. Butler translated it (chap. 6 of *Unconscious Memory*) to support his own theory of memory, though in chap. 10 he objected that Hering extended his theory into areas in which it is not applicable.

I start early Thursday morning, having sent my last sheets to the press & absolutely completed my book. I don't think I could write another page without being knocked up with it. It is called "Unconscious Memory," and will I believe form a good third to my two last.

After a few days rest I am to begin at another [1] to be finished if possible by October, but my friend Jones is to do part of it as time presses, & I am to illustrate it with 50 illustrations some full page, some half & some small. I shall have my hands full, but it is a commission,[2] & if it succeeds will lead to more, & not a little more either. It is to be about the Italian villages I go to on the slopes of the Alps & I have hit on a title which I think will do, to wit "Verdi Prati." [3] ⟨&⟩ It will contain not one word of philosophy [4]—nothing but pure gossip & illustrations. Having failed so often at exhibitions I am glad of an opportunity of getting some black & white work before the public & seeing what the verdict is.[5]

The heat here is intense today, & the weather looks much more settled. I cannot give you an Italian address yet, but believe it will be Sant' Ambrogio, Poste Restante—but I don't know the post town & provin[c]e. Sant' Ambrogio is mid way between Susa & Turin, under Monte Pirchiriano—and I expect great things of it.[6]

Letter 33:

[1] *Alps and Sanctuaries,* published in November, 1881.

[2] David Bogue, who published *Evolution, Old and New* and *Unconscious Memory* at Butler's expense, offered him £100 for a book on travel in Italy; but when the manuscript was done Bogue declined to take it, probably because his publishing house was about to go bankrupt (Boase, IV, 446).

[3] Butler changed his mind about this title from Handel's opera *Alcina,* but he always accociated it with northern Italy. Seven years later he wrote: "We might almost fancy that Handel had it [the country around Varallo] in his mind when he wrote his divine air 'Verdi Prati.' Certainly no country can be better fitted either to the words or music" (*Ex Voto,* p. 27).

[4] Butler was hardly able to refrain from including "philosophy." See, for example, pp. 26–27, 42–46, 47–54, and 86–92, of *Alps and Sanctuaries.*

[5] The illustrations were well received; the reviewer for the *Athenaeum,* for example, complains only that the process by which they were reproduced was poor. He also approves the text, though questioning the worth of a curiously large number of gratuitous references to Handel.

[6] See Butler's account of the Romanesque abbey above Sant' Ambrogio in chaps. 7–8 of *Alps and Sanctuaries.*

I was very sorry to hear poor accounts of the Bathers, & hope their outing will set them up. I hope also that my father's cough is better for his trip and that he is well. If you have occasion to write before you hear—address Poste Restante, Turin, or if you can manage to get a line to reach me tomorrow night I shd be glad of it, but shall go before post time on Thursday. With my best wishes to you all three I am

Yr. affte. brother
S. Butler—

34. *Butler to May*

Text: Chapin Library MS.

Sant' Ambrogio (di Susa)
Piemonte, Italy.
Frid. July 16. 1880—

Dear May

Thank you for your's of the 7th. I am not at Sant' Ambrogio, but at San Pietro 1,300 or 1400 feet above it; a lovely place upon little table land of meadows & chestnuts some 300 or 400 ft. below the Santuario. The Santuario is stupendous—& I am getting many sketches from it. I shall have however to leave some for another year, or by [*sic*] my book would be about nothing but this place.

The sketch I send ⟨you⟩ my father was much reduced—the original was 7 in. x 5 in. & what I am doing now are for the most part 10 x 6½ inches—or 7 x 5.

My landlady at Sant' Ambrogio was something like Anne [1] —though more in disposition than actually in personal appearance, though there was something even of this: I thought her one of the most fascinating people in the world. It was *very* primitive—not a jug nor a bit of carpet nor a washing jug on the establishment, and the most maddening fleas conceivable. Here the inn though also primitive is more

Letter 34:
[1] Anne Wade.

advanced the other: [2] they have less flea & more washing jug: they are very nice people here too, but the landlady down below is enough to spoil one for any one else.

I stop here 4 or 5 days longer, & then go to Vicè of which I expect great things. I do not think it is [in] Murray or Bädeker, but was told of it by a priest with whom I travelled —a most delightful person who was very kind & took a great interest in England. When he found I did not like Gladstone he said Bravo! Bravo! & was quite satisfied. He seemed quite to understand the late elections & to attribute the result to a general malaise in consequence of bad times.[3]

The post office people at Sant' Ambrogio are to be trusted so please address there till further notice.

With all best wishes to you both I am

Yr. affte. brother
S— Butler—

35. *Butler to May*

Text: Chapin Library MS.

15. Clifford's Inn E. C.
Nov. 22 1880.

Dear May,

I was extremely sorry to hear of Mr. Bradshaw's [1] death & write a few lines to Mrs. Bradshaw by this post. I shall always think of him as one of the best men that I have ever known, & regret greatly to think that I shall not again see him. I shall be glad to hear any further particulars that may reach you.

[2] Butler is apparently mimicking the landlady's English, as he does that of his guide in *Alps and Sanctuaries* (p. 263).

[3] Butler was of course displeased by Disraeli's defeat, which came about in part because of a serious failure of the 1879 harvest and heavy military expenditures in Africa. In *Alps and Sanctuaries* (pp. 88–89) he notes that this priest was well read on English politics, and sound (i.e., conservative) on all issues except the Irish question. Butler explained that question to him "as well as I could, and found him very willing to listen to our side."

Letter 35:

[1] John Bradshaw. (See note 6 for Letter 31.)

I am very well, but cannot quite shake off a cold & my eyes are rather troublesome—weak—but nothing much amiss. The weather here is bitter, & it looks uncommonly like a third hard winter—I hope it may not turn out so, but we have had one good thing so far—*no fog*, and only Londoners can appreciate this.

I have had an extremely kind letter from the Bishop of Carlisle,[2] about my book. I showed it my publisher—he said "that is very strong." I sent him a copy of the book because I had quoted & referred to his article in the Nineteenth Century [3] but of course did not write to him. Other news of it as yet I have heard none, but there was a flaming leader in the Times yesterday about Mr. Darwin; [4] very disgraceful considering what he has done, but the Times always is disgraceful. However, we shall see what the next three months brings forth. I hear his line concerning me is "I can't think why Mr. Butler attacks me in this way. I'm sure I must have done something very dreadful, and if I only knew what it was &c." This from one to whom it was said, & whom Mr. Darwin knows to be an intimate friend of mine.[5] He knows as well as I do. I don't know whether he has yet seen my new book; it was not out when this was said.

I see the Town Hall was burnt down,[6] fancy the town

[2] Harvey Goodwin (1818–1891). Butler's reply to this letter commending *Unconscious Memory* is printed in *Memoir*, I, 344–345. On the bishop's death Butler wrote: "I cannot say that I respected him or admired him as more than a man who knew very well how to play his cards," (MS Notebooks, IV, 131).

[3] "The Philosophy of Crayfishes," *Nineteenth Century*, 8 (October, 1880), 622–637. In *Unconscious Memory* (pp. 198–199) Butler quotes and enthusiastically agrees with the position that Goodwin takes against the foolish obscurity of scientific language.

[4] The third leader on November 20, 1880, is extravagant in its praise of Darwin's book on the similarities between plants and animals, *The Movements of Plants*. Darwin's work is compared to Newton's; the book is said "to mark an æra in biological science."

[5] Butler's Notebook identifies his informant as Miss Arabella Buckley (1840–1929), formerly secretary to Charles Lyell, at this time a lecturer in natural science. "She had been," Butler writes, "to dine and sleep at Down [Darwin's home] (Oct. 1880) and I saw her in the Museum afterwards" (I, 79).

[6] The top floor of the Shrewsbury town hall was destroyed by fire on November 19, 1880. The Shrewsbury fire brigade had to call for engines from neighboring towns.

having no fire engine: so the papers say at least, but it must surely be a mistake.

I have finshed my account of Oropa [7] for my Italian book, & shall now do ⟨Oropa⟩ Sammichele.[8] I still grind away at German; it will be no good to me till I can read it fluently: this I cannot yet do, but it is coming, & then I think I need learn no more languages: a good job.

Do you mean that Jack Lloyd is going to Kansas? [9] I dare say he is quite right, but it will be a rough place; still if he doesn't mind that & if he has a good sound head on his shoulders I shd think he was right. Very glad to hear of my father's being able to walk so far—but don't let him over do it—only that there is no stopping him. I have had a proposal made to me from Kegan Paul the publisher to edit *Hudibras* & write a short life and introduction to the poem—say 20 pp. for £5. The proposal entirely from him. I declined it, after consultation. I could not do the thing properly in a month, and had better do my Italian book instead. Besides, it looks as if I wanted to connect myself with my namesake,[10] & though unwilling to turn money away, we concluded on the whole that it would be a mistake for me to do it.

Yr. affte. brother
S— Butler.

36. *May to Butler*

Text: British Museum MS.

Wilderhope.
Feb. 27. 1881.

My dearest Sam

Thank you very much for your kind little letter, and you will like to hear that both of us are fairly well, though I think

[7] See chaps. 14–15 of *Alps and Sanctuaries.*

[8] See chaps. 7–8.

[9] *Alumni Cantabrigienses* indicates that John Bucknall Lloyd (1853–1932), son of Butler's cousin, Thomas Bucknall Lloyd, spent some time in Kansas.

[10] The earlier Samuel Butler (1612–1680), author of *Hudibras,* was not related to Butler.

both of us feel the strain that is upon us. Papa went to Harnage [1] one day last week, & walked 6 miles so you see his foot is right again.

The matter of the guardianship [2] was to have been settled last Wednesday, I believe—but there has been no letter as yet from Mr. Jeffes [3] who has been very good and kind in keeping Papa informed—In any case it is all in good train. The advocate to whom that woman first applied has thrown up her cause in disgust, and she has now put her affairs into the hands of another lawyer, & one probably less scrupulous, but Mr. Jeffes seems to have no anxiety whatever as to the result of any proceedings she may take. Meantime she is keeping us here in a state of suspense by intending to come over to England, & have an interview here. I suppose she thinks she can extort money from my father, either by threats of exposure here, or by some disclosure true or false which she will profess to have held back. She wrote a week ago to the chief constable here—asking whether Papa was now residing here, but he brought the letter straight here, & she got no reply. Since then we hear from Etta that she is known to have expressed an intention of coming, & a persuasion that by so doing she could obtain her end—and this morning brought a letter from the post master here, enclosing one from her saying to *him*, that "serious family difficulties would oblige her to come here, & as she knew no one in England to apply to, and was not sure whether the Rev. T. B. was still residing here—could he be kind enough to give her his address." Papa will consult Mr. How, & probably get him to write to her, & say that the police know something of her, ⟨& that⟩ —and that any communication must be made to Mr. How.—

At Brussels things seem going outwardly smoothly, & Etta

Letter 36:

[1] Property owned by Canon Butler, a few miles southeast of Shrewsbury.

[2] In the autumn of 1880 Butler's brother Tom was discovered to have been living with a prostitute in Brussels. His father (with Butler's approval) took steps to see that Etta, Tom's wife, and her four children would receive the income from Tom's inheritance. (Correspondence in the British Museum.)

[3] Thomas Edward Jeffes, British vice-counsul at Brussels.

& the children are very brave, but I am afraid there is not much to hope for else.

Be sure that I will let you know if anything important comes, but it is slow lingering work.

We were very much amused & interested in your account of the Puicernas. It was a much prettier name. Do you remember at all *when* they became Butlers—it would be curious to try & trace some reason for the change, whether it was with any view to disguise or concealment or a quarrel with the original stock.

In turning out all his boxes Papa came upon all the clues he has to our family history. They are very imperfect, but I have been working at them, & have brought them into something like order, & making them out into a clear genealogical shape as far as can be done. Papa got me two big bits of paper to do them on, as he said he thought you would like a copy of it all.

It is snowing at intervals today, but there are crocuses out. I hope you will keep better, & am glad you have got through your row. I hate rows. With very best love I am ever

Your affectionate sister
May.

Henry Bather [4] was here yesterday he showed us an amusing little note he had from some tenant or some such thing—apologising I think for being a little behind to the collector Mr. Sotherne. It was *pretty* well written & spelt till he came to the P.S. when his feelings evidently overcame him, & he ended thus "as youshel Sotherne's tong—" That was all the P.S.

[4] Henry Bather, land agent for Butler's father.

37. *Butler to May*

Text: British Museum MS.

[15 Clifford's Inn]
April 22. 1881.

My dear May—

Did you also see that Carlyle died [1] worth £35,000 all made from his books after years & years of waiting? And Herbert Spencer has just given evidence that after 15 years he was £1200 out of pocket by his books, but has now recouped himself & is making a moderate profit? [2]

I dislike both these men heartily—and am glad to see the counter blast is full blow against the former—but their careers tend to show that after a time persistent writing does force its way. I never was so much abused before as now. Bogue says he never had a book yet which has been so much abused as my last.[3] I cannot but think that there will be a turn in the tide ere long—for not one reviewer has called me to task for a misstatement, or even argued with me seriously. I called on the editor of the St. James' Gazette the other day, and asked him why there had been no reply to my rejoinder to one of the bitterest & most unscrupulous attacks upon me.[4] The editor said his reviewer had wanted to reply "but I told him he had no case, & had better let it alone." This sort of thing *must* tell in time.

We are here all grieving about Lord Beaconsfield.[5] I never felt the loss of any public man before as I do his. We have nobody comparable to him for a moment. That is the worst

Letter 37:

[1] Carlyle died on February 5, 1881.

[2] Spencer lost heavily on *Descriptive Sociology*, a multi-volume study begun fourteen years earlier. In a "Notice of Cessation" included with the eighth part in 1881 he stated that loses of £3000 on this project alone were forcing him to abandon it.

[3] The most unfavorable review of *Unconscious Memory* was written by George John Romanes (1848–1894), a disciple of Darwin's, in *Nature*, 23 (January 27, 1881), 285–287.

[4] The review appeared on December 2, 1880 (p. 13), and Butler's reply on December 8, 1880 (p. 5).

[5] Disraeli died on April 19, 1881.

of these exceptionally great men—there is nobody to take their place.

With all best wishes to you all I am

Yr. affte. brother
S. Butler.

38. *May to Butler*

Text: British Museum MS.

[Wilderhope]
Dec. 10. 1881

My dearest Sam

We should like to hear that you were keeping well. I hope you did not think us very foolish to be afraid of you, but independently of any *danger*, it is such a horribly *tiresome* thing to get into a house.[1] But we should like a line to say that you had not caught it. I hope your friend is better by this time. —We have not had, & are not at all likely to have any further letters, and I think the money will be let alone.[2]

I have not seen any review of your book.[3] Tell us if there is any good one.

On Thursday afternoon I went over the factory here with Miss Downward. I had no idea it was so large or so important —it sends thread and twine to every part of the world, & you can't buy any of it in Shrewsbury. It was rather nice to see all my factory girls at their work, & gave one a homelike feeling with them.

On Monday night I have to play at a little concert & reading of Mrs. Bentley's here, for the school and clothing club,— & have just come from practising in the big dark school room by the light of two little candles— It is so cold but not so dark as the papers today describe London!—

Letter 38:

[1] Jones was ill with what was believed to be scarlet fever (see next letter).

[2] May is referring to an attempt by Tom to keep the income from his inheritance from Etta and the children.

[3] *Alps and Sanctuaries.* Butler received the first copy on November 22 (*Memoir,* I, 362).

Last Saturday I was at Lichfield on some business with Mrs. Madagan and went all about the Cathedral. The front will be so beautiful; they are filling in the statues fast. There are some very beautiful modern monuments there, beautiful enough as far as I can judge to admire in any old sculpture gallery, and the last, the memorial to Bishop Selwyn [4] is the most beautiful of all. It was rather a tiring day more especially as I did not change at Stafford coming home, & to my horror found 'Crewe' staring at me from the lamp glasses, just when I thought I was getting to Wellington [5]—so I didn't get home till 10:30. We have lovely Chrysanthemums, and I have seen a little pot of Dutch tulips out today, & the Bishop's study at Lichfield was full of little Roman hyacinths. I wonder whether you have any yet.

Harrie will be here about the 20th, I think—

Goodbye dear Sam. With my love I am your affectionate sister

May

39. *Butler to May*

Text: British Museum MS. *Extracts published: Memoir,* I, 364.

15. Clifford's Inn
E. C.
Dec. 17. 1881

Dear May

I have been hindered from writing all the week & shall now, I fear, hardly catch the post. My friend Jones continues very ill & we are anxious about him, but he is certainly better today. The scarlet fever part of the story was very mild, but

[4] As part of a comprehensive plan for the restoration of Lichfield Cathedral, memorials were constructed to honor illustrious churchmen. In January, 1881, a statue of George Augustus Selwyn (see note 4 for Letter 4) was placed in the cathedral. A Melanesian boy clings to his feet.

[5] May had continued on toward Liverpool, and at Crewe was about 25 miles farther from Shrewsbury than she would have been if she had traveled the same distance to Wellington.

it has been followed by rheumatism, & other complications: I do hope however that the present improvement will be maintained & not lost as it has been on three or four past occasions.

My rib is now much better. For a long while it seemed to get worse & worse, but the last three days there has been decided improvement each day. I had a small bottle (a homeopathic round bottle) of Worcestershire Sauce in my pocket to eat with my lunch which I had in my pocket with me. Getting over a stile on a wet slippery day & with an umbrella in my hand I slipped & fell with all my weight on the top rail but so that all the weight bore on the homeopathic bottle: this did not break the bottle but it cracked the rib.

There have only been three notices of my book yet—It is still early for them. A very complimentary not to say flattering one in "Truth" for Dec. 15. and another equally complimentary in "The Bookseller." In Punch, (this week's) however there are two lines "Alps & Sanct. &c By S. B. rather dry: not a bad thing when you've far to go: no umbrella required." [1] This and nothing more. I have no doubt it's all right but beyond the fact that they mean to say the book is dry I don't understand them. I will send the favourable reviews if my father wd like to see them.

Mr. Garnett [2] of the Museum is evidently much pleased with the book, & the fathers at S. Michele are *delighted* with it. I sent them a copy, & they are evidently very much pleased. One man a barrister complained to me quite seriously that the book was written in a very sympathetic spirit towards the church of Rome,[3] & said he hoped I was not thinking of joining: absurd nonsense; I hope however the Romanists in

Letter 39:

[1] *Truth*, December 15, 1881, p. 792; *The Bookseller*, December 2, 1881, p. 1207; *Punch*, December 17, 1881, p. 285. Two other generally favorable reviews appeared later: *Athenaeum*, December 31, 1881, p. 898, and *Academy*, 21 (January 21, 1882), 39–40.

[2] Richard Garnett. (See note 4 for Letter 31.) *Unconscious Memory* is dedicated to him.

[3] Chap. 9, "The North Italian Priesthood," compares the personal qualities of the priests favorably with those of the English clergy, but Butler shows no sympathy for the doctrine of the Roman Catholic church.

England may think what my barrister friend did, for they will buy my book if they do—and my own impression was that they wd not think ⟨the book⟩ it one that was likely to do them much good. With love to my father

Yr Affte brother
S. Butler.

40. *May to Butler*

Text: British Museum MS.

Wilderhope.
March 4. 1882.

My dear Sam

It is *such* a long time since I have written to you—I do not like to think of it, but I know you have been hearing of us through my father,[1] and I have been very full of work ever since Christmas.

Do you know that I am starting a little Childrens' Home here? It is a very sad one in some ways, for it is meant especially for such children as cannot be received into ordinary schools or industrial homes, for fear of the harm they might do others—their own knowledge of evil being so sad,[2] but it is very bright in other ways, for children so soon get happy & bright. It is a nice little house toward Sutton, about half way between here & Meole, & Martha, our nice housemaid is installed as matron, and my first child, an Islington child, came a few days ago, & I expect another next week. I hope to get about 8 by degrees, & they will scour & wash & cook & sew and have a little garden, & by degrees drift off into carefree little places. I was in London last week, if I had had any time that I could reckon on I should have let you know, but I was out from morning till night, literally, seeing various 'homes' with a view to learning all I could that might be

Letter 40:

[1] There is a considerable amount of correspondence between Butler and his father at this time, most of it very cordial.

[2] May's home was for illegitimate children.

useful. I spent a good deal of my time in Ratcliffe Highway and Stepney! and saw sides of London life which one had never seen before out of books—and longed for an interpreter to explain things as I came through the city, & to go into the Tower as I passed it. It is a disgrace never to have seen the Tower—I was at London House,[3] & with Gertrude.

Our Bishop here *set* me starting the little home, which is supported by subscription through an appeal, partly from him, so I have not much difficulty or anxiety, only the superintendence & management. And Papa is very much interested about it, & it has been a pleasure to him I think.

I did not do a single thing else but business in London—except to make acquaintance with a telephone, and to be somewhat disappointed with electric light. It is very brilliant just on the spot, but its light seems to go such a little way, & it is so dark between the lamps. I was delighted to find that in all classes & opinions Mr. Gladstone seemed getting into disgrace, but what is Northampton about? [4]

I saw Dick Worsley [5]—& hope the accounts of Clifton [6] are really better, but it is strange they cannot find out the cause of four cases of typhoid in a house.

May & Elsie & Etta with them, have been to a dance. Papa sent them lovely flowers, & they seemed to have enjoyed it immensely, the girls dancing every dance.

Papa heard yesterday from Mr. Woodcock that Tom was letting the sale of Kenilworth go on,[7] so he is still in Brussels. Papa is going to post this as he goes up in town, so goodbye. My best love—

Your affectionate sister
May.

[3] The home of the Bishop of London.

[4] Gladstone opposed a committee of Lords which was to investigate the operation of the Land Act. At the same time Charles Bradlaugh, M.P. from Northampton who had been rejected by the Commons on the grounds that as an atheist his oath was invalid, was overwhelmingly re-elected.

[5] A cousin, son of Philip Worsley. (See Biographical Sketches.)

[6] Clifton, Bristol, home of John and Sarah Worsley, brother and sister of Butler's mother.

[7] Tom had a contingent interest in the Kenilworth property and could have prevented its sale.

41. Butler to May

Text: British Museum MS. *Extracts published: Memoir,* I, 375.

Aosta [Italy]. Augt. 30.
1882.

Dear May

I have had no letter since I left England and rather think one must have miscarried. I wrote to my father from S. Pietro. I came here a fortnight ago and have sketched all day, & every day since, the place & neighbourhood are singularly rich, and the weather has been good. One castle I have found about 10 miles off [1] which must wait to be done thoroughly another year, but which I think beats all I have ever seen: full of X⟨I⟩Vth Century frescoes and the frescoes as usual all written over from 1560 downwards to the present day. There are *two* sets of walls round it, & when I got inside and went upstairs to a huge wooden gallery which runs round the court I found the only tenant an old woman spinning at a spinning wheel. I have accumulated a large stack of notes, and I see very well it will end in another Italian book. Jones is with me, and we have decided to go to Milan tommorrow. Jones is not well, and cannot walk much so I have determined to take him to Milan, and thence to Bergamo, [*one or two illegible words*] Padua, [*one or two illegible words*] for a couple of ⟨days, and⟩ so to Venice. Where please address to the

Hotel Luna
Venice.

I have seen few English people since I left & none of them striking.

I am very tired and have been so every day, and expect I shall be till I get back to England. With all best wishes to you all

Believe me
Yr. affte. brother
S. Butler—

Letter 41:

[1] Butler collected many notes about the Castle of Fénis, a late fourteenth- or early fifteenth-century castle above Aosta, intending to incorporate them in another book like *Alps and Sanctuaries* (see *Ex Voto,* p. 192), but he never finished the book.

42. Butler to May

Text: British Museum MS. *Extracts published: Memoir,* I, 383.

Mar 15. 1883
15. Clifford's Inn E. C.

Dear May,

I hope this bitter weather is doing no harm either to yourself or to my father; good it can hardly do to any thing except the land, and not being a field myself I find it hard to look upon the good side of such East Winds as we are having. I have chillblains & my hands are chapped—really cracked—in some places—true I have been working out of doors, but that has made me feel the winds all the worse.

I have had no events except a call from a man who made me one of the most surprising propositions I ever had made to me in my life: he was a stranger to me, and called sending in his card; he wanted to introduce me to a certain Jew who was deeply interested in the return of the Jews to Palestine, and who had an idea which I was to work out for him, &c—&c. by means of which not the poor Jews only but the Rothschilds & Oppenheims wd be induced to leave England & settle in Palestine.[1] I will not mention the name of the gentleman('s name) who called on me, & I had rather you said nothing about it, for you & I & he have friends in common, (on the strength of which it was that he called) and it might come round, but, as I have said, I think this was the wildest of the many wild schemes which have been presented to me at one time & another. I was very civil but quite inexorable. This happened a couple of days ago.

I have also heard a good story of a boy who was asked by an Examiner "what (were) are the postulates?" He replied

Letter 42:

[1] The Zionist movement gained force at this time because of anti-Jewish riots in Russia. Butler says in his Notebooks (I, 180; Shrewsbury *Note-Books,* p. 240) that on this occasion he was approached because he was a writer of reputation who could propagandize the movement. He had brusquely refused such a request ten years earlier (MS Notebooks, III, 42).

"There are three postulates: firstly things that are equal to the same are equal to one another: secondly things that are greater than the same are greater than one another, & thirdly things that are less than the same are less than one another." [2]

You asked me if I like Rosetti's [*sic*] pictures: [3] I dislike them extremely: in fact they have made me so angry that I cannot see any good in them at all, but there was a very beautiful Titian and a lovely Marco Basaiti in the same exhibition. With all best wishes to my father & yourself

Believe me
Yr. affte. brother
S. Butler

43. *Butler to May*

Text: British Museum MS. *Extracts published: Memoir*, I, 385.

15. Clifford's Inn
E. C.
Mar 29. 1883.

Dear May

I returned from my Easter outing on Tuesday evening, having been to Guildford and had some very pleasant walks, but I find this continued East Wind very trying and am watching the weather cock more carefully than I think I ever did before: I have been painting out of doors today but after an hour & a half found my hands so cold that I could do no more. I am sending in four pictures to the Academy, as good I think as any I have done, but I am too old now to be sanguine about getting them in or to be much disappointed if I am turned out, though of course I should like to be in. I

[2] Cf. MS Notebooks, I, 179; *Further Extracts*, p. 97.

[3] A year after his death, the Royal Academy held an exhibition of the paintings of Dante Gabriel Rossetti. In the same exhibition were works by the Old Masters; including Titian's "Caterina Cornaro" and Marco Basaiti's "St. Jerome in the Desert."

send two London subjects one suburban one and a knight in armour with a landscape background, a more ambitious performance, which requires all the time between now and Monday to complete.[1]

I have thought of the wedding today and wish the young couple all happiness: the sun has been brilliant here all day and I doubt not all has gone off as brightly as a wedding should do. I suppose you have had the house full, if the Crees are not gone please remember me most kindly to Lucy.

Thank you for telling me about Bishop Tozer's [2] speaking warmly of Alps and Sanctuaries. It is not the bishops and archbishops I am afraid of; men like Huxley & Tyndal are my natural enemies, and I am always glad when I find church people recognising that the differences between me & them are, as I believe myself, more of words than of things.

My French review does not come off: I doubt not that it will do so for the man who was to do it wrote to me about it himself [3] and said it would appear in February in Le Parlement. I know nothing whatever about him, except that he is a well known writer, and both February and March are nearly gone; still I expect it will appear sooner or later.

Jones and I have taken a composing fit. I have done two minuets and Jones quite a lot of gavottes bourrées & gigues.[4] He writes very well and we think of publishing a small collection together some day when we have got enough done, but this must wait for a long time, for it is only at odd times that we do anything. I will bring my minuets when I next come down to Shrewsbury.

This is a very stupid letter, but I am afraid it must go for

Letter 43:

[1] Butler later noted on his copy of this letter: "All were rejected, I should think rightly."

[2] William George Tozer (1829?–1899), retired from active church work at this time; he had most recently (1880–1881) been bishop of Honduras.

[3] On his copy of this letter Butler identifies the man as James Darmesteter (1849–1894), a French orientalist, and says he thinks the review never appeared because of Darmesteter's failing health.

[4] *Gavottes, Minuets, Fugues, and Other Short Pieces for the Piano* by Butler and Jones was published in 1885.

lack of a better—With all best wishes to my father and yourself I am

Yr. affte. brother
S. Butler—[5]

44. May to Butler

Text: British Museum MS.

Wilderhope.
Sep. 11 [1883]

My dearest Sam

I think you must be come back again, on a dismal rainy day, if it was like our's yesterday, and I send you a line of welcome. I am so glad you had a pleasant time, and I am sure the selling of your sketch must have made it pleasanter. I should like to have seen Mt. S. Michel and the jolly little boys & the gracious landlady.

I have not yet got Alice Hall.[1] I think she is waiting for Edward [2] to go but I hope to have her in October. Harrie is going to be with us a big piece of this winter from November to February I hope.—My father is well, but for a scrap of cold, nothing much. He walked 9 miles one day not long ago, not feloniously, but he missed a train, and it did not seem to hurt him, though I do not like him to do so much. He is just now deep in the life of Professor Palmer [3]—a brightly written

[5] Butler's note, dated December 17, 1901, on his copy of this letter reads: "I suppose that seeing how ruinous writing was I must have gone back to painting more seriously than I had remembered. This must account for my having no book published (except the Selection book) between Alps & Sancts in 1882, & Luck or Cunning in 1886." Though dated 1882, *Alps and Sanctuaries* was published at the end of 1881; *Luck or Cunning?* dated 1887, actually appeared late in 1886.

Letter 44:

[1] See note 3 for Letter 4.

[2] Edward Algernon Hall, Alice Hall's brother.

[3] Edward Henry Palmer (1840–1882), professor of Arabic at Cambridge, fellow of St. John's College; he was murdered in Egypt while on a confidential mission for the British government. His friend Walter Besant brought out a laudatory biography soon after Palmer's death.

& interesting book. He must have been such a nice "all-round" man. I don't get on very fast, but I can do what I have to do, and the experienced all tell me that they *felt* their weakness more a good bit after than *just* after such an illness. The only moral is not if possible to do it again.

The new greenhouse is now complete with its stand in, and we have some pretty new flowers, some from Ceylon, seeds of Ernest's, one of them the most brilliant velvety sky blue—convolvulus. Poor Edith is still very delicate, & ordered to the South for the winter. She will go to Torquay or Bournemouth I think.

We hear very good accounts of Charlie[4] who seems working well and steadily. Amy Cree was here lately—I think it must have been before I wrote last, that she broke her right wrist, falling over a little step in St. Mary's—it was very painful.—I have been writing a number of necessary letters today—and am rather tired—so I won't go on—only as I suddenly remembered that you come home on the 11th I did not want to leave you without a line. With my love, your ever affectionate sister

May

45. *Butler to May*

Text: British Museum MS. *Extracts published: Memoir,* I, 391–392.

15. Clifford's Inn E. C.
Sep. 12. 1883

Dear May

Thank you for your's received this morning. I got home on Monday morning after a delightful journey from Havre with the sea as smooth as glass. I am *very* much better, and for the last two days sneezed quite freely with only the least bit of the old pain remaining. I had begun to fear that I shd not get rid of it, but I can see it will go unless I do too much again now; I hope it will not be necessary, but if I find it

[4] Charles Butler, Tom and Etta's son.

slipping back I shall take another fortnight somewhere before the winter begins—I did not like Normandy really a bit—all the time I was comparing it with Italy—very ungrateful & very wrong—but I cd not help it. I don't like the French character, & at Lisieux on my way back the boys threw stones at me as I sketched. I never had the smallest trouble with Italian nor yet with English boys. Fortunately an old lady watched the boys from her window, & scolded them: I never budged: I cd'nt, I was too well fixed up, & besides, that was what the boys wd have liked—so I kept my ground & took no notice. Then the old woman came down & routed the boys effectually, & I was grateful. I have done the best sketch I ever did in my life—this my sketch—during which the boys stoned me. By the way what I sold was not a sketch—it was a picture worked on for several days. I cd not have sold it otherwise. It has encouraged me & done me good—not so much for the money as for the finding some one like[d] my work well enough to buy it. Today I have been painting in London, but somehow I have not succeeded, & am down in the mouth about it for I had meant capping my best sketch, & I don't know why it hasn't come right. That's what plagues me most of all—when I know the work is wrong, but don't understand how & why, & wherein the error lies, but I generally find out in a day or two.

I am very sorry you do not gain ground faster; my own experience is that one is not aware of gaining ground much while one is gaining it, but suddenly one day one finds oneself pretty well. This is how it has been with my head this time, & how it always is every year when I go abroad. It was not till I was at Verona last year—after I had been 5 weeks out & did not feel to have gained at all, that it stole upon me that I was all right again—but *change*, if you can stand it, & if you can get it is the best restorer. A change is to a person's life what a cross with fresh blood is to an animal or a plant,[1]

Letter 45:

[1] Compare the prescription of the eminent physician for Ernest's melancholia after he rids himself of his wife and children (*The Way of All Flesh*, chap. 79). Butler was writing this section of the novel at the time.

but of course one must be strong enough to stand it. It rests by giving the mind other objects, & therefore even though it fatigues there is a gain. Pardon this preaching. I am sorry my father has a cold, but hope it will be all right soon. I did not think I ever saw him look better than when I saw him in July.

Believe me yr. affte. brother
S Butler—

46. *May to Butler*

Text: British Museum MS.

Wilderhope.
Nov. 1. 1883.

Dearest Sam

I have got back one of my children,[1] who had made her way to London—& is at this moment housed in the jail, on remand till Monday—when we hope to have the other two.

Yes, I am glad, for I hope to do something for them still, & in any case it is far the best lesson for the children at the Home. She succeeded in quite captivating the detective who brought her back! & to whom she told no truth at all.—

I have had a good deal on my hands just lately, for two ladies came from different quarters, one for two nights & the other for one, both of whom are starting similar homes in different directions and wanted all the information they could get, & by the time I had talked of nothing else for 48 hours I did most heartily wish to smother all the children, & go to the opera!—

We have had—& also, lost—the loveliest little cat that ever was seen. A little grey Persian which Hodgkins [2] sent us from Derbyshire. It ran away, and I fear we shall see it no more, & we are very low.

I will tell you a nice sentence of a French lady's at a table

Letter 46:

[1] One of the children in the home for illegitimate girls.

[2] Hodgkinson was butler to the family.

d'hôte "I am so glad I do not like asparagus, for if I did like it I should certainly eat it, & I can't *bear* it."—

Maysie comes to us on Tuesday, & Harrie very soon afterwards. It is getting very wintry here, true November fog & damp, but not cold.—The last news I heard from Whatton was of the very sudden death of Mr. Miles [3] who has been ill for some time. How wonderfully the whole district has changed. Edward [4] has sailed for America.

We have had squabbles in the kitchen & have given the tall cook Margaret, notice—much to her indignation—and I have my choice of 3 nice young girls whom I can order about & not be afraid of. I like your cookery book, & am going to get it; I will send yours back very speedily.

With my love, I am always

Your affectionate sister
May—

47. *May to Butler*

Text: British Museum MS.

[Wilderhope]
Thursdy. Dec. 6 [1883]

Dearest Sam

My father's cold which did not seem at all serious yesterday morning—(he was in the drawing room doing his plants) has developed into bronchitis, and he seems gravely ill.—He has slept much, but takes all the nourishment ordered, which amounts to a good deal. We think you should know, but we will of course send a card after the doctor has been this morning. He saw him yesterday aftn. first.

Your affectionate sister
May.

[3] Robert Henry William Miles, rector of Bingham. (See note 5 for Letter 28.) He died on October 25, 1883, at the age of 64.

[4] Edward Hall. (See note 3 for Letter 4.) There is a letter from Hall to Butler from 208 Fifth Avenue, New York, dated January 8, 1884. (Correspondence in the British Museum.)

48. *May to Butler*

Text: British Museum MS.

Wilderhope.
Dec. 24. 1883.

My dearest Sam

I send a line by a midday post today in hopes that it may greet you tomorrow morning & wish you a happy Christmas.

My father goes on capitally, is getting hungry, & intends to walk 'round his bed' this afternoon, and he is really able to read a little tiny bit now, & is very cheerful & bright, & I think he begins to realize how ill he has been, & will be careful, at least for a time. He has been considering two bottles of sugarplums for the Home children! and is anxious about the welfare of cinerarias & chrysanthemums. I am getting quite well again & am enjoying this most lovely day, which is like sunny spring.

With Harries' love & mine I am dear Sam

Your very affectionate sister
May.

49. *Butler to May*

Text: British Museum MS. *Extracts published: Memoir,* I, 403.

15. Clifford's Inn E. C.
Jany. 9. 1884.

Dear May,

I have missed the post, but will keep this open, and by me to add a line tomorrow in case anything turns up.

I was very glad to receive your letter written on Sunday. Please again congratulate my father from me; I hope now that as this mild weather continues he will pick up fast, & be caught looking not only at the stairs but at the outside of the hall door before so many days are over, but we must be careful how we put imprudent ideas into his head.

I forgot to say that Tom did write to Jones as usual for his dividend,[1] but he desired them to be sent to himself at an address in a Flemish part of Brussels, and not to Louis Loos, Rue des Petits Carmes, as before.

I sent a copy of his note at once to Etta. There was nothing to be made out of it except that he was still in Brussels. He may still have the business or he may not.

Some 13 or 14 years ago I gave a couple of pounds for a picture purporting to be by Reynolds [2] at an auction in Oxford Street. I thought it was one, & so did Heatherley,[3] whom I got to come & look at it before I bought it. I have had it ever since, & in the Autumn seeing there was to be a Reynolds exhibition [4] I determined to send it on loan. They have accepted it as so writes their secretary, "an indisputable Reynolds" and hung it so I now figure in the catalogue as having lent them a Reynolds. It is not in a very good state, but it can be restored, and if ever I want to sell it, now that I can give it a character and appeal to its having been in the Grosvenor Reynolds exhibition. I think it shd be worth something, so I am rather pleased.

By the way Harrie was kind enough to talk of sending me some eggs—will you say please that while thanking her none the less I can now get *capital fresh* eggs as the French new ones have come in, as cheap as she can buy them in Shrewsbury. From now to the middle of May really good eggs can be got as easily in London as any where.

I am very well. My head is now perfectly well. I cannot feel the slightest trace of mischief remaining.

Letter 49:

[1] Butler was executor of the trust fund from which Tom received dividends; Jones acted as his solicitor.

[2] Jones identifies this as a portrait of the Countess of Egremont (*Memoir,* I, 403). Walter Armstrong lists the painting as by Reynolds in *Sir Joshua Reynolds* (1900), p. 204. Ellis Waterhouse, however, rejects the authority of Armstrong's book and that of the Grosvenor Gallery in accepting the portrait as genuine; "I should say the odds are against its being a genuine Reynolds and against its being Lady Egremont," Professor Waterhouse writes in a personal letter dated November 14, 1955.

[3] Thomas Heatherley. (See note 2 for Letter 8.)

[4] The Grosvenor Gallery exhibition of Reynolds, December 31, 1883–March 29, 1884.

I am to bring out at Easter a book of extracts—the best chapters—from my first six books [5]—to keep me before the public a little until I can get the book out [on] wh: I am now engaged [6] ready. This will be a matter of time for it is much the most arduous task I have yet undertaken & necessitates my being well up in all the latest information.

On second thought I will not keep this open so conclude with every good wish for my father's complete recovery & to him & both of you—Believe me

Yr. affte. brother
S. Butler—

50. *Butler to May*

Text: British Museum MS.

15. Clifford's Inn
E. C.
Jany. 16. 1884

Dear May

Thank you for yrs. received this morning. Again congratulate my father from me (I hope you *do* congratulate him, but as you never say you do & he never sends any message I am left rather in the dark unless I write straight to him which I suppose it is a charity not to do just now)—I am sure Dr. Burd is quite right about the boots especially if the weather with you is as raw and cold as it is here today.

Will you also ask him if he knows the silver beech as a tree singularly sulky and mindful of injury? I was in Kensington gardens a few mornings ago, and my eye was caught by seeing 1813 cut in bold clear letters on the trunk of a tree. The tree looked so young ⟨that I⟩ and the cutting so clean that I cd not believe it to be a genuine date & went up to the tree to inspect. I found it covered with names cut *from the dates 1717 & 1736* both very clean & perfectly unmis-

[5] *Selections from Previous Works, with "A Psalm of Montreal" and Remarks on G. J. Romanes' "Mental Evolution in Animals."*

[6] *Luck or Cunning?* It appeared almost three years later.

takably genuine to the present day. I found 4 more of these silver beeches close by & in each case the cutting lasted with a freshness far beyond that of any other tree I ever saw. Common beech is not that I know of particularly retentive of injury, but if you so much as scratch the silver beech it never forgives you.

Another curious sight I saw this morning. I was going to the British Museum and saw a crowd outside the corner house of the street going from Gt. Russell Street to Russell Square. It was a curious shaped crowd & a curiously behaving crowd. I cd see in the distance that it was not a fight, nor a fire, nor a man being taken up & I kept thinking to myself what an *odd* behaving crowd it was—all the time I drew nearer. The people walked up to the area, looked down—talked a little and went on. When I came up I found that *two horses* had found their way into the area. One had shied, swerved from the road and falling against the iron railing had knocked it down & tumbled down the area. The other was blind & went where its mate went, and there they were. They said one was hurt but the other not. The area was so narrow that there was no room for them to turn round so how they are to be got out I know not.

So Hal [1] is in love. I wish him joy. I shall never marry myself, I think that seems ⟨quite⟩ decided. It is quite clear that every one cannot do so, and I am not sure that I do not deserve well for standing aside & making room for others—but those things come of themselves—bachelorhoods are made in heaven quite as much as marriages. Any way I wish him & all of you joy though I suppose the event is not going to come off immediately. And I am *very* glad you are looking out for another billet for him; it is cruel work where he is [2]—

Yr affte. brother
S. Butler.

Letter 50:

[1] Henry Thomas Butler. (See Biographical Sketches.)

[2] See note 2 for Letter 61.

51. *Butler to May*

Text: British Museum MS.

[15 Clifford's Inn]
Sunday evening.
Jan 20, 1884

No. Silver birch will not do at all—I mean silver beech. There are seven trees in all in Kensington gardens of this kind wh: is a variety of the beech, throwing up a long straight smooth *white* trunk to a good height; not spreading out pretty soon with inter twining, inter growing branches & brilliant green trunk as the common beech does, but as soon as the boughs have begun to part from the trees they keep more clear of one another. The bud is like that of the common beech. I think the tree is rare, for I told Mr. Salter [1] of it a few days ago & he did not know it—

Very glad of your good account of my father

S. B.

52. *Butler to May*

Text: British Museum MS. *Extracts published: Memoir,* I, 403–404.

15. Clifford's Inn E. C.
[February 1, 1884]

Dear May

Thank you for your's received yesterday. I am very sorry that my father must still remain a prisoner, for I know how much he must feel it, & how much I shd feel it if I were in his place, but I dare not say a syllable that shd encourage rebellion, so can only express my sympathy.

I have got a very bad cold—or rather have had, for today I am much better, but am still in that uncomfortable state in

Letter 51:

[1] Samuel James Augustus Salter (1825–1897), by profession a dental surgeon; he shared Butler's interest in botany.

which a heavy cold leaves one. I go about however much as usual.

I am very sorry for the black cat. I am sure animals feel very jealous of a new inmate when they have had everything their own way for some years. I hope however that her age & experience will make her able to hold her own & shall be glad to hear that the two have found a modus vivendi. I shd think the old black cat carried as many guns as most cats do, & will find ways of saying nice little nasty things if the new one does not fall into her proper place.

I see advertised a book called "The Sagacity & Morality of Plants." [1] It is to appear shortly. What are we coming to? And what will the vegetarians do? You know perhaps that Mr. Darwin in his later years edged strongly towards giving intelligence to plants, though he never went so far as to say so point blank. I shall be very curious to see this book. I wonder whether the writer will say that carrots are passionate because they have such a red root.

I saw this advertised in last week's (or the week before) Athenaeum.[2] In last weeks's I had a letter challenging Mr. Romanes for having given a wrong reference.[3] He said Canon Kingsley first advanced the theory connecting Heredity & Memory—& did so in Nature Jan. 18th 1867. I went to Nature to see what Canon Kingsley had said, & found that Nature did not begin to appear at all till nearly three years after

Letter 52:

[1] "Science Gossip" in the *Athenaeum* for January 26, 1884, announced the forthcoming publication of this book by John Ellor Taylor. The book begins by quoting Darwin on the similarity of plants and human beings and then develops the analogy. One chapter, for example, is entitled "Social and Political Economy of Plants."

[2] The announcement of Taylor's book appeared in the issue of the previous week. The same issue contains Butler's challenge of Romanes which he mentions below.

[3] Rankling under Romanes' unfavorable review of *Unconscious Memory* (see note 3 for Letter 37), Butler wrote to the *Athenaeum* (January 26, 1884, p. 124) pointing out that Romanes' attribution of the phrase "hereditary memory" (in his *Mental Evolution in Animals*, p. 296) to Charles Kingsley (1819–1875), the novelist, was wrong—that the volume of *Nature* which Romanes cited does not exist. Butler claimed that the phrase was his, but actually the phrase occurs in an earlier article by Kingsley in *Fraser's Magazine*, 75 (June, 1867), 808, though, as the title of the article, "A Charm of Birds," suggests, not in a scientific context.

this date & that there was nothing from Kingsley in any way bearing upon the subject. So I wrote in the Athenaeum & asked for the correct reference—very civilly—assuming that Mr. Romanes had made a slip. Romanes has not replied,[4] & I could see by the smile on the editor's face when we discussed the matter that he did not expect him to. I shd have thought he would have done so.

The editor of the Athenaeum announced my book of Selections very prominently in the preceding week,[5] I thought he had done it by chance, but it was not so for he said "I gave your announcement an exceptionally good place." When I was so unpopular after writing Evolution Old and New, the Athenaeum & Academy both declined to announce my two next books Unconscious Memory & Alps & Sanctuaries. As they have both given prominence to my new announcement I flatter myself that I am making way. I think that Mr. Darwin's being no longer alive will make a great difference to me.

What a lot I have written about my books—but then my books are to me much the most important thing in life. They in fact are "me" much more than anything else is. The magnum opus is at a stand still while I am putting this stop gap through the press & touching up the remarks which it will contain on Mr. Romanes's new book.[6]

With all best wishes believe me

Yr. affte. brother
S— Butler.

[4] Romanes admitted the error in the *Athenaeum* for March 8, 1884 (pp. 313–314), not in reply to Butler but in reply to the review of his book in the *Athenaeum* for March 1 (pp. 282–283) which includes some of Butler's charges.

[5] The fourth item of "Literary Gossip" is a discussion of Butler's forthcoming *Selections from Previous Works* (*Athenaeum*, January 19, 1884, p. 89).

[6] *Selections from Previous Works* contains a chapter, "Remarks on Mr. Romanes' *Mental Evolution in Animals*."

53. *Butler to May*

Text: British Museum MS.

15. Clifford's Inn
E. C.
Feb. 12. 1884.

Dear May

Thank you for your's received this morning. I am very sorry my father cannot go out yet—but I again dare not do more than express my sympathy, for of course we all know that Dr. Burd will let him but the first moment he dares. I am glad to hear he is so patient. Does he come down to breakfast and stay up to supper? I presume he does, but I shd like to know.

I have got rheumatism in my left arm today & can hardly lift it—the remains of my cold which hangs about & has pulled me down a good deal. I don't think I ever had such bad rheumatism before—but I have been to the Museum all day as usual.

I went to dine at Chester Terrace on Saturday. I thought my uncle looking remarkably well and *quite* recovered from his illness of the early winter. I also went to dine at the Beales [1] a few days ago. We are all wondering who will be the new editor of the Times. I did not like the old one, but am glad to see that the Times has gone very much against the government these last few days.[2] I went to hear Romanes lecture at the Royal Institution on Friday last.[3] I never heard a worse lecture nor one worse delivered. I did not want to go—I said there wd be no fun in it—but my friends said I ought to go so I went. I got no good by it, but am glad I went for I saw the man, & know what he is like, and besides know he said

Letter 53:

[1] See note 3 for Letter 22.

[2] On February 11, 1884, Thomas Chenery (b. 1825), the editor of the *Times*, died and was succeeded by George Earle Buckle (1855–1935). Since November the *Times* had been critical of Gladstone for allowing the French to increase their power in Egypt, and was at this time becoming increasingly critical.

[3] "The Darwinian Theory of Instinct." The lecture is printed in *Notices of the Proceedings, Royal Institution of Great Britain*, 11 (1884–1886), 131–146.

nothing whereas if I did not know what he had said I might have thought I might have missed something. As for lying—the text is a very simple one. ⟨Does any one⟩ people set up for being better or more agreeable—or more clever—or in any way ⟨a⟩ bigger swells than their neighbors? if they do they will tell lies & be guilty of petty meannesses. If they don't they won't go far wrong—& if they do tell a lie some time it will be one that hurts no body.

Believe me Yr. affte. brother
S. Butler—

54. *Butler to May*

Text: British Museum MS.

15. Clifford's Inn
E. C.
Feb. 22. 1884.

Dear May

I am glad my father continues to gain, and if this mild weather lasts shall expect to hear ere long of his having been well wrapped up & put into the close[d] carriage & taken out for a drive. I shall be very glad when I can hear of this, and am sure that I shall do so the first day that it can be allowed safely.

My rheumatism is gone, & so is my cold. I rubbed in kewts [*sic*] horn & oil & it did me a great deal of good.

Ashamed of one's country! Yes indeed I feel ashamed of it, and yet at the same time I feel that it is ever so much better than any other. I think we shall have a change before so very long, & am sure I hope so.

I am glad Harry is coming to you. I hope Miss Dedington will keep him dangling on for some years so as to stop him from marrying any one else, & then throw him over just when he is becoming resigned to a bachelor existence.[1]

Letter 54:

[1] Butler later noted on another letter that Hal did not marry Miss Dedington.

I heard the other day of two couples who came to be married & it turned out they had had their banns given out wrong, the wrong couples having been announced by mistake. They were very angry & went away, but presently returned, saying that as they had come intending to be married, it was a pity that nothing shd come of it, so they had exchanged *fiancées*, and wd be married as the banns had been read out—& married they were.

My book of selections will be out next week. Through Mr. Garnett I set Moss Kingsley on to ask Kingsley's widow whether she knew of his having said anything anywhere of the nature of what Mr. Romanes said he had said,[2] but she knew of nothing, & we think the whole thing is [*one or two illegible words*]. Of course I have given it Romanes pretty hot. Kegan Paul, Romanes's publisher came up to me in the Museum as I was at my seat a few days ago & tried to pump, but I was on my guard & said nothing.

I saw Trübner,[3] my publisher a few days ago, & found him most effusive. I saw he had lost faith in me when I returned to him from Bogue's & that though we were excellent friends he no longer had the same expectations wh: he had a few years before. I did not care: I knew very well how & why it was. It was because Romanes had published a book with him under the signature Physicus,[4] & of course had run me down. Now he is all the other way again, because he went to dine with Professor Mivart[5] the other day & he had spoken very warmly of my books, & had run down Romanes. Trübner knows less about literature than I shd say Hodgkinson or Dr. Burd does & of course only goes by what people with names say. "But" said Trubner "though he likes your books so much he is very much offended with you." "Why?" said I—"Because

He did, however, marry Ada Wheeler (see note 3 for Letter 115) and become a citrus grower in Florida. Butler corresponded with Hal regularly and left him a considerable share of his estate.

[2] See note 3 for Letter 52.

[3] Nicholas Trübner (1817–1887), with whom Butler published most of his books.

[4] *A Candid Examination of Theism* (Trübner & Co., 1878).

[5] St. George Jackson Mivart (1827–1900).

he sent you a letter & a review & you never answered his letter." The fact was I never received either letter or review & knew nothing about it—I wrote at once to Professor Mivart & said what Trubner had told me, & then it all came out that three years ago he had sent me a long review he had written of my three books on Evolution—*most sympathetic*—in an American Roman Catholic Quarterly [6]—but that some how or other it had never reached me. He sent me his own copy at once on loan & the misunderstanding is now removed—but it is very vexatious, for Professor Mivart is one of the few men I can look to in the scientific world for anything like an alliance & support, & when he had made an advance to be supposed to be rude enough to take no notice of it is a piece of pure bad luck. However it is all right now.

With best wishes to you all

Believe me
Yr. affte. brother
S. Butler.

55. *Butler to May*

Text: British Museum MS. *Extracts published: Memoir*, I, 410.

15. Clifford's Inn E. C.
Wed. evening.
Ap 9. 1884

Dear May,

I send a few lines as I shall leave town tomorrow returning on Monday evening. We are going to Shoreham,[1] but letters will be sent from here to me, I hope however that there will be none to send—still I never like quite cutting myself off from my base of operations.

I am afraid you are not very well by your being ordered

[6] Mivart, a Roman Catholic convert, treats Butler as the best of the theorists who see evolution to be a result of some conscious design (*American Catholic Quarterly Review* [Philadelphia], 6 [July, 1881], 385–433).

Letter 55:

[1] The home of Charles Gogin. (See Biographical Sketches.)

to do no home work. I hope a little change will do you good. Perhaps we can arrange a meeting at Etta's or at the National Gallery, but I dare say you will wish to be as quiet & do as little as you can so shall not be surprised if I do not see you. I am very well myself, and have not felt even the smallest trouble in my head since the little scare I had three weeks ago. A stitch in time &c—

Herbert Spencer's letter is to my mind the most important thing in the whole controversy.[2] It assures me that I was already aware of & had not missed his most important passages [3]—and those he gives do not enable him to claim more, even himself, than to have done the thing "by implication." As a matter of fact no one understood him to mean what he now implies that he did mean. The editor thought his letter (to use the editor's own words) "without definite aim" so that I need not reply and I was very glad not to do so; so the matter will drop—but in an appendix to Life & Habit later on I will say what I think advisable.[4] I am so glad to find that none of my opponents have been able to catch me napping—of course I have known all along that I was writing with a halter round my neck. The matter is at an end for the moment, but you may be sure that it is in reality only the beginning & not the end. They will never be content to leave it as it stands, but will go for me in some other paper. The positions are reversed. Heretofore it was I who wanted to draw them & cd not get them to break silence—now they have been well drawn & it is I who am holding my tongue, & the more I hold it the more they will try & draw me, & the more the really influential people will incline towards me.

[2] Spencer's letter to the *Athenaeum* (April 5, 1884, p. 446) concluded the argument between Butler and Romanes. Romanes and Ray Lankester (see note 4 for Letter 32) wrote that Butler's work on evolution was worth considering only insofar as it reflected other writers, particularly Darwin. In his letter Spencer defends Butler and points out that Butler's theory relies heavily on his, Spencer's, *Principles of Psychology*, a book published five years before *The Origin of Species*, and one to which Spencer feels Butler amply acknowledges his debt.

[3] In Spencer's *Principles of Psychology* (1854).

[4] Butler included a discussion of Spencer's position in his next book, *Luck or Cunning?* (1886), chaps. 2–3.

My collector[5] called a few days ago with his accounts (quite satisfactory). When we had gone through them, he asked me if I were writing another book. I said "of course I am—I am always writing books," & shewed him a lot of Manuscript. "Dear dear me" he said "and is that Manuscript? I have often heard of manuscript—and is that really manuscript?" I was very much pleased—it was like Monsieur Jourdain on discovering that he had been talking prose all his life without knowing it.[6] You remember Mme. Jourdain on Latin? "Scavez vous Latin?" said the instructor "oui" said Mme. J. *"Mais faites comme si je ne le scavais pas."*[7] I think there is a c in Old French for "savoir" but cannot trouble to look.

Mr. Tylor[8] says the moon was a small planet that came within the sphere of the earth's attraction. Perhaps we sucked her atmosphere away from her—but I don't know about that. He told me a lot about the tides—very simple & intelligible, & there was a pluvial period as well as a glacial, & during the glacial period the level of the sea was sensibly lowered by the vast quantity of water frozen up as ice, and the skull is an epitome—well—I will tell you about the skull another time. I am very glad of this fine weather for my father's sake as well as my own. I hope it will last. Believe me

Yr. affte brother
S. Butler.

[5] The collector of rents for Butler's houses in Battersea.

[6] *Le Bourgeois Gentilhomme*, Act II, scene iv.

[7] *Monsieur* Jourdain says: "Ouy, mais faites comme si je ne le sçavois pas" (II, iv).

[8] Alfred Tylor (1824–1884), a geologist. Butler dedicated *Luck or Cunning?* to him, giving him credit for instigating it.

56. *Butler to May*

Text: British Museum MS. *Extracts published: Memoir,* I, 416.

15. Clifford's Inn
E. C.
May 5. 1884.

Dear May

It is some time since I had any Shrewsbury news, & since I wrote, but doubtless both sides have taken the view that your visit is much the same as a letter. I hope⟨d⟩ you liked Jones but we are afraid by your going away without waiting to say good bye to him that he had not made so deep an impression as he cd have wished.[1] We have both of us done a lot of music since you were here, and are each [of] us well pleased with the progress of the work [2]—which however will certainly not be complete before next Xmas. It is quite certain to be done [3] by about then shd life & health permit.

I hope you have not over fatigued yourself during your outing & will reap the benefit of it on your return.

We are writing our own words as well as the music & imitating the style of Handel's librettist Dr. Morell.[4] We are surprised to find that the style is one which lends itself singularly well to adaptation to music, & think that much better poetry would not have been half so well suited for the particular purpose that Handel had in view. We have to cover a sheet of foolscap with trial rhymes before we get the right thing, but what we have got so far will suit us very well. At present I am engaged on a fugal chorus & Jones on a song which I think perfectly lovely.

I have been wracking my brain to think of anything that will amuse or interest any of you, & have sat so long without

Letter 56:

[1] In the *Memoir,* Jones prints most of this letter, but he omits this paragraph.

[2] Butler and Jones were at work on *Narcissus,* which Jones says was practically finished at this time (*Memoir,* II, 37).

[3] Butler noted on his copy of this letter: "By 'done' I must have meant 'completed.' It never has been 'done' in the sense of being performed, and I fear never will be in Jones's & my life-time."

[4] Thomas Morell (1703–1784).

thinking of anything that I will conclude rather than pad. I am very well & hope you are all the same, with all best wishes believe me

Yr. affte. brother
S. Butler—

57. *Butler to May*

Text: British Museum MS. *Extracts published: Memoir,* I, 411.

15. Clifford's Inn E. C.
May 13. 1884.

Dear May

Thank you for yours of the 6th from which I am glad to learn that you are all well. I have very little news. I was at Mr. & Mrs. Salter's [1] last night, they being up in town for a few days—Mrs. Salter told me that Miss Burd [2] had gone over to the church of Rome & that Dr. Burd was very much cut up—I am extremely sorry to hear of this—it is really very sad. I hope the nice Miss Burd whom I met at the Salter's won't go too, but I shd be sorry to trust her not to.

I was at the Tylors [3] on Sunday. They are the people who know the queen. It was all explained to me that it arose through a certain Mr. Allen who with the then Archbishop of Canterbury were left guardians to the queen by the Duke of Kent's will, but what the relationship between Mr. Allen & Mr. Tylor was was not explained to me. They asked me to bring Jones & were exceedingly kind to ⟨me⟩ both of us (for Jones went) and treated us very well. I like the old gentleman very much—⟨but the queen (I mean Mrs. Tylor) bullies him a good deal.⟩ Their daughter married a son of John Bright's [4]

Letter 57:

[1] See note 1 for Letter 51.

[2] Daughter of Henry Edward Burd. (See note 14 for Letter 31.)

[3] See note 8 for Letter 55.

[4] John Bright (1811–1889), still very active in Liberal politics at this time.

not long ago & I think I told you another daughter married a son of Canon Morse's [5]—

There was also there a Mr. Horsburgh [6] assistant secretary of the Royal Institution, and one of the enemy's camp—I mean an intimate friend of Mr. Romanes. He asked me if I knew who wrote the articles in the Athenaeum, (re myself & Romanes) and this it seems to me was not a right thing to do. Of course I assured him that though I believed I knew who did them, it was a man whom I had never seen, nor ever had any communication with direct or indirect, & he didn't seem as if he alone half believed me. I was glad to have met him. And then Mr. Salter last night told me a delightful piece of scientific scandal against Mr. Ray Lankester how he misbehaved about a Medusa found in a water tank in the Botanical gardens [7]—I was so pleased.

The Tylors told me of a brother of Mrs. Tylors' who lived near Croydon & got into a new house. They had 23 servants and when they got into this new house the servants fell to fighting & there was a great to do. They cd not fall into their proper departments & were all upset by the change. So the master & mistress announced their intention of going away at once for a week to Brighton—to give the servants time to settle matters among themselves—on their return they found everything as quiet as possible—it had all settled itself much better than they could have settled it.

[5] Francis Morse (1818–1886), vicar of St. Mary's, Nottingham, known to the Butlers during the last twelve years Canon Butler was at Langar.

[6] Probably James Macdonald Horsburgh, 30 years old at this time. His official connection with the Royal Institution of Great Britain is not listed, but the Post Office Directory for 1885 gives the Institution as his address.

[7] Four years earlier, Lankester (see note 4 for Letter 32) wrote to *Nature*, 22 (June 17, 1880), 147–148, to report that he had discovered a new variety of medusa in the water lily tank in the Botanical Society pool in Regent's Park. Then, in the issue of June 24 (pp. 177–178) he admitted that George James Allman (1812–1898), an elder scientist of great reputation, had previously done a great deal of work on this jellyfish. Lankester offered to give up the name he had given it—"craspedacuata"—and allow Allman to name it. Allman, unimpressed by this offer, proceeded to attack the accuracy of Lankester's description of the medusa. The affair ended when the editors of *Nature* printed a grudging and unconvincing statement (August 19, p. 361) that they had misprinted Lankester's description.

Our composition [8] is going on capitally. I allow myself two hours every day at it. Jones does not get anything like so much, but he works more quickly. I have *completed* one air & broken the neck of another—and am getting on with my chorus. We have got sketches for most of the choruses.

With all best wishes to you all believe me

Yr. affe. brother
S. Butler

58. *Butler to May*

Text: British Museum MS.

15. Clifford's Inn
E. C.
May 29. 1884.

Dear May

I have solved the mystery of Jones's baby. It was my cousin Reginald (who *entre nous* is one of the worst narrators of a story that I know) who is supposed to have spoken of Jones's baby—& not me—wh: is all the more amusing as it was *he* who told me that *I* was supposed to have said it. It arose thus. He was telling the story of the child that said it did not like the kitten because it had pins in its toes. It was a *neighbour of Jones's* who had this child—the neighbour dropped out—the child became a baby—and thus the story has assumed its present awful shape.

This is a good example of the way in which inaccuracy turns the most innocent thing all wrong—& shows also how much better it is to write to people at once & give them an opportunity of explaining before rushing to conclusions. I wrote to Etta last evening & got my explanation this morning. Believe me

Yr. affte. brother
S. Butler—

[8] *Narcissus.*

59. *Butler to May*

Text: British Museum MS.

15. Clifford's Inn
E. C.
June 20. 1884.

Dear May

I am afraid you are still a good deal out of sorts, but hope that change of scene and air will ere long produce the good effect upon yourself which they always hitherto have produced on me. I have no news—am rather done up, but able to rub along. This is the time of year when I always am rather done up. I am still at work on my chorus—it is *very* difficult but it is nearly done now, and will, I think, do. I shall never have such trouble with another—and indeed see my way comparatively clear now. Airs are much easier than chorusses—but then this chorus is a good long one.

I have been exercising my rights as a free and independent voter this morning in respect of the Mid Surrey Election [1]—I have a few houses in Battersea which give me a vote—which I have duly given on the Conservative side, of course.

I am to dine at Mrs. Danvers's [2] tomorrow & take her to the health exhibition [3]—which I have not yet seen, & shd not, I believe, have gone to if I had not been caught unawares & made to go by Mrs. Danvers. I suppose on the whole it is good for me to go—but I got on very nicely without the fisheries exhibition last year. I have not even been to the Academy yet—but shall go soon, in fact I have done nothing but write all the morning till about one & then compose all the afternoon.

I got a very good musician whom I know a little to come & hear what we have done, the other night, and both Jones

Letter 59:

[1] The Conservative candidate was returned to office.

[2] Mrs. Augustus Danvers, whom Butler met first at Verona in 1882 (*Memoir*, I, 376).

[3] The National Health Exhibition in South Kensington, one of the most popular attractions in London during 1884.

& I were quite satisfied with the effect produced. He complained of its being comic, & said that the music was much too good for the words—but then that is what we intended, and to do what we are doing except by way of a jeu d'esprit wd be simply impossible. To do the whole thing in a serious spirit wd be [to] fly much too much in the face of the tendencies of music at the present time. It is a case in which we can blurt out a truth with a laugh & a joke which cd never be said gravely. We thought of all this beforehand & stick to our original scheme.

I really hope you will be better soon—don't trouble to write unless & until you are in the humour & believe me

Yr. affte. brother
S. Butler—

60. *Butler to May*

Text: British Museum MS.

15. Clifford's Inn
E. C.
Wed. Augt. 6. [1884]

Dear May

A line before I start to send my address—which for the moment will be Hotel Caspar Badrutt St. Moritz, ober Engadin, Suisse. Jones's mother & sisters are there & we travel thither together. He is better & taking his holiday now will I doubt not set him up. I shall leave Jones almost immediately with his mother & sisters & go over either to Maloja or Bernina, I have not yet decided which, but letters will be forwarded. I am in a very good state to be benefited by a holiday—not too much done up to start with, but it was time I went somewhere.

I saw Elsie on Saturday evening when I called on Etta to say good bye, & was glad to have good accounts of you all. I hope you will do as nearly nothing as you can.

I start tomorrow morning at 10. a. m. taking a 45 day

return ⟨to⟩ ticket to Basle, where I ought to arrive on Friday morning at about half past six. I shall go straight on to Coire & sleep there Friday evening. Thence next day to St. Moritz. I think I have done everything I have to do except actually put my things into my bag & portmanteau, but as I have made an inventory of everything I want this is not a long business. However I must set about it, so no more except that I hope I may find you all well on my return—and am

Yr. affte. brother
S. Butler—

61. Butler to May

Text: British Museum MS.

Soglio [Switzerland]
Sep. 7. 1884.

Dear May

Yours of the 3rd ⟨of the⟩ reached me yesterday evening—so quickly do letters travel now even to out of the way places like this. Thank you very much for it. Tell my father that I have not seen a ghost of a woodsia. In fact I will venture to say that they do not grow about here. I have some seeds of the mead tiger lily—if he wd like some of them. [*One or two words illegible*] to sow some about Kent, as also some blue Sabina seeds.

I am glad there is a talk of Harry's emigrating.[1] If he doesn't mind it, it is much the best thing he can do. A railway clerkship wd be only the Queen [2] over again. It cannot do him any harm learning a little blacksmithing & carpentering, but I wd put in a plea for his learning the mystery of keeping accounts by double entry.[3] A week wd teach it to any one once

Letter 61:

[1] See note 1 for Letter 54.

[2] Jones noted in pencil on this letter that Harry had been a clerk for the Queen Insurance Company.

[3] Butler added a note dated February 1, 1902, to his copy of this letter: "I taught my nephew how to keep a/cs by double entry myself."

for all, & it is never forgotten when once learnt. If I had known this not very difficult art when I was in New Zealand it would, I am sure, have saved me many a pound, indirectly, if not directly. At any rate it is like being armed with a weapon of precision as against one of very uncertain accuracy. I don't want him to learn anything else at all.

I am extremely sorry about Charley's thumb. I hope he will recover it by & by, but it sounds rather bad, & I shd have thought he ought to have got some feeling into it by this time.

Harrie must mind, please, & let me have one of my father's photographs.

I am getting a lot of black & white pen & ink drawings—much—very much—better than my last—so much so that I cannot think how I let the others go. These ought I think to come out very well. I have not done much oil. I shall probably stay here till next Thursday & then return to Coire. I shall spend a few days at Sargans, & expect to reach London about the 20th or 21st. I think you had almost better not write till you do so to Clifford's Inn unless you shd have occasion to say something that will not well wait—but ⟨either⟩ Poste Restante, Coire, Grisons, Suisse will find for ten days from hence, & I shall probably be at the Hotel National, Bâle abt the 19th where a letter wd find me.

Jones tells me that a man named Browning came to stay at the hotel where his mother & sisters are, ⟨&⟩ as also a young lady [4] who is staying with them. It was reported that this was Mr. Browning the poet—the young lady, however said this was impossible for the poet had such a much grander head than this man, & ⟨that⟩ this man would not do at all—but it *was* Browning the poet all the time.[5]

My two young ladies are gone over the mountain to Cresta, but the Baroness who is *charming*, & her husband who is also very good indeed remain—as do also the Italian family.

If you can fancy a still young & extremely beautiful Italian

[4] Edith Paine (Butler's note).

[5] There is some confirmation of Jones's report in Mrs. Sutherland Orr's *Life and Letters of Robert Browning* (1908), p. 343.

Mrs. Miles, with a less beautiful Italian Jenny Miles along with her, you have the Italian lady & her daughter.

With all best wishes to you all believe me

Yr. affte. brother
S. Butler—

62. *Butler to May*

Text: British Museum MS. *Extracts published: Memoir,* I, 437–438, and *Further Extracts,* pp. 171–173.

15. Clifford's Inn
E. C.
Dec. 20. 1884.

Dear May

I write a line to say that I shall leave town on Tuesday morning for over Xmas returning on Saturday or Sunday—and as Jones & Reggie [1] will be with me & I shall have no one to send letters on whom I can rely, for Mrs. Doncaster's [2] writing is most uncertain—I shall not have any letters sent on. I feel sure I may cut myself adrift safely and we can move about so much more freely if we have not said we wd be at such & such & there at such & such a date.

I have just come back from an at home at the William Rossettis.[3] I did not know them, but Mrs. Rossetti sent me an invitation & said her father Madox Brown, the painter, wd be there & wd much like to see me. I used to know the Madox Browns but found that if they gave me a bun at all they wanted me to climb the pole too much & too often to get it so on my return from America I did not call & let the acquaintance drop. In the mean time Oliver Madox Brown [4]

Letter 62:

[1] Reginald Worsley. (See Biographical Sketches.)

[2] Butler's laundress.

[3] William Michael Rossetti (1829–1919). His wife, Lucy Madox Brown (1843–1894), was the eldest daughter of Ford Madox Brown (1821–1893), the painter to whom Butler refers.

[4] Son of Ford Madox Brown by his second wife. The Pre-Raphaelites considered him a most promising novelist and poet. He died in 1874 at the age of 19.

had died, & I was supposed not to be as sorry as I ought to have been the fact being that I hardly knew him at all beyond ⟨the fa⟩ his calling on me sometimes & reading me his M.S novels which I particularly disliked; I don't mind reading my own MS.S. to people, but I don't like being read to, & I did not like either young Brown or his novels—and did not feel his loss so acutely as I ought to have done.

However two years or so ago old Madox Brown the father wrote me a letter asking if I had any letters of his son's as they wanted them for a biography. I don't believe he ever wrote me a letter; at any rate I had none, but I took the opportunity to write prettily about the loss literature had sustained etc., & the old man wrote me back an answer saying something about "silent equivoques" [equivokes] [5] whc I did not quite understand but it was rather touching, for I knew ⟨the old man⟩ he had been very proud & hopeful about his son. So when Mrs. Rossetti wrote me thus I thought I ought to go & did & there was old Madox Brown so I went up & said how glad I was to meet him again but he had forgotten all about it & evidently did not know me from Adam, nor care two pence whether he saw me or not—and his being so glad to see me was a *wicked hoax*—I was very much amused & rather comforted. The Rossetti's (he is brother of the painter) belong to a set from which it is perfectly hopeless for me to think I shall get any good—the ultra aesthetic cultured & scientific people & I don't mean to follow this up. The Tylors & Mr. Seebohm [6] are their very opposites and I will cultivate them to the best of my power. I saw Mr. Tylor last Sunday at Carshalton & Mrs. Tylor says he wd like to see me again tomorrow so I shall go—he is sinking fast & I fear cannot last long. I am extremely sorry. An old lady a Mrs. Sims has sent me a card also for an evening at home early in January. I like her very much—she is very good indeed, so I shall go. What a long story I have

[5] Butler's brackets.

[6] Tylor (see note 8 for Letter 56) asked Butler to attend his lecture at the Linnaean Society on December 4, 1884. At this lecture he met Henry Seebohm (1832–1895), an ornithologist. Butler visited both men, and often saw Tylor at his home in Carshalton during December; after Tylor's death on December 30, he saw little of Seebohm (MS Notebooks, II, 106–108).

made about nothing. I hope you are all pretty well & feel sure you are or I shd have heard. I send my best & my good wishes to you all & am

Yr affte brother
S— Butler—[7]

63. *Butler to May*

Text: British Museum MS.

15. Clifford's Inn
E. C.
Dec. 30. 1884.

Dear May

I found your letter of Saturday waiting me on my return on Sunday evening—very cold & rather tired—I also found a telegram from Carshalton saying that Mr. Tylor was "very anxious" to see me, so I had to go off to Carshalton again then & there and did not get back till nearly midnight. The poor old man did not want anything of importance but one never can tell what may happen—& receiving such a telegram I cd not do *otherwise* than go. I found they had sent up Skerbekly to find me in the afternoon if they could. I had promised to inscribe my new book to him [1] & to call attention to his experiments in the inscription, & this so pleased him that I must come at once. I got there at about nine & found him ⟨scarcely⟩ only able to speak very little; it really was heart breaking for he is so good & so patient. However I hear from Mrs. Morse his daughter, this morning that he is better and "a little more

[7] After modifying the account of his evening at the Rossettis' for his Notebook (further emphasizing what he took to be the deliberate rudeness of the Rossettis), Butler commented: "I have added to the letter as I wrote it to my sister, but all I have said here is correct. May wrote back, 'I very much sympathise with you in your objection to the ultra-aesthetic Rossetti school. It must have been rather fun to let them see you saw they did not really want you.' I did not 'let them see &c.,' nor say I had let them see. I did my best to conceal it.

This [from May] was meant as a snub for me, it was her way of saying 'you have been to the Rossetti's indeed, but you must not think much of that, they did not really want you at all.' "

Letter 63:

[1] *Luck or Cunning?* is dedicated to Tylor.

encouraged about himself." I am afraid however that there is no chance of his recovery. Of course I feel in a very strange position going so much at such a time to people whom I hardly know, but I never go unless upon such a message as makes it absolutely imperative—and they are very good people who perfectly see that I shd not come if I could help it. They say his father had a very lingering illness before he died.

The music book is not done.[2] We took our M.S to Novello's immediately on my return from Shrewsbury to have it corrected, & have only got it back yesterday. There are no important corrections—I mean no consecutive fifths or any thing of that sort, but he has made a ⟨great⟩ good many very small ones, not as correcting something absolutely wrong, but as slightly more elegant. Many of these we take gladly enough, but others we think mistaken. We shall return it in two or three days & then it will be out as soon as Novello's choose to let us have it. Of course we take all suggestions that we do not think absolutely damaging.

I enjoyed my outing—but shd have enjoyed it more if it had not been so cold. I brought back 8 beautiful new laid eggs which I got for 8 a shilling & thought I had done well. I am very glad you give so good an account of my father—thank you for being so much more full; it makes me feel that I really understand how he is. I hope you will like the new man. I am afraid I have caught cold—I think that bitter Carshalton journey did it, but I will stave it off if I can. I am to see Elsie & Charley on Thursday. They are going to tea at Reginald Worsley's along with Amy & Teddy, & Jones & Uncle John [3] are to be there too, & uncle John will smoke a cigarette & sing a comic song. I don't think I have anything else that will interest you. You never admired my duet—I hope you liked it. All good to all of you for the new year

Yr. affte. brother
S. Butler—

[2] *Gavottes, Minuets, Fugues, and Other Short Pieces for Piano* by Butler and Jones was published by Novello, Ewer & Co.

[3] John Worsley. (See Biographical Sketches.)

64. May to Butler

Text: British Museum MS.

Wilderhope.
Feb. 1. 1885.

My dearest Sam

I want to send you a few lines myself, to thank you for thinking about me so kindly, & to tell you that my cold has passed off as quickly as it came. The mild weather of the last day or two has been very much in its favour. On Friday I thought it was going to be real bad, but now I am down stairs again, & a robin is singing outside our closed shutters, and the snowdrop clumps are coming up fast.

I am so glad your leg has righted itself quickly.

Papa has been to church, to a long full service, this morning, & seems not at all the worse. He did not cough much, Harrie says, & it was a great pleasure to him to get out again, and he has liked being at the Museum.

One has been so glad to hear the little we heard from Mr. Jeffes,[1] & I do think it seems as if people had shewn all the kindness & care strangers could. I don't know whether any one told you that Dr. Burd seemed to understand exactly the course of the illness, & looked on it as an aggravated form of dysentery. He says that if it was as he understood it, no doctor could have done anything after that collapse.

How one wishes one could be always gentle. Somehow one begins to see that however much in the wrong people ⟨p⟩ may be, there is always much one wishes one had not done or said or thought when any softening comes, & one is sorry now to think how ready we all were—even I,[2] for I am speaking for myself as much as any of us, to think some evil of this silence

Letter 64:

[1] Tom Butler died in Corsica on November 30, 1884; he had disappeared from Brussels some time before. News of his death did not reach the family until the middle of January, whereupon Butler's father asked Mr. Jeffes, the vice-consul in Brussels, to send him whatever details he could obtain.

[2] Butler inserted "who am so exceptionally sweet," at this point.

—or that if the end had come, it might have come in some far *more* sad way.[3]

Harrie & I wish that it could have been arranged for the *clothes* not to be sent, but I fear it is too late. Dr. Burd says there is no *risk* if it is as he thinks, but they would probably be much worn, very difficult to dispose of in any comfortable way, & perhaps the most trying sort of thing for Etta.

Goodbye, dear Sam—my love, & I am your very affectionate sister

May.

The new man seems to do.

65. *Butler to May*

Text: British Museum MS. *Extracts published: Butler-Savage Letters,* pp. 357–358, and *Memoir,* I, 442–443.

15. Clifford's Inn
E. C.
Mar 4. 1885—

Dear May

I ought to have written before to thank you and ⟨Ma⟩ Harrie for your letter. I attended Miss Savage's funeral on Saturday [1]—a very sad business. I find she died of blood poisoning after an operation for cancer, and I am told also that she was suffering from creeping paralysis. She did not happily suffer during the short interval between the operation & her death, and made all those about her believe that she fully thought she was going to recover, but she would do this whatever she thought. The day before she died she said the first thing she should do when she got out would be to support the School board, for the noise the children made had, she said

[3] Butler noted: "I don't know what she means. I thought Tom's silence meant that he was dead—& he *was* dead. I did not think anything else."

Letter 65:

[1] Miss Savage died on February 22, 1885, and was buried on Saturday, February 28.

prolonged her illness for at least forty eight hours and she was determined to crush all the vitality out of them in future—this which of course was playfully said was the nearest thing to a complaint she made & the sisters who attended said it was a pleasure to have anything to do with her she was so cheerful & grateful. Towards the end she began to wander, became unconscious, and died most tranquilly. For herself this is no doubt best, but to those who knew her as I did the loss is simply irreparable. I do everything just as if nothing had happened, but in reality I can think of nothing else. However I will say no more upon this, and I would again ask you & Harrie not to do so.

I am glad you like your new man servant. I am struggling with a cold and am keeping warm and quiet today. Last night I dined at Chester Terrace to meet Mr. & Mrs. Arthur Darbishire who Alice wrote wd like to see me. My uncle was pretty well & Alice I thought a good deal better than when I saw her last.

We have returned all our revises but cannot prevail on Novello's people to let us have our books. Jones has one fugue which is I think of great beauty and very pathetic so we have had it headed *In Memoriam E. M. A. S.* which are Miss Savage's initials.[2] Jones admired Miss Savage almost as much as I did though he did not know her nearly so well. I was anxious to connect her at once with the best thing I could get—and I could not have written so good a piece even if there had been time, but I will write the best I can for our next collection, should this one encourage us to repeat what we have now done. I saw the man who corrected the press a few days ago, and questioned him a little, as well as I could. He said he had been much struck with the pieces, & that nothing at all of a similar

[2] Jones explains (*Memoir*, I, 448): "Butler was consciously planning to associate Miss Savage with his own work, that is with our album of *Gavottes, Minuets, Fugues*, etc. . . . [But] there was nothing of his that had any feeling of sadness, so we chose what we used to call my 'miserable fugue' in C. We never thought it worthy of her, but we wrote at the head of it 'In Memoriam E.M.A.S.,' and there was only just time to do so, for the book was all but ready for publication." The dedication is on p. 26.

character had come under his notice. I said I thought it was many years since any one had published a collection of pieces frankly in the Handelian manner. He said "not in fact since Handel died," which is true, and I was glad to hear him say it: please note however that this does not for a moment pretend that the pieces will bear comparison with what Handel did himself or with other collections written in different manners —it only refers to the style of the pieces. I am very glad you can give a good account of my father. Sir J. Lubbock[3] is no friend of mine. He was closely intimate with old Darwin, & is sure to view me and all my works with disfavour—

Believe me Yr. affte brother
S. Butler—

I will come down, please towards the end of this month.

66. *Butler to May*

Text: British Museum MS.

15. Clifford's Inn
E. C
April 2. 1885.

Dear May

We changed our plans at the last moment and are going by the excursion steamer from London Bridge to Boulogne—They take us *there and back* for 12/6 and we think the change will be greater and do us more good and we shall get a whiff of sea—so we have decided to go and shall stay at Boulogne without moving about till Tuesday evening when the boat returns and brings us back to London on Wednesday morning.

My address will be Hotel de Paris Boulogne—but I shall not expect to hear till after Easter now. I am very glad you can give such a good account of my father—with the warm

[3] John Lubbock (1834–1913), at this time well known as a Liberal politician and as a writer of popular science books. As a young man Lubbock lived near Darwin, at Down, and received much of his scientific training from him.

weather ⟨now⟩ coming on he ought to do well now for some time. I am certainly brain fagged and my eyes are troublesome. I mean I cannot use them to the same extent as heretofore even for reading & writing. I don't like going for more than eight weeks at full swing without a broken week. I have often done it and always been sorry for it—this spring I have been close on 13 weeks and this is more than is good for me.

We have had one friendly little notice in "The People"[1] but no more. I will send it but have not got it at present. It said very little, but was not spiteful.

Also Mivart has been referring to Life & Habit with some fulness[2]—for though I am only mentioned expressly in one passage the whole article is against Life & Habit—or rather against what he chose to say is Life & Habit. His article is stupid & unintelligible, but it will do me good. It is in this month's Fortnightly Review.

I have finished my minuet and shall take the chorus with me to Boulogne in case there is a piano & it is wet—but I hope for every one's sake that we shall have a fine Easter. I hope Harry will enjoy himself & have good weather too.

Our boat leaves about midnight, but we shall go on board at 9.30 & go to bed—as they have good sleeping accomodation on board—the voyage takes from 10 to 12 hours. I hope you will all keep well till my return—and as much longer as possible—and am

Yr. affte. brother
S. Butler—

Letter 66:

[1] A short notice of *Gavottes, Minuets, Fugues* which commends their "musicianly grace and generally tuneful character" (*The People*, March 29, 1885, p. 10).

[2] Mivart attacked the theory that there is an "unconscious intelligence" directing the process of evolution, and cited Butler's *Unconscious Memory* and *Life and Habit* as carrying "this hypothesis of unconscious intelligence to its last consequences" (*The Fortnightly Review*, 37 *n.s.* [March, April, 1885], 323–337, 519–531).

67. Butler to May

Text: British Museum MS.

15. Clifford's Inn
E. C
Apr 15. 1885

Dear May

Thank you for your letter received Monday morning. I am glad the opening of the Museum [1] passed off so well and I am also spitefully glad (and the luxury of small spite is a very pleasant one) that my father did not think Sir J. Lubbock [2] particularly successful. I do not like him and am sorry that the Bank holidays shd have come from him & not from our side. However that is only more small spite. At any rate I am glad the opening was such a success and am much obliged to you for sending me the paper. I keep catching colds & sore throats wh: are new things with me. I have had a cold off and on ever since the end of December when I went to see poor old Mr. Tylor that bitterly cold night & cannot shake it off— I think myself this spring has been a very trying one and wish I could see the weather cock point towards the S. West again— nor is my head right, by any means. I don't mind a cough shaking it a bit—what I don't like is its coming back again after it is all gone—when I have once got it into this state I find it very troublesome to get rid of. ⟨However⟩ I mean I don't like the jar & temporary headache caused by a cough subsiding & then coming back again in full force without any new cough, a minute or so afterwards. I got this first about two years ago & never got rid of it till I stayed at Wilderhope during my father's illness & did nothing for a fortnight. Then I lost it, & have not had it since till it came on the morning after I got to Shrewsbury a fortnight ago, and now I suppose I am in for it till the Summer—I have seen my doctor about it. He says it is brain fag—but evidently does not con-

Letter 67:

[1] The Free Library and Museum of Shrewsbury, purchased by public subscription, was formally opened on April 9, 1885.

[2] See note 3 for Letter 65. Lubbock was chiefly responsible for the Bank Holidays Act of 1871, Liberal legislation.

sider it serious. I don't get on with my chorus or rather have not got on till yesterday when at last I settled satisfactorily a passage which I have written & rewritten till there seemed no end to it & now I hope I shall get on faster. We hear nothing about our music—Novello's man told me he had seen a very favourable review somewhere, but could not tell me where—which was vexatious, but he says they are selling fairly well. I am also very busy & deeply interested with my second volume of Life & Habit,[3] which I think all will like who liked the first volume.

Pray remember me most kindly to Alice Hall.[4] If ever she gets a chance of pumping Sir Arthur Sullivan about our Gavottes &c. I wish she would, but am afraid by his not acknowledging the receipt of them that he did not estimate them so highly as we do. I am sorry to hear of poor old Miss Hall's death. I am very glad my father keeps so well and am

Yr. affte. brother
S. Butler—

P.S. I believe it is settled now that the earth is *older* than the sun—and all the planets also older except Uranus & Neptune which rotate on their axes the other way to what all the other planets and the sun do. It has been a great puzzle why they shd do this & now people say they know: I don't quite understand it, but no doubt it is all right.

68. *Butler to May*

Text: British Museum MS. *Extracts published: Memoir*, II, 19–20.

15. Clifford's Inn E. C.
June 30. 1885

Dear May

Thank you for your's received on Friday— By this time doubtless my father has got home and I am glad to think he had finer weather during the latter part of his outing; I am

[3] *Luck or Cunning?*
[4] See note 3 for Letter 4.

sure it must have done him a great deal of good. Please ask him whether he can give me a bed for a few days on Tuesday June [July] 14th till the following Saturday. If he can I will come down. Not that I have any thing to say or business of any kind but I shall be going somewhere for my holiday at the end of the month or early in next and unless I go then shall not be able to do so for some time.

I went to an old acquaintance's [1] on Sunday evening or should have written then. He is secretary to the Joint Stock Bank of London and writes mildly broad church books. He had made what I am sure was a plant to bring me & one of my particular foes Grant Allen together. I had said I would go, and late on Saturday night—too late for me to get out of it, Grant Allen was sprung upon me as to be one of the company: so I must either make a good deal of fuss, or go & be civil. Of course the second alternative was the proper one—at the same time I did not like it, for Grant Allen had behaved badly by me,[2] & I had given it to him pretty hot in two of my books.[3] However I went and did the thing handsomely assuring him how glad I was to have the pleasure of meeting him and behaving as though there had never been the smallest row of any kind between us—this is literary etiquette: to do him justice he behaved very well too, so it all went off smoothly. There were a lot of other literary people (& scientific) people there and I derived more of an impression that last year's *Athenaeum* row [4] had been working than I have done on any oc-

Letter 68:

[1] Jones identifies this "old acquaintance" as Edward Clodd (Memoir, II, 19). Clodd (1840–1930), a banker by profession, had wide intellectual interests and admired Butler; but because of his close friendship with Grant Allen (1848–1899) —one of Butler's chief scientific "enemies"—Butler never considered him a friend.

[2] Allen reviewed *Evolution, Old and New* in the *Academy*, 15 (May 17, 1879), 426–427: "[The book] is very characteristically Erewhon, or in other words Nowhere, spelt backward, and spelt backward incorrectly." The accuracy of the paraphrase that Butler gives of Allen's review a few sentences below suggests the strong impression it made on him.

[3] Butler answered Allen's review in an appendix to the second edition of *Evolution, Old and New* (1882), pp. 339–342. This was the only *book* in which Butler quarreled with Allen, and when Jones printed part of the letter he silently corrected Butler's error so that the text of the letter reads: "in *one* of my books."

[4] The dispute with Romanes and Lankester about the source of the phrase, "Hereditary memory." (See notes 3 and 4 for Letter 52 and note 2 for Letter 55.)

casion since the row—but it disgusted me in a way too to hear Grant Allen praise Evolution Old and New so warmly and say of what great use he had found it and all the rest of it—which indeed is true ⟨enough⟩ for it has appeared clearly enough in his books—& to remember that when it came out he laughed at it & sneered at it as "leaving the reader without a single clear idea upon any subject whatever," and did it more mischief than anyone else I know—and all the time I had had his first book his "Colour Sense" submitted to me by Trubner in its sketch state, and did all I could to induce Trubner to take it—which indeed he did.[6] However what it comes to virtually is that Grant Allen wanted to make peace & I let him—and I dare say it is as well—

With all best wishes to you all believe me

Yr. affte. brother
S. Butler—

69. *Butler to May*

Text: British Museum MS. *Extracts published: Memoir,* II, 22, and *Butler-Savage Letters,* pp. 361–362.

15. Clifford's Inn
E. C.
July 24. 1885

Dear May

I arrived safely & without adventure on Saturday evening, and yesterday severed the last material traces—or rather I shd say devoured the last material traces—of my visit by [*illegible word*], finishing the excellent cream cheese my father was good enough to give me. It was very good indeed. By the way can my father spare Gretton's [1] little book "ferrago libretti" which I saw in the dining room. If he can, please send it me by

[6] *The Colour Sense: Its Origin and Development* (1879), Allen's second book, the only one published by Trübner.

Letter 69:

[1] Frederick Edward Gretton. (See note 6 for Letter 17.)

book post and I will return it in a day or two. Also I have your Paradisio Sonatas, or rather they are at Jones's—shall I get them & send them to you? You will gather from this that I am having my great annual tidying & cleaning up. I generally do this on my return from abroad, but this year have taken it into my head that I shall enjoy my outing better if I feel that I have left everything very trim & shipshape—You know it was said that no one could *be* as wise as Lord Thurlow looked.[2] I want it to be that no rooms can look as tidy as mine are. Among other things I am arranging in proper order and dating poor Miss Savage's letters & as many of mine to her as have reached me. This is a very painful business but no one can do it except me and the letters must have all the care bestowed upon them that I can bestow upon them. I should burn mine to her but they explain hers so much—when there are any—that I cannot do this. I do not find I miss Miss Savage any less than I did when I heard of her death. She kept all my early letters and all my latest ones, but for some years there are none returned to me. I destroyed her letters at first and did not take to keeping them till about thirteen years ago since which time I kept every scrap she wrote. How I ever came to burn her earlier ones I cannot conceive—but enough of this. I shall not go abroad till I have done all I have to do to those I have kept.

Did you read Tennyson's poem about the Princess Beatrice's marriage? [3]

I hope my father is well—indeed this weather he is pretty sure to be so. I will add no more and am

Yr affte brother
S. Butler—

[2] "On one occasion, during the progress of Mr. [Warren] Hastings' trial, Mr. [Charles James] Fox, struck by the solemnity of Lord [Edward] Thurlow's appearance, said to the Speaker, 'I wonder if any man ever was so wise as Thurlow looks' " (George Pellew, *The Life and Correspondence of Right Hon. Henry Addington, First Viscount Sidmouth* [1847], I, 155).

[3] "To H.R.H. Princess Beatrice," a short poem in honor of her marriage to Prince Henry of Battenberg on July 23, 1885, appeared in the *Times* on that day.

70. Butler to May

Text: British Museum MS. *Extracts published: Memoir*, II, 22.

Hotel Croce Bianca
Varallo Sesia, Novarese [Italy]
Augt. 23. 1885.

Dear May

Thank you for yours of the 16th [1] to which I have been unable to reply till this evening I find myself quiet for a little while. I left Sargans on Monday evening last—slept at Coire; left next morning at 5.20 a. m and crossed the S. Bernardino to Bellinzona. At Bellinzona I lunched in company with the monk who is parroco of Soazza. I knew him and laughingly reminded him of how he wd not let me finish a study of a festa & I had to go away without finishing it; he had heard of Alps & Sanctuaries & wanted me to send a copy to Soazza. I again laughed & said I wd only send one on condition that he wd let me make a sketch upon a Sunday. He saw he was caught & gave me a pinch of snuff at once.

"Io dico niente," said he laughing, "ma siamo intesi," [2] so, I suppose I must send him a copy. I had behaved quite rightly for I had asked leave & on being refused had not done the study so we parted amicably.

Then I went on down the Laggo Maggiore reaching Arona on ⟨the⟩ Wednesday evening late. There I found the Albergo d'italia my favorite inn closed and the Zanettas gone. Next morning I went to Varallo by a series of small cross country diligences & arrived about six in the evening. Friday I outlined, and the evening brought Miss Thomas & Miss Zimmern.[3] We three represent so far as we can see the whole

Letter 70:

[1] In a letter to Jones dated August 19, 1885, Butler says that he received a letter from May reporting that it was difficult to get Canon Butler to take proper exercise. Butler thinks May's letter indicates that his father is weaker.

[2] "I will say nothing, but we understand each other." For an account of Butler's first interview with this monk, see *Alps and Sanctuaries*, chap. 17, p. 181.

[3] Butler met Bertha Thomas through Miss Savage, who worked as a governess for Miss Thomas's uncle, John Sumner, son of the Archbishop of Canterbury. Helen Zimmern (1846–1934), known as a translator of Lessing and Schopenhauer, had

foreign element that has come to do honour to Gaudenzio Ferrari.[4] Yesterday we took a small vittura between us to Valduggia where Gaudenzio Ferrari was born. Valduggia is abt 10 miles from Varallo in a Valley breaking off from the Val Sesia a few miles below Varallo. The country is enchanting and the festa went off exceedingly well. The town clerk of Varallo is an old & very particular friend of mine of some 15 years standing, & he took the greatest care of us seeing that we were well feted and we had to sign our names, as among those who had assisted, in the records of the paese, as we have had to do again at Varallo today. We rather like this, it is so charmingly incongruous. Today there was nothing done till after two since which we have been in a whirl of *discorsi* and flags flying and processions in which we took part of course, & tonight the town will be illuminated and there will be fireworks in the giardino publico. Of course I had much rather be sketching quietly without any *festa* at all; but the *festa* had to be gone through according to a long standing promise and after all I don't dislike it, and am gathering lots of notes. There are to be two more days of it and then I shall be able to paint again. I have chosen three excellent subjects and shall stay here another week at least as I want to do them. I think what I did at Sargans was abt. the best I have ever done, and hope to get some nice studies here. I think I shall have to give up the Valtellina this year and stick between here and Varese and Bellinzona till it is time for me to come back, at any rate I shall be (another) week here; I know a good many people here and feel as though I were rather regarded as among the institutions of the place, having been known now a good many years, at any rate they know I like them and make me feel as though they like me, so it all goes very nicely. They know Alps & Sanctuaries & keep pressing me to write a book like it

just completed her biography, *Maria Edgeworth*, and was beginning a series of books on Italy.

[4] Gaudenzio Ferrari (*ca.* 1470–1546), a painter whose work is extensively represented in the churches at Varallo, especially the Sacro Monte. (See *Ex Voto* [1888], *passim.*)

about them, & I expect I shall have to do it when I have done the one now in hand.[5]

I am very glad to hear my father keeps so well, and heartily hope he will continue to do so. Very sorry that John [6] does not gain faster. Believe me Yr affte brother

S. Butler—

71. *Butler to May*

Text: British Museum MS.

Dear May

Hotel Riposo, Sacro Monte
Varese, Italy
Sep 9. 1885

Your's of the 5th [1] reached me yesterday. I am very sorry you cannot send me a better account of my father, but after a cold one must always expect the cough to be worse for some little time, and I hope your next letter will bring a better account. I am also extremely sorry to hear of Rhoda & Bessie Bather's accidents, but hope that in neither case there will be any permanent mischief. I left Varallo on the 6th having I think made a very fair impression, but I was more or less an old friend to start with— I got to Varese town the same evening and here next morning. As usual it was a gran festa, but Alas! it was dreadfully wet both Monday & Tuesday, and the poor people, who came none the less, got such a drenching as many of them I am afraid will not soon forget. At five I got up & looked out of window—there they all were in thousands filling the broad road up to the Sanctuary, under a

[5] Butler was working on *Ex Voto: An Account of the Sacro Monte or New Jerusalem at Varallo-Sesia.*

[6] John Worsley. (See Biographical Sketches.)

Letter 71:

[1] In a letter to Jones dated September 8, 1885, Butler says that he received a letter from May reporting that his father had not been able to leave the house and had had a bad coughing fit.

sea of "humble brothers." Today it is lovely and the mountain tops being covered with snow I think it bids fair to settle down. I am finishing a picture begun 3 years ago, but then left incomplete through the break up of the weather which ended in the Verona floods. On the whole I am painting better than I have ever done yet, the last three or four summers I have hardly painted at all except the picture I am doing now & one at Mont St. Michel; I drew almost exclusively instead. This year I am not drawing at all except to outline, and I seem to have rather turned a corner. I expect the black & white has done me good, any way I think there is considerable difference between what I have done before and what I am doing now. The camera saves a lot of trouble.

This is much the most beautiful of all the Italian Sanctuaries quâ place, and it is the most delightful place to stay at imaginable. There is a very nice Italian family here, an old gentleman his wife & daughter. The wife reminds me a little of Aunt Bather and the daughter is really very like Elsie. The old gentleman said to me today—"Why shd one take walks at such a place as this? è inutile—it is enough to sit here in a chair without going so far as to say that it is quite useless to take a walk at all. I do think that this is about as good as any thing North Italy can do. This morning I saw Monte Rosa—Monte Viso, the mountains above Genoa and the Apennines as far as Bologna with Novara shrines (or whatever they shd be called) Milan and the lakes of Varese, Gallarate & the Lago Maggiore [2] all seen through chestnut trees & vineyards. I do not know any such panorama as this—& then on the other side the marvellous Sacro Monte.

I am better than when I left, but did rather too much at Varallo and my head is still not quite right. I shall stay here some days so you had better address here—then Jones will join me and I shall go so far with him on his way to his mother at

[2] Butler, standing in a semicircle formed by the Alps, was looking over the Po valley. Behind him to the northwest was Monte Rosa on the Swiss border. To the southwest at a distance were Monte Viso and the mountains above Genoa; directly below him, the lakes of Varese and Gallarate; in the valley, Novara and Milan, and further on, the Apennines, which stretch southeastward toward Bologna.

Vicenza which I have long wanted to see, & which is close to Castelfranco about which Miss Thomas & Miss Zimmern have rather set my head on fire. Then about the 24th I shall begin to turn homewards. If I go from here before letters reach me they will be forwarded directly—these are most excellent people, and both feed me well and charge me little—the monde is exclusively Italian—no English ever stay here. Events I have had none since the baton affair [3]—With all best wishes to you all I am

Yr. affte. brother
S. Butler—

72. *Butler to May*

Text: British Museum MS.

15. Clifford's Inn
Fleet Street E. C.
Oct. 12. 1885

Dear May

I had meant to have written before post time but have been hindered by small interruptions. I was very sorry to hear from my father that you had had one of your bad turns and am afraid this really bitter weather is not in your favour. I do hope, however, that you may be better; I am afraid I think that you do a good deal more than you have strength for: so indeed do I, and cannot help it—but I fear you overtax yourself more considerably than I do, it is no use however preaching to any one on this head. I am very well, but as usual find getting into harness tells on me at first—this is always so & it always wears off after a fortnight or so—it is my eyes that feel it most—so long as I don't read & write much they are perfectly right, but they will not stand the amount of con-

[3] Butler tells Jones, in a letter dated August 26, 1885, about attending a performance of a new composition in the church at Sacro Monte. The composer, Antonio Cagnoni, conducted, and Butler was so taken with his skill as a composer and conductor that as a sign of his admiration he asked for his baton—and was given it (*Memoir,* II, 23–24). See also *Ex Voto,* chap. 17, p. 194.

secutive using they once would; printing does not try them at all—it is writing which they most object to.

Please thank my father for his very kind letter. I am very sorry to think that he must now be rather a close prisoner for some little time, but am afraid there is no help for it—please tell him I will send my Athenaeum letter when it appears.[1] I have written it, but am keeping it till Jones returns. I got him to go to the Brera on his way home—& see whether he agreed with me—he writes that he has no hesitation about it, so I am tolerably easy, for I impressed it on him to be sceptical. He will be back now in a week, and as soon as he has seen my letter I shall send it. It seems to me quite a pious act to give those two good men their portraits again—and such perfectly comfortable satisfactory portraits too. I cannot understand how any one can have wished to disturb them, fortunately the new theory which I am combatting [2] breaks down too completely to admit of being resuscitated, for it requires us to believe that a man who was not born till 1510, painted as young men two men who were painted as in middle life or elderly in 1507, & again in 1514: so I think I may say there is an end of that.

I have written a very pretty minuet which came into my head while I was abroad, and am now doing the little that remains to be done to my share of the Cantata [3]—which I do hope will now really get done before Xmas. I have not yet resumed my book,[4] but shall do so immediately now. I don't think I have any news that can interest you—I saw Etta one

Letter 72:

[1] The letter, "Portraits of Gentile and Giovanni Bellini," appeared in the *Athenaeum* on February 20, 1886 (p. 271). In it, Butler attempts to show that a painting in the Louvre attributed to another artist was a portrait by Gentile Bellini of himself and his brother Giovanni; as evidence he cites two very similar heads (which he says must be those of the Bellini) in a painting by Giovanni in the Brera in Milan. The letter is reprinted in the Shrewsbury Edition, XIX, 151–155.

[2] J. A. Crowe and G. B. Cavalcaselle, in *A History of Painting in North Italy* (1871), I, 133–134, maintained that the painting was not by Gentile but by Cariani and that the heads were not those of the Bellini.

[3] *Narcissus.* According to Jones, they had made enough progress on it to have some of it performed in May, 1886 (*Memoir*, II, 37).

[4] *Luck or Cunning?*, which appeared about a year later.

day last week: she seemed fairly well, and Maysie was all right; I did not see Charlie. I dare say I shall get a letter from some one or other of you in a day or two and am

Yr affte. brother
S. Butler—

73. *Butler to May*

Text: British Museum MS. *Extracts published: Memoir,* II, 27–28.

15. Clifford's Inn
E. C
Oct. 21. [1885] [1]

Dear May

Thank you for your's of the 14th. how fast the time slips by —I can hardly believe it is 9 days since I wrote. I hope you are better and that my father keeps well—this weather is nice for him here.

No—I will not have any Persian cat—it is undertaking too much responsibility. I must have a cat whom I find homeless, wandering about the court & to whom therefore I am under no obligation—there is a Clifford's Inn euphemism about cats which the laundresses use quite gravely: they say people come to this place *"to lose"* their cats: they mean that when they have a cat they don't want to kill & don't know how to get rid of they bring it here and drop it inside the railings of our grass plot and go away under the impression that they have been "losing" their cat. Well this happens very frequently and I have already selected a dirty little drunken wretch of a kitten to be successor to my poor old cat. I don't suppose it drinks anything stronger than milk & water but then, you know so much milk & water must be very bad for a kitten that age—at any rate it looks as if it drank, but it gives me the impression of being affectionate, intelligent and fond of mice

Letter 73:
[1] This letter is dated 1886, apparently by Butler at a later time, perhaps by mistake in trying to clarify the last numeral. The contents clearly date it 1885.

—and I believe if it had a home it wd become more respectable, at any rate I will see how it works.

Grant Allen has brought out his Darwin and has made a handsome acknowledgment of Evolution Old & New in his preface [2] [*three or four illegible words*] to do this two years ago. Also the Athenaeum sent or rather personally offered me the book to review—this was the first time they ever asked me to review a book, but I declined on the ground that I had seen it and shd cut it up if I reviewed it, and I did not think this [would] look well considering how savagely Grant Allen had cut up mine. I was *very* sorry not to review it, but I make no doubt I was right. It is however a sign that I must have gained ground lately for they would never have done this two years ago.

My letter about the Bellini will probably appear in next week's Athenaeum—I think it is all right.

Last night Jones & I both went to dine at Miss Thomas's to a "pranzo sociale" to meet Miss Zimmern,[3] play Narcissus & talk Italy—it was very pleasant. Also I have at last done what I have threatened for some time past, and bought one of those new & cheaper Columbia type writers. I cannot yet write as fast with it as with the pen, but even now it is a great comfort. It saves all fatigue of eye, and then one can see so well what one has got. I have only had it a week, but I already feel I shd be lost without it, and it will save its cost twice over in a single book, for I can see my book in type before sending it to the press, and correct it so much better that I ought to have very little corrections in future to pay for. I have written my

[2] "There are, however, three persons in particular from whom I have so largely borrowed facts or ideas that I owe them more special and definite thanks. . . . From Mr. Samuel Butler, the author of 'Evolution Old and New,' I have derived many pregnant suggestions with regard to the true position and meaning of Buffon, Erasmus Darwin, and the early essentially teleological evolutionists—suggestions which I am all the more anxious to acknowledge since I differ fundamentally from Mr. Butler in his estimate of the worth of Charles Darwin's distinctive discovery of natural selection" (Charles Grant Allen, *Charles Darwin* [1885], p. v).

[3] See note 3 for Letter 70.

Athenaeum letter with it, and use it for all writing except for letters to intimate friends. I hope Elsie is all right and am sure you will find her [a] help to brighten the house— With all best wishes to you all believe me

Yr. affte. brother
S. Butler—

74. *Butler to May*

Text: British Museum MS.

15. Clifford's Inn
Fleet Street E. C.
Dec. 22. 1885

Dear May

Thank you for your's received Saturday morning. I send this to say that I shall leave town on Thursday morning & return on Sunday evening—let me have a line on Thursday morning if you can manage it, and if it gives a good account of my father, as I have no doubt it will, I will not have letters forwarded: for that short time it really does not seem necessary & Mrs. Doncaster is very stupid about it. I have not yet settled where to go but it will be somewhere close at hand.

I am extremely sorry about Mrs. Bather's hand. As for the shilling the man stole & he did not steal—this is one of the not uncommon cases in which a contradiction in terms is the most legitimate statement of the facts. If you choose to look at the "steal" side of the matter you can see it to the exclusion of the other: if you choose to look at the "not steal" side you can do the same: the sides are so nearly equal in value that neither distinctly overbalances the other: this being so, a preponderance (with consequent formed opinion) is only obtained temporarily by looking at one side rather than the other.

We find Jones's head is *not* ring worm—it is what is called Alopecia Areata, and is not catching nor connected with ringworm in any way. He went to a specialist who at once declared it to be what I have said above only I don't know whether the first Latin name has two l's in it or only one. Fortunately whatever it was the hair has begun to grow again. The doctor said it was the result of a nerve-storm—but we neither of us were aware of any particular disturbing cause; still a nerve-storm sounds rather grand. He went out to dinner the other day and heard a lady sing a song—a French song—so the lady's mamma told him—but to Jones it seemed as though it were about some Indian potentate whose name was Sir Cussha Sweesong Twar.[1] The mamma said the lady had such a beautiful Parisian accent.

Wishing you all a happy Xmas I am

Yr. affte. brother
S. Butler—

75. *Butler to May*

Text: British Museum MS. ***Extracts published: Memoir,*** II, 29.

15. Clifford's Inn
E. C
Dec. 29. 1885

Dear May

One line to say that we returned on Sunday evening as per programme. I think I must have caught cold; at any rate I have a very heavy one now, the first I have had this winter, and am fit for nothing—Tuesday is more particularly my day for going round my houses [1] & I ought not to have gone this morning, but went, and this evening am paying the penalty of my imprudence. Tomorrow unless better I will lie up. Curiously enough like all unimaginative people I have a fancy that every one else has a cold, as soon as I get one myself,

Letter 74:
[1] *Ce que je suis sans toi* (Butler's note).

Letter 75:
[1] The houses he owned in Battersea.

whereas until I had caught one I fancied that really no one was at all likely to have one; I hope the fancy is groundless so far as all you are concerned.

There has come out a very angry and untruthful version of my quarrel with Darwin in a German book by Dr. Krause [2]—most unfair—but as it is in German I shall take no notice of it: they would not dare to say the same in English; I am angry, of course, but ⟨I⟩ think I shall probably do most wisely by taking no notice unless the book is translated. I am getting on with my book,[3] but never wrote one which I had to rewrite so much: it will probably be all the better for it.

Please ask my father if he remembers a line in Horace "Nec mihi res sed me rebus componere. . . ." [4] Does he remember the last word—it sounds as if it ought to be "conor" but I have a half fancy that the o in Conor may be short; if he remembers ask him to supply the missing word; if he doesn't I will look through the Epistles & Satires of Horace. I want the passage as summing up the Lamarckian system, according to which modification is effected by animals & plants adapting themselves to their surroundings as well as they can, and as the surroundings gradually changed—changing too—

[2] Ernst Krause, *Charles Darwin und sein Verhaltnis zu Deutschland, Gesammelte kleinere Schriften von Charles Darwin*, I (Leipzig, 1885), 185–186. The passage summarizes Krause's view of the following events: In February, 1879, Krause (1839–1903) published a sketch of Erasmus Darwin's life in the German periodical *Kosmos*. *Evolution, Old and New*, in which Butler praises Erasmus Darwin as opposed to his grandson, appeared in May. In November, Charles Darwin published *Erasmus Darwin*, which he claimed was a translation of Krause's biographical sketch, but which actually contained additional passages directed against Butler's position in *Evolution, Old and New*. Butler objected on the grounds that he was being refuted without being acknowledged an opponent. For Butler's view see *Unconscious Memory*, chap. 4, pp. 41–56.

[3] *Luck or Cunning?*

[4] Nunc in Aristippi furtim praecepta relabor,
Et mihi res, non me rebus subiungere conor.
(Book I, Epistle 1, ll. 18–19)

Butler adapts and uses these lines in *Luck or Cunning?* (p. 79): "According to Charles Darwin 'the preservation of favoured,' or lucky, 'races' is by far the most important means of modification; according to Erasmus Darwin effort *non sibi res sed se rebus subjungere* is unquestionably the most potent means; roughly therefore, there is no better or fairer way of putting the matter, than to say that Charles Darwin is the apostle of luck, and his grandfather, and Lamarck, of cunning."

I hope you are all none the worse for this bitter wind and am

Yr affte. brother
S— Butler—

P. S. How is poor Mrs. Henry Bather's hand?

76. *Butler to May*

Text: British Museum MS. *Extracts published: Memoir,* II, 29–30.

15. Clifford's Inn
E. C
Jan 18. 1886

Dear May

Thank you for your's received this morning—please tell my father from me that I am extremely glad to hear he is so much better; ere long now we may consider the neck of the winter broken and on the whole he is getting through it very well. Pray again congratulate him from me.

We were much shocked yesterday to find that a poor old man who keeps a public-house near Dartford, where we generally take our beer with our sandwiches when we are in that neighbourhood, had been horribly murdered by a discharged soldier about ten days ago.[1] The soldier murdered a customer, who was sitting before the fire, and then murdered the landlord apparently without any reason. He was apprehended immediately.

A man named Vianna de Lima has been writing a book in French, *Les Theories Transformistes de Lamarck, Darwin, et Haeckel.* It is only just out, but the Museum had received it and got it for me before it has appeared in the catalogue. I was pleased to find a perfectly satisfactory and unsnubbing reference to *Life and Habit* [2] as though to quite a standard

Letter 76:

[1] On January 1, 1886, the keeper of the Greyhound, near Dartford, and one of his lodgers were murdered by an army pensioner.

[2] Arthur Vianna de Lima, *Exposé sommaire des theories transformistes de Lamarck, Darwin et Haeckel* (Paris, 1885), p. 106.

book—so I set this off against *The Athenaeum* and Dr. Krause.[3]

I am getting on fast with my book which I shall call *Luck or Cunning as the most important means of Organic Modification?* The short title will be *Luck or Cunning?* which I think will do very well.

Yesterday at last I found "Pousse"[4] and having fixed it do very well.

I hope you are better. I am pretty well all right again now, but had a long cold. I think the worst of the winter is over. I hope Harrie will get good by her outing, and am

Yr. affte. brother
S. Butler—

77. *Butler to May*

Text: British Museum MS. *Extracts published: Memoir*, II, 34.

15. Clifford's Inn
E. C
Mar 24. 1886

Dear May

Thank you for your letter received this morning. I am very glad to hear that you are so much better and hope that with this fine weather you may keep free from a return of neuralgia. You say it is a long time since you wrote to me, and indeed I cannot deny that I had been expecting to hear from one or other of you; ⟨for some day's post's⟩ considering how ill my father still was when Harrie last wrote I confess I do not understand why either you or she did not write sooner. If I had not heard from Etta on Saturday that my father had

[3] See note 2 for Letter 75. After Charles Darwin's "translation" of Krause's article appeared, Butler outlined his case in a letter to the *Athenaeum* (January 31, 1880, p. 155). There was no reply, and Butler felt that the *Athenaeum* intentionally shut off debate.

[4] Jones noted on this letter that "Pousse" is a corn salad, which the French call "mâche."

come down to breakfast on the preceding day, I should have been anxious, uneasy & uncomfortable for some days past.

My kittens came and alas! went—one after another died for want of sufficient nourishment—this being their poor mother's first confinement she had forgotten to make the milk necessary to feed her offspring & so one after another starved in spite of what I cd. do; I had found homes for three out of the four—and was very sorry to lose them. They were exceedingly pretty while they lasted, but none of them lived as long as four days. The cat came & told me that things were not going right frequently & I soon found out what the matter was, but I could not do anything.

You say perhaps I shall try for the Slade Professorship again.[1] My friends advise me not & I think wisely. They think I am all right as I am & that a good many are saying I ought to have had it & that there the matter should rest. I ought not to give them the chance of refusing me a second time. I hear from Etta that Middleton is "in a galloping consumption," but no matter when a vacancy occurs I should make a mistake if I stood again.

Jones and I have begun to score 'Narcissus;' it will be a long tedious business, but the difficulties like all others in connection with the work, prove mere bogies when attacked—in fact there is no difficulty about it. We are only scoring it for 5 stringed instruments, Horns, Hautbois, & Bassoons, for this is probably the band that will perform it. It will probably be performed (privately) next winter—indeed, unless unforseen accidents occur, this will be so.

I need not say I was very glad to get so good an account of my father; I think now the cold weather must be pretty well over—and am pleased to think that he will soon be able to enjoy more liberty. Here the weather is simply perfect. I am sorry to hear that uncle John seems somewhat seriously

Letter 77:

[1] Butler entered the competition for the Slade Professorship of Art at Cambridge, left vacant by the resignation of Sidney Colvin. On March 10 it was announced that J. H. Middleton (1846–1896) was the successful competitor.

failing, I thought him a good deal aged when I last saw him.

With all best wishes to you all believe me

Yr. affte. brother
S. Butler—

78. *Butler to May*

Text: British Museum MS.

15. Clifford's Inn
E. C
May 27, 1886

Dear May

Thank you very much for your letter of May 21. I saw a few day's afterwards the announcement of John Bather's death as having happened on that day. I am very sorry for them all and for poor Mrs. Bather to whom under the circumstances the blow must be doubly painful. I had not heard of John Bather's being ill, so conclude he had a sudden attack. Let me know about it please when first you write.

I am very glad it is settled that Harry [1] is to emigrate, but am also very glad that no responsibility in connection with his going there attaches to me. I should think it was a nice step to take, and if I was a young man should certainly emigrate myself but I think I should go to the N. Island of N. Zealand or to Australia. ⟨myself.⟩ I am very glad to hear he has been so exemplary in putting by money, not only for his own sake but from an avuncular point of view; a pecunious nephew is so far more agreable in every way than an impecunious one.

There is to be a Shrewsbury dinner on the 23d. I cannot say that I want to go—I look upon my school days as matters of ancient history—all very well in their way and doubtless exceedingly interesting once, but no longer seriously concerning me: still I suppose I ought to go—at least people tell me I rather ought so I have said I shall do so.

Letter 78:

[1] Butler's nephew. (See Biographical Sketches.)

Jones almost collapsed after the fatigues of the 18th; [2] for some days I thought he was going to be ill, but it has passed and he now seems all right again. Reggie Worsley said next day "well I've attended a great many rehearsals but I never saw one more successful." He said the players were applauding all the while between every piece—which neither Jones nor I knew; it seems the way they do it is to pat their violins, & this makes so little noise that it was lost in the clapping &c—of our small audience. At any rate I was very glad to hear they had done so. A tame oratorio is a delightful pet but he is something like a tame elephant and would eat Jones & me out of house & home if we did not keep him in his proper place. As for printing it—we might just as well throw our money into the sea.[3] Nevertheless we shall go on with the chorusses as fast as we can, but I have announced my book [4] for October and have still more to do to it than I like. I imagine that this book will do very well.

I am very glad you can send such good accounts of my father & hope that you & Harrie keep fairly well.

Believe me yr. affte. brother
S— Butler.

79. *Butler to May*

Text: British Museum MS. *Extracts published: Memoir,* II, 37–38.

15 Clifford's Inn
E. C
June 3, 1886

Dear May

Thank you for your's of the 28th. I am very sorry my father has had toothache and hope that it was a loose old stump & that the dentist chloroformed his gums well, in

[2] Jones writes: "We had made sufficient progress to have a rehearsal of some of it [*Narcissus*] on the 18th of May in Gogin's studio in King Henry's Road, followed by supper in the studio of another painter, Joseph Benwell Clark, on the floor below. Butler's cousin, Reginald Worsley, who knew many violinists and other players, got the band together . . ." (*Memoir,* II, 37).

[3] It was printed by Weekes & Co. in June, 1888.

[4] *Luck or Cunning?*

which case the operation is not a serious one; I wish it had been the Grand Old Man [1] instead & in that case I confess I should not have cared how tight the stump was in, nor how little chloroform was given him. However it seems as though his political days are numbered and that being so we may perhaps allow him to keep his teeth in peace. I really do think it looks as if the rejection of the Irish bills was pretty safe now,[2] and over and above my desire to see them rejected on grounds of public welfare I want them to be so because from the first I maintained that the house of Commons could never pass them—or at any rate never would, and I like being right. However the matter is not settled yet & we must wait and see.

I have no doubt you are wise in closing your home.[3] I am afraid in that matter I am on the side of the political economists & regard all such attempts as you are making with distrust—not as doubting that they are often successful in individual cases but as believing that the same amount of money and trouble can probably be turned to better account in other ways—and of course what one aims at is making the most of what one can command.

Jones and I went to a Philharmonic concert last night; [4] we went to the shilling places behind the orchestra and sat close to the drums so we could see each instrument & hear what it was about. I do wish people would not make their movements so long. We have resolved that all our movements shall be of reasonable length. I am afraid I liked our own music a great deal better than Beethoven's, but then, of course if we had been devoted admirers of Beethoven we should have founded ourselves on him and imitated him as we have imitated Handel. Narcissus's successor is to be called Ulysses [5]—

Letter 79:

[1] Gladstone.

[2] The Irish Home Rule Bill was defeated on June 7, and the Conservatives were returned in the general elections which followed.

[3] May was giving up her home for illegitimate girls.

[4] Butler gives a more detailed account of this performance in Shrewsbury *Note-Books*, pp. 129–131.

[5] Butler noted on his copy of this letter: "Here, then, is the beginning of a deflection on to Odyssey & Iliad, which I little foresaw, but over which I now rejoice. S.B. Feb. 26, 1902."

and is this time a serious work dealing with the wanderings of the real Ulysses—and treating the subject much as Hercules or Semele were treated. We think we could get some sailor choruses & some Circe & pig choruses & the Sirens, & then Penelope and her loom all afford scope. I made up my mind about it when I read Charles Lamb's translation of parts of the Odyssey in Ainger's book [6]—but please don't say anything about it.

I don't believe in Florida. I do believe in emigration—and shall not be sorry to hear when Henry goes out there that he has gone to some other state or even to Canada, or Australia or New Zealand. I hear that the climate for 5 months in the year is very unhealthy. Has young Atkinson [7] actually made money? Is he receiving an income or is he only going to make it? & has he spent a summer in the place?

I hope you are all pretty well & am

Yr. affte. brother
S. Butler—

80. *Butler to May*

Text: British Museum MS.

15. Clifford's Inn
E. C.
July 21, 1886.

Dear May

Thank you for your's received this morning—yes I will come on Monday by the usual train leaving Paddington at

[6] Alfred Ainger, a friend of Butler's cousin Henry Bather, published *Charles Lamb*, a short life, in 1882. Butler read it while visiting Shrewsbury in 1886. Ainger's book does not contain Lamb's "translation of parts of the *Odyssey*," but suggestive criticism of the *Odyssey* from Lamb's Preface is quoted (pp. 67–68). Jones says that this brief mention of the *Odyssey* inspired Butler to begin his *Ulysses* (Introduction to *The Authoress of the Odyssey*, Shrewsbury Edition, XII, xvii–xxiii), and he is supported by Butler's note (MS Notebooks, IV, 87, July 6, 1891): "People will say it is odd that I who must have known the Odyssey so well &c. should have departed from it so widely in my libretto of Ulysses. The fact is I wrote the libretto & my 5 songs without looking at the Odyssey, & only looked at the original when the work was nearly done as far as I was concerned."

[7] Henry used letters from a friend, Atkinson, who had emigrated to Florida, to convince his family that he should go too.

10 & reaching Shrewsbury at 2.45. I called on Harry on Monday afternoon and learned that he and Elsie meant going on the following day (that is to say on Tuesday next) so I shall see something of him, which I shall be very glad to do. I wish his eyes did not look so congested—Maysie's & Charlie's eyes do the same—if Dr. Burd happens to call while Harry is there I wish you would get him just to look at them and give him a few hints how best to humour them. With *me* congested eyes always mean more or less brain fag. I know that there are people whose eyes are always like that and it does not seem to matter much, but, as I said, if Dr. Burd puts in an appearance I think I would ask him to look at them.

I am very glad my father seems to have enjoyed his outing, at the same time I am sure he will be very glad to find himself at home again. He does not like late dinners, & the strain of visiting in other people's houses is always more or less fatiguing, so I shall not be surprised to hear that he has returned tomorrow, painters or no painters. Besides the Langar neighbourhood cannot but reawaken old associations that having now long been dormant cannot be revived without something near akin to pain—so I shall be glad when he is back & shall wish him fine weather for his Wales outing. I think the summer seems likely to be a fine & hot one. I hope it will for political reasons if for none other—a few good harvests would make things much easier for the new government.

I am glad I did not prophesy a coalition [1]—I was a good deal tempted to do so—for I did think it the most sensible & reasonable thing under the circumstances & fully hoped it would have come about. I suppose Lord Hartington & Mr. Chamberlain hope to regain the liberal party when Mr. Gladstone retires, & think their having served with a Conservative Government will do them harm. I think their wisest plan would be to throw in their lot once for all without more

Letter 80:

[1] After the results of the general election were known, Lord Salisbury was asked to form a new government, but there was still the possibility (which did not come about) that Lord Hartington, leader of the Liberal Unionists, and Chamberlain, leader of the Radical Unionists, would join Gladstone in a coalition government.

delay with the Conservatives, but I suppose they know their own business best—any how they must help us as long as Mr. Gladstone leads the opposition.

Veracini was an Italian writer of the first half of the last century [2]—he was twice for a short time in England but did not prove much of a success. He was a man of unbounded conceit & once all but killed himself by throwing himself out of [a] window because some one played better than he did. I have heard Piatti [3] play some, or at any rate one, suite of his & believe I liked it at the time but have forgotten it.

If I were you I would take my outing as soon as I could.

Yr. affte. brother
S. Butler—

81. *Butler to May*

Text: Garnett, pp. 213–215.

15 Clifford's Inn,
Sunday evening
[August, 1886] [1]

Dear May,

I am sorry to have let so long go by without a few lines, but ever since my last I have been working exceedingly hard and have really had no events. I did the head of little Pollie Morris for the Wades,[2] and made it much better than the other. I sent it yesterday, and they seemed pleased. The other certainly was very bad; much worse than I thought; but I

[2] Francesco Maria Veracini (1690–1750), better known as a violinist than as a composer. Butler greatly underrates his success in England.

[3] Alfredo Carlo Piatti (1822–1901), a cellist who spent most of his adult life in London. He too was a composer, but Butler means that he heard Piatti play a suite by Veracini.

Letter 81:

[1] Garnett dates this letter "probably 1887" because in it Butler refers to his new book on "heredity and instinct." But though dated 1887, *Luck or Cunning?* appeared in November, 1886; actually, the letter seems to have been written before Butler left for a holiday in Italy in mid-August, 1886.

[2] The family of Anne Wade, nurse to the Butler family.

was thoroughly played out when I did it, and indeed should not have done it at all at that time if I had not known how much Anne was looking forward to getting it.

I have not yet written to Miss Brooke. Every bit of spare time I get goes to my new book on 'heredity and instinct,' which will be out, I hope, before Christmas, and which will, I hope, do great things for me; but I assure you I am worked hard, and even such a matter as the correspondence necessary in the matter of Tom's settlement [3] wears me. Do you see my letters to my father? If so, you could, I am sure, do me a good turn by making him understand exactly what the hitch is, which by his last letter to me he did not seem to have got hold of. I hope he is well and enjoying himself; certainly he won't have it too hot if the weather there has been what it is here. Where is he gone after Mentone? He has not determined to have an adventure and gone to the seat of war,[4] has he?

As an example of how coincidences sometimes very nearly come about, but happily fail to do so entirely, let me tell you the following. My friend Pauli went, ten days or so ago, to Mt. St. Michel to see to the tombstone over his sister's grave. The driver of the diligence attempted the road across the sands before the tide was sufficiently down, and there was evidently great danger. Suddenly he remembered that it was the anniversary of his sister's death (she was drowned by the tide on those very sands). For the first time in his life he felt superstitious, but sat still, when fortunately all the other passengers rose against the driver and by main force made him put back.

I heard a funny thing to-day. A man told me at St. Albans, where I have been for the day, that one of the English Queens

[3] In his will (of which Butler was an executor), Tom tried to settle "what money he could on his children's quondam governess, and away from his own family" (MS Notebooks, II, 176, May, 1886). Butler was trying to frustrate this settlement.

[4] The Treaty of Bucharest in March, 1886, brought only nominal peace to the Balkans, and during the summer of 1886 England watched with great interest a series of events that threatened war.

lived there, but he said that at the moment he could not remember whether it was Boadicea or Anne of Bolaine [6]—or Bow Lane, as he pronounced it—he could not remember.

Your affectionate brother,
S. Butler.

82. *Butler to May*

Text: British Museum MS.

Faido
Ticino, Swiss
Sep. 9, 1886.

Dear May,

Thank you for your postcard of the 4th with good accounts of you all; I sent my father some Edelweiss on Monday, but having unfortunately posted the post card without addressing it it was returned to me & only went next day. Mrs. Danvers [1] & her son have been here since Sunday—they go on today, & I stay here two days longer going on to Bellinzona on Saturday evening. Please address "Hotel Bellinzona, Bellinzona, Switzerland." I am quite well and am enjoying my outing very much. The Danvers's were quite good and did not bore me more than it is desireable that I shd. be bored from time to time.

Yr. affte. brother
S. Butler

[6] The man, a "barman" in MS Notebooks, I, 216, confuses Boadicea, who sacked St. Albans during a revolt against the Romans, and Anne Boleyn, who lived 1,500 years later and had no connection with the town.

Letter 82:
[1] See note 2 for Letter 59.

83. *Butler to May*

Text: British Museum MS.

Hotel Bellinzona
Bellinzona [Switzerland]
Sep. 13 [1886]
Address to: Hotel Riposo
Sacro Monte, Varese
Lombardia, Italy—

Dear May—

Thank you for your post card wh: came this morning. Please also thank my father for his letter of two days earlier—glad the Edelweiss came all right—I left Faido yesterday. The Bishop of Chichester [1] and one of the Prebends were at Faido on Saturday & Sunday and were very civil to me. I was fortunate enough to say something which pleased the Bishop very much, but it is too long to report: I put them on to the Woodsias & Alternifoliums, and altogether it was rather a success. I am finishing an old study here, and on Wed. afternoon go on to Varese where I shall finish two more studies. Jones will join me there, & I shall then turn homewards. I quite surpassed myself in painting at Faido—expected to get on swimmingly here, but can not hit it off. Glad my father is so well—[*last few words and signature illegible*]

84. *May to Butler*

Text: British Museum MS.

Wilderhope
Oct. 1, 1886

My dearest Sam

You will like to hear that we had a lovely still warm afternoon yesterday, and that the stone-laying went off very nicely and pleasantly. The Bishop gave a good address, & spoke pret-

Letter 83:
[1] Richard Durnford (1802–1895).

tily to Papa afterwards, & *he* was very well and did not cough at all. The building committee gave him a very pretty trowel —with his name &c. engraved. Today he has gone to Harnage. It came on to rain soon after he started, and I hope he will not be the worse.[1]

Harrie is just starting back on her way to Ventnor, where she left all the Glover party.[2] She had not intended coming back so soon as this, only could not resist the stone laying.

I am very glad that the outing has done you good, & almost sorry to think of you in London again. I do hope you did not find the poor old woman very bad! [3] I'm afraid no one will have tried during your absence to get her into the workhouse. Etta says she would go directly & willingly if you promised to see that she "had a funeral."

I suppose you will soon see their house. I shall like to hear your impressions of it all—

Did I tell you that Mr. Moss [4] was going to be married. Mr. G. Hall [5] says he is very proud of himself, & cracks little jokes, & comes out in quite a new phase.

Bessie Bather's operation is over, in Edinburgh, & the accounts so far are very good. The doctors hope for a very complete & successful recovery, but she must be there some weeks. Edward Bather was married yesterday.

Our love, dear Sam—I wish you could have spirited me to Chiavenna. It is a place I dearly love.

Your very affectionate sister
May.

Letter 84:

[1] In a note on this letter, Butler says that he cannot remember whether this was the visit to Harnage that brought on his father's fatal illness, but he recalls Rogers, the butler, telling him that his father returned from Harnage one day, wet through and reluctant to part with his wet clothes.

[2] The family of Frances Caroline Glover. (See note 2 for Letter 24.)

[3] Mrs. Doncaster, Butler's laundress.

[4] Henry Whitehead Moss (1841–1917), headmaster of Shrewsbury School; he married Frances Beaufort on January 6, 1887.

[5] George Thomas Hall (1843–1931), senior assistant master at Shrewsbury School.

85. Butler to May

Text: British Museum MS. *Extracts published: Memoir,* II, 40–41.

15 Clifford's Inn
E. C.
Oct. 2, 1886.

Dear May

Thank you for your's received this morning. I am so glad you had a fine afternoon for your foundation laying—and that the bishop was nice. I think bishops generally are rather nice. I know I am terribly afraid of ⟨anything under⟩ an archdeacon, or I may say of a Dean, but am generally set quite at my ease by a bishop—when I have anything to do with one—which is not very often.

I stuck to my plan; spent Tuesday & Wednesday copying Holbein in Basle [1] and leaving Wednesday night got here on Thursday evening. I found my kittens well and strong but as wild as little tigers, through not having been habitually caressed. They spat and swore and altogether behaved abominable—now, though only 48 hours have gone by, they are quite tame and very pretty.

I had a scare at Basle about my theory concerning the Holbein drawing I have been working at. My theory was blown to atoms in a way which seemed to leave no doubt whatever that I was mistaken [2]—I was very meek—gave it all up and went immediately on the other tack—ere long however I had the pleasure of finding the evidence in favour of which I had retreated, break down hopelessly, and was able

Letter 85:

[1] A drawing, "La Danse des Paysans," which Butler maintained was by Holbein, in a letter to the *Academy,* 30 (October 23, 1886), 282–283.

[2] Butler's case for this drawing as an original Holbein rested largely on some faint marks in one corner. When he returned to Basel on this occasion the marks which he had seen earlier were gone. He contended that the directors of the Museum had obliterated them to disprove his theory. The fullest account of his position is his article, "L'Affaire Holbein-Rippel," *Universal Review,* 5 (November, 1889), 377–392, reprinted in Shrewsbury Edition, XIX, 173–192. Recent scholars consider the drawing a copy of Holbein by Nikolaus Rippel (1563–1631). See Heinrich Alfred Schmid, *Hans Holbein der Jungere,* II (Basel: Holbein-Verlag, 1948), 348–349.

to get important confirmation of my original opinion which I am now convinced was right—I shall write about it to the Athenaeum.

I am to lecture at the Working Men's College in December on the principles underlying the subdivision of the organic world into animal and vegetable.[3] I do not like it, but it is good for me to learn the use of my tongue. I shall do as I did before & speak my lecture not read it.

I am much better, but have never been free of my book which is now nearly printed. I have still to write the last chapter—some fourteen or fifteen pages—this I hope to do next week, and then nothing remains but the index. I shall be very glad when it is done—and shall be curious to see what kind of reception it meets with[4]—nothing, we may be sure, very startling—still I make no doubt that my position is greatly stronger than it was. I hope my father will take no hurt from the shower and am

Yr. affte. brother
S. Butler—

86. Butler to May

Text: British Museum MS.

15. Clifford's Inn
E. C.
Oct. 10, 1886

Dear May

I meant to have written yesterday, but the post slipped by and I was very busy finishing my last chapter which I have

[3] The lecture was postponed and given March 19, 1887. It is reprinted in Shrewsbury Edition, XVIII, 235–256.

[4] The reviews of *Luck or Cunning?* generally regretted its contentious tone but found it a clearly stated argument for Butler's position on evolution. In a spirited review (*Pall Mall Gazette*, May 31, 1887, p. 5), George Bernard Shaw applauded the book because it set out after Darwin (one of the "graven images" the English tend to set up) so directly; regardless of the validity of Butler's science, Shaw approved of his "skilfull terseness and exactness of expression, his frank disdain of affected suavity or imperturbability, his apparently but not really paradoxical humour, his racy epigrams, and the geniality of his protest against 'a purely automatic conception of the universe as of something that will work if a penny be dropped into the box.' "

now despatched. I am pleased to see that Trubner's people place my book first in their circular of autumn announcements, and in their advertisements, which means that they consider it their most important book; of course I have nothing to do with this, but it is another of the many little indicators which show me that my position is getting stronger—no doubt in great measure through the Athenaeum support given me two years ago.[1] I have sent the Athenaeum a letter [2] of about the same length as the one I sent in the spring, about a drawing of Holbein's hitherto said to be a copy but which I have I believe, conclusively shown to be an original. I have shown that the painter to whom it is ascribed in the Basle catalogue was not born till many years after the work he is supposed to have copied had been destroyed, and from internal evidence of paper, and collateral evidence of a photograph from Holbein's original sketch have made a very good case. The editor has promised me that the letter shall appear next Friday so I suppose it will. The Basle people gave me their only copy of the photograph on which my case mainly rests and said they would get another for themselves, but they did not like having it shown to them that their ascription was an impossible one. The drawing was bequeathed to them with the ascription it now bears and it never occurred to them to go into dates, and worry the thing out. Holbein is a man who is supposed to have been so exhaustively studied, that it is no small thing to get him another and very important work; indeed I am more pleased with this discovery and with giving the Bellini back their portraits [3] than with anything I have ever done. I only hope I shall not get jumped upon in a way I do not expect now, but Gogin [4] and other competent judges entertain no doubt that I am right.

I have sent away one of my kittens and shall not be al-

Letter 86:

[1] See Letters 52 and 55.

[2] The *Athenaeum* questioned Butler's letter about the Holbein drawing, and he quickly withdrew it and sent it to the *Academy*, where it appeared on October 23, 1886 (pp. 282–283). (See Letter 87.) For an account of his letter on the Bellini, which had appeared on February 2, see Letter 72.

[3] See note 1 for Letter 72.

[4] Charles Gogin. (See Biographical Sketches.)

together sorry to dismiss the other, lovely little beast though she is—she is arriving at a noisy mischievous age and is somewhat disturbing.

I am extremely glad to hear that Mrs. Bather is doing well, but I am afraid she must be very much shaken and broken down with such a long course of pain and shock as she has lately suffered—I am very sorry for her. I am very glad my father keeps so well and make no doubt that when the colder weather comes he will keep closer at home. I am sure that every effort will be made to induce him to do so. I have not been able to get to Narcissus yet, and dare say it will be some days before I can manage to do so, but I shall as soon as ever I can—Jones comes back this day week—Believe me yr. affte. brother

S— Butler—

87. *Butler to May*

Text: British Museum MS.

15. Clifford's Inn
E. C.
Oct. 19, 1886

Dear May

Thank you for your's received yesterday morning—very glad to have good accounts of my father and hope Harrie's cold will not be serious. The Athenaeum set up my letter, sent me proof & the understanding ⟨clearly was⟩ was perfectly clear that it was to appear on Friday—Friday came, but no letter, so on Monday I sent and found that the Athenaeum art critic had got hold of Maccoll,[1] the editor, and frightened him, calling the Basle drawing "rubbish," and utterly pooh-poohing my theory: I told Maccoll that there was nothing in it, but he naturally preferred to stick to his own man—& I therefore pointed out to him that I must take my letter to

Letter 87:
[1] Norman Maccoll (1843–1904).

the Academy if he would not publish it. This he evidently did not like, but I had no alternative, and, therefore, without offence, & with many expressions of regret on both sides I took my letter away. The Academy have promised me faithfully that it shall appear on Friday, but whether it will or no I cannot of course say—I told them it had been to the Athenaeum and that the Athenaeum art critic had said [it] was all wrong—at any rate we shall see whether they keep to their promise; if they do I am preparing my supports—and will see at any rate that the matter is thrashed out—I do not much care whether the drawing is by Holbein or no; but I care a good deal about finding out which way competent opinion most inclines.

I am *very* busy, but also close upon the very end of my work: still just now I am hard pushed & this Holbein letter has taken some time also. I see the Darwins' book [2] is not to be out till the end of the year; they are probably waiting to see whether I give them an opportunity. I dare say I shall have given them a good many—perhaps they also may give me one. By the way I hear it semi-officially that Uncle John died with £30,000, Uncle Philip getting the largest share, then Uncle Sam & then Aunt Sarah,[3] but Reggie, who told me, did not know the proportions. This tallies with what Phil gave me to understand in the spring. With all best wishes to you all believe me yr. affte. brother

S— Butler

[2] *The Life and Letters of Charles Darwin*, ed. Francis Darwin. Butler suspected that Francis Darwin was waiting to see what *Luck or Cunning?* (published in November, 1886) contained, but when Darwin's book appeared in 1887 it did not mention *Luck or Cunning?* and contained only a brief, restrained account of Butler's reaction to *Erasmus Darwin* (III, 220).

[3] Butler himself received £25, though in the spring he had thought he might inherit as much as £75 (letter in the British Museum dated May 4, 1886).

88. *May to Butler*

Text: British Museum MS.

[Wilderhope]
Oct. 30, 1886.

Dearest Sam

We meant to have sent you a line by last night's post, but you will get this this evening, I hope.

Papa is quite convalescent again, & came down to breakfast this morning—he will not get out just yet, but we are having an All Saints' little summer—so all things are in his favour. Harrie does not throw off her cold so well, and does not seem very well altogether, but she is up & about, & will I hope get stronger when she gets out. I uphold the credit of the family at present—

The old church has nearly disappeared. All but the tower which looks horridly unsafe, & as if it might come down with a rush. On Wednesday we are going to have a Bottesini concert [1]—but somehow I don't feel impelled to go & hear him. People say he is very wonderful, but his picture was sent round with the programmes, and that didn't seem like a first rate advertisement.

I see Mr. Romanes has been writing a new book.[2] There was a long review of it in this week's Guardian [3]—fairly favourable.

With our love, I am dear Sam, your very affectionate sister

May.

Letter 88:

[1] Giovanni Bottesini (1821–1889), a singer, at this time on a concert tour of England.

[2] Romanes began to sum up his position on evolution with respect to Darwin's in an article, "Physiological Selection," in the *Journal of the Linnean Society* (July, 1886).

[3] A very long review of Romanes' article appeared in the *Guardian* (October 27, 1886), pp. 1603–1604; the reviewer attempted to evaluate Romanes' contribution to evolutionary theory.

89. *Butler to May*

Text: British Museum MS.

15. Clifford's Inn, E. C.
Nov. 4, 1886.

Dear May

Thank you for your note and Harrie for hers with stamp edgings which are very acceptable—that will be enough for some time. Neither of your notes ought to make me at all uneasy about my father, and I do not suppose there is any serious mischief; still, I cannot help fearing that he has had a rather sharp attack, & that he is hardly rallying as rapidly as usual. Has there been any return of that paraplegic mischief of a few years ago? Reggie Worsley, & Jones and I mean going to Guildford or Godalming [1] or somewhere close by for Saturday and Sunday leaving Saturday forenoon and returning Monday evening—let me therefore have a line on Saturday morning before I go.

I am to dine with Sir Julius & Lady Von Haast [2] next week one evening, but have no other dissipation on hand. I have been up to Etta's this morning and have got promise of assistance from them in the matter of copying Narcissus, or rather of inking my pencil score. This will be a very great help to me and we shall get along much faster. We are making plans for a performance of the whole work on the 27th of May next,[3] and this, so far as we can look ahead for such a considerable time, will probably come off—but it will be all we can do to get the chorus singers drilled, and the whole thing sufficiently rehearsed in time: nevertheless it will probably be done, and it is something to have even fixed a date. If by the end of February we find we cannot manage this it must stand

Letter 89:

[1] Towns just outside of London.

[2] John Francis Julius von Haast (1824–1887), German-born geologist who did extensive exploratory work in New Zealand during the time Butler was there.

[3] Parts of *Narcissus* were performed at Shrewsbury School on June 24, 1887, but the whole work was never performed.

over till the following winter or spring, but I expect it will get done—

Mrs. Tylor has sent me Mr. Tylor's book [4]—it is beautifully got up and they have done their best to run me & my books. Dr. Dudgeon [5] has got Luck or Cunning, & declares himself delighted with it so far. The Athenaeum also has it, but no one else yet. Dr. Dudgeon will tell me if there is any gross blunder from a scientific standpoint, and if there is anything to necessitate it I must have an *erratum* pasted in, but I do not think it likely that I shall have to do this—

Professor Conway [6] (the Liverpool man) has written a line of thanks for the photographs, but did not say a word as to whether he agreed or disagreed—he will probably do this when he returns them [7]—but I am fortified by too many confirmatory opinions to be disturbed if he differs—which, however I do not think he will. I shall await tomorrow's Academy [8] with interest. I am getting up a card with the two photos reduced and mounted on it above a few paragraphs of explanation. I shall thus, probably, get the matter settled one way or the other. I hope Harrie is better, and yourself keeping fairly well—and that I shall have a comfortable account of my father on Saturday morning—Yr. affte. brother—

S— Butler.

[4] *Colouration in Animals and Plants*, published posthumously in 1886. Tylor writes that Butler's theory of inherited memory "smoothed away the whole of the difficulties we had experienced, and enabled us to propound the views here set forth with greater clearness" (p. 9).

[5] Robert Ellis Dudgeon (1820–1904), homeopathist, Butler's doctor.

[6] William Martin Conway (1856–1937), professor of art at University College, Liverpool. He wrote to Butler on October 23, 1886, in response to his letters in the *Academy* about the Holbein drawings, and asked if Butler had photographs of the drawings (British Museum).

[7] In a personal letter to Butler dated December 12, 1886, Conway said that it seemed to him that the Basel drawing was an original; but in opposition to Butler, he thought that a similar drawing in Berlin was only a copy (British Museum).

[8] Nothing relevant to Butler appeared.

90. Butler to May

Text: British Museum MS.

15. Clifford's Inn E. C
Nov. 9, 1886

Dear May

Thank you for your letter received Saturday morning & for your post card of this morning. I am very glad my father is so much better. Could he give me a bed for a few nights next week if I should want it? I have written to Mr. Moss [1] asking him whether he would play a piece or two from Narcissus at his next school concert; (he said he would in the summer) and if he assents to this I said I would at once come down, bring the score, see his musical instructor, and see what modifications would be necessary to adapt the pieces to his orchestra. He may have already settled his ⟨orchestra⟩ programme, & in this case I would not come down for a fortnight, but if he assents I should like to come next week.

I am to have copies of my book tomorrow. I got Dr. Dudgeon to read it while there was yet a little locus pœnitentia[e]: he found four small mistakes—very small—which I have made into *errata,* and thus corrected, but declared himself quite satisfied with the scientific part. It will take me some time to fully recover from this book, but it is done and is not more than a week later than the date I had fixed for it to appear. Any time before Nov. 15 is all right. Very glad Harrie is better

Yr affte. brother
S. Butler—

Letter 90:

[1] Henry Moss, headmaster of Shrewsbury School. (See note 4 for Letter 84.)

91. May to Butler

Text: British Museum MS.

[Wilderhope]
Nov. 10. [1886]

Dearest Sam

We shall all be pleased to see you whether you come next week, or whenever you like. I think from your note that you are probably under an idea that there is a School concert in the winter. It is only at midsummer, but I hope you will come down shortly all the same.

Papa keeps well; he twisted his heel a little bit afresh, so is not tempted to go out in this very damp weather, but he is using hot vinegar & salt which does it good.

I heard this morning from Alice Hall,[1] who says the Duke has given £500 for Granby [2]—& they hope to have it opened in the spring.

Sarah Heatly is just dead. You will remember her—

I hope you remember to congratulate Mr. Moss.[3] He likes congratulations very much, I believe. The wedding is to be at Christmas.

We shall like to see any ⟨criticisms⟩ reviews on your book—I am glad you have done with the hard work of it.

Your very affectionate sister
May.

Letter 91:

[1] See note 3 for Letter 4.

[2] All Saints' Church, Granby, Nottinghamshire, was extensively restored at a cost of £1200 and reopened in 1888; it was in the patronage of the Duke of Rutland.

[3] In his letter to Moss, dated November 9, 1886, Butler did not congratulate him on his forthcoming marriage but dealt only with the performance of *Narcissus* which he proposed be given at Shrewsbury School (British Museum MS).

92. *May to Butler*

Text: British Museum MS.
Postcard.
Postmark: Shrewsbury No. 30, 86; *address:* S. Butler Esq. / 15, Clifford's Inn / London / E. C.

Dr. Burd says it is nothing serious, only internal disarrangement and faintness—He has bruised himself badly, & grazed one arm a good deal, but is very bright, and Dr. Burd says it was *certainly* nothing of the nature of seizure or paralysis.

He is to sleep in the spare room tonight & have Rogers,[1] but only as a precaution—

He is *really* quite bright & fairly well, only of course tired & shaken.

M. B.

93. *Butler to May*

Text: British Museum MS.

15. Clifford's Inn
E. C.
Nov. 30, 1886.

Dear May

I thought of you all & of my father more especially on Sunday,[1] and was very glad to hear from Harrie yesterday what I take to be a better account, but between ourselves I could make very little out of what she said. She said "Dr. Burd does not think very gravely about my father's foot," & this may mean either that he thinks gravely about it though not by any means despairingly, or that he thinks it a matter of very little importance. Moreover then she infers that I am not to expect to hear unless the foot "gets seriously worse." I hope that one or other of you will find time to send me a line

Letter 92:
[1] Rogers succeeded Hodgkinson as butler at Wilderhope House.

Letter 93:
[1] Sunday, November 28, 1886, was Canon Butler's eightieth birthday.

to say how my father is going on at not infrequent intervals until he is out of this present mess—which, happily, I fully believe will not be long.

He seems ⟨a little⟩ low about himself—as he drove up with me to the station, but taking him all around & judging by his little ways I should say he has a considerable reserve of strength still remaining & if he is careful may get through the winter a good deal better than he appeared, from what he said to me, to expect. I therefore am not seriously uneasy about him—but shall be glad to hear, if even by post card—how he is going on—& especially whether his appetite is improving. If I was his doctor I should insist on his taking more stimulants.

I don't think anything of a little swelling in the left foot, & think you will find the other probably right itself shortly, but until it has taken a decided turn for the better more or less uneasiness is inevitable.

Did I leave behind me a small common ivory paper knife about 9 or 10 inches long by an inch wide? If I did, kindly wrap it up and send it by post.

Believe me yr. affte. brother
S. Butler—

94. *Butler to May*

Text: **British Museum MS.**

15. Clifford's Inn
E. C.
Dec. 1, 1886

Dear May

I am glad to gather from your post card that my father's illness is less serious than both the matter & manner of Harrie's letter had led me to suppose. At his age, however, severe bruises & grazes, and the shock from falls, cannot but be serious, especially seeing that he is still below par; Dr. Burd of course, & rightly, minimises the mischief, & I am especially glad to learn that there are no paralytic symptoms; still an internal derangement which makes an infirm old man of 80 lose consciousness, & fall down is hardly less serious than paralysis itself, and until I hear of my father's being up & about again it is impossible that I should not be more or less uneasy. In the meantime I rejoice to think that he is going on favourably—pray tell him so from me.

I am afraid both you & Harrie must be very much upset by what has happened, but fear that there is nothing I can do to make matters easier for either of you. Believe me

Yr. affte. brother
S. Butler—

95. *May to Butler*

Text: British Museum MS.

[Wilderhope]
[Morning,] Dec. 1. [1886]

Dearest Sam

We are always so anxious to tell you the truth about my father as far as we know it, that I think Harrie's letter must have made you more doubtful about his foot than she at all intended. Dr. Burd was not at *all* uneasy about it—& tho' we have not seen it yesterday or today—on Sunday & Monday the swelling was very much gone, & it is really sufficiently well to be dismissed as any cause of anxiety. I think Harrie, like yourself, had been more uneasy about it than I—who had seen it when even more swollen. He did not have a very good night—because he cannot lie comfortably except on his back—his bruised side & grazed arm are in the way but he is what people call "well in himself" & bright—& though at his age one is sorry for the bruises &c—& they may be slow in getting quite right—everything is getting quite right, & he is going to get up & sit up. Rogers will be in his room for a night or two. You shall hear daily till he is quite out of the wood. Indeed he is scarcely *in* a *wood!*

Nothing known of your paper knife

Your very affect. sister
May.

His appetite does not improve much, but one could hardly look for that just now.

96. *May to Butler*

Text: British Museum MS.

[Wilderhope]
[Evening,] Dec. 1, 1886

Dearest Sam

My father has not seemed quite so bright since he was up as he did when I wrote this morning,—though we think he is better this evening than this morning, and he has just announced that he thinks he will be better tomorrow. He has been sitting up in his dressing gown in the arm chair most of the day. His arm is going on *quite* nicely—& shows no sign of doing anything but heal[ing] rapidly & well. The worst trouble is his side, (the other bruises are all quite unimportant) but that has bruised the pleura to some extent, Dr. Burd says, & caused a little congestion or inflammation there, and he is to have a strong plaster (of the diachylon nature) put over the side & a broad bandage, which Dr. Burd thinks will make it much easier. It is not *very* bad because when amused with his story book he can cough rather badly without taking any notice of it. If he is not amused, he grunts if he coughs much—

I think he feels the general *shake* more today than yesterday but that is not unnatural.

Dr. Burd did not speak as if *uneasy* about him, though he did not think him quite so well. But for his age I should not be uneasy at all, and my own feeling & hope is that he will be decidedly better in a day or two. He is eating very little—but there is still a little stomach derangement to make that difficult, but he is taking his rice &c—& tonight I think Dr. Burd is going to give him something to help his sleep. A real good night would do more than anything. I think Harrie thinks a little more gravely of his side than I do.—The thing I am most sorry for was the original *faint*—more than the hurts, & yet that was not unnatural between the shock of his first fall, & something disagreeing.

He must not be made nervous about himself, so will you either send him a little line enclosed, or such a letter as we might read to him—

With much love your very affectionate sister

May

Of course we would tell you at once if there occured [*sic*] the least right reason for your coming.

97. *Butler to May*

Text: British Museum MS.

15. Clifford's Inn
E. C
Dec. 2, 1886

Dear May

I have taken your hint & sent my father a few lines direct, which you will doubtless see, but there is nothing in them. Anxious of course we must all of us be; *any* illness is serious when a man is over 80. I am very much afraid my father's first idea was right—& that he has fractured a rib. Mine four years ago had been fractured a fortnight before I knew that it was so—and there being any congestion in the pleura suggests that the rib must have had a very heavy blow. If so I am afraid he will suffer not a little discomfort for about a month from the time of the injury—

I am afraid you & Harrie will be very much tired by the

events of the last few days, being neither of you too well or strong—of course if there is anything I can do you will at once let me know.

Yr. affte. brother
S. Butler— [1]

98. *May to Butler*

Text: British Museum MS.

[Wilderhope]
[December 4, 1886]

Dearest Sam

If you come, don't go to the George [1] before coming down here. My father is better today—& we think to tell him you are here. The kindness & attention would please him we think, but we wait first to see that you do come.

We can quite well take you in here—& the servants never, as you know, think you anything of a trouble, but a pleasure.

Yr. very aff. sister
May— [2]

99. *May to Butler*

Text: British Museum MS.

Wilderhope, Tuesday morning.
Dec. 7, 1886

Dearest Sam

I think my father quite keeps the ground he was gaining when you left. Yesterday he wrote a letter or two, settled

Letter 97:

[1] In a note on this letter, Butler says that May sent him a letter on December 2, reporting: "My father seems really much better this morning, slept well all night (with help [i.e., an opiate]) ate his breakfast nicely this morning, & is merry."

Letter 98:

[1] An inn in Shrewsbury.

[2] Butler noted on this letter that he arrived at the George late on December 4 and was asked to go to his father at once.

accounts, saw Mary Lloyd,[1] and Mrs. Fletcher[2] & Dr. Burd, and seemed pretty bright all day tho' tired at night. He had a good night & is now getting up. His cough is more troublesome but he is now taking no opiate, and he must feel these rapid changes of temperature. Now it is only *just* over freezing with scads of snow & cold rain. Appetite much the same—Dr. Burd thought him certainly rather stronger yesterday—& the arm going on quite right.

His cat has a cold, so they must not be companions at present.

With our love, dear Sam. I am glad you came & have seen him for yourself—

Your very affectionate sister
May.

100. *Butler to May*

Text: British Museum MS.

15. Clifford's Inn E. C
Dec. 8, 1886.

Dear May

Thank you for your letter received last night & post card this morning. I am very glad my father is so much better, and hope that he has now sufficiently turned the corner to warrant the expectation that he will be ere long down stairs again—but an invalid he must I am afraid, at best, remain, at any rate until the summer.

Please tell Harrie I have looked everywhere for her letter & cannot find it so suppose I must have burnt it as I have been doing with a good many letters lately. I had a perfectly eventless journey down and have not a shred of news that I can think of—I am *very* glad I went down when I did.

Letter 99:

[1] Canon Butler's niece, daughter of his sister Harriet.

[2] Probably Agnes Crawfurd Fletcher (d. 1922), wife of William Henry Fletcher, vicar of Holy Trinity Church, Shrewsbury.

We had a severe hail storm this morning with violent wind, & it looks as if it was going to be colder this evening—

Pray give kindest messages from me to my father & believe me

Yr. affte. brother
S. Butler—

101. *May to Butler*

Text: British Museum MS.

[Wilderhope]
Wednesday morning
Dec. 8, 1886.

Dearest Sam

My father still continues much better. The change in him yesterday was most marked—he is gaining strength very decidedly—& we no longer feel afraid of leaving him alone a little. I think he eats rather better too. We shall not write again tonight—unless some very unlooked for change takes place. But he quite seems now going on steadily toward a real recovery.

Yr. very affectionate sister
May.

102. *May to Butler*

Text: British Museum MS.

[Wilderhope]
Saturday morning
Dec. 11, 1886

Dearest Sam

My father still continues to improve. He does not come down stairs yet, but is very bright, & eats very much better, sleeps well, does not cough much—has no attempt at [*sic*] faintness—& though weak, is very fairly well, & Dr. Burd is satisfied even with his arm, which is still inflamed & hot. Vaseline is said to produce that in people whose skin it does not suit, & you know he almost always has trouble with any break of skin, but Dr. Burd thinks nothing of it, & it is now being treated with zinc ointment which he likes. He is going on so well, that we shall not write till Monday without special cause.

We are well, & I played at a temperance concert last night. What did you do about your working men? [1]

Your very affectionate sister
May.

103. *Butler to May*

Text: British Museum MS.

15. Clifford's Inn E. C
Dec. 12, 1886

Dear May

Thank you for your's received yesterday evening. I am very sorry to gather from it that my father's arm has been troublesome, but your account is on the whole so good that it is impossible not to hope that he will now come nicely round. I am especially glad to hear that he has been eating better—with this and some good nights' rests he is sure to gain in strength. I am glad he has not yet come down, for I am sure he is better kept as quiet as possible. I know that whatever can be done is being done, and am glad to think there seems so fair a prospect of its being attended with a good result. Please tell him from me how glad I am that he is better.

They have put off my lecture till March. I told them I had gone to Shrewsbury & was very uncertain of any movements, but left it to them either to take the chance of my being able

Letter 102:

[1] Butler's lecture at the Working Men's College, scheduled for December 11, 1886, was postponed till March. (See note 3 for Letter 85.)

to lecture, on yesterday, or to put me off at once & they chose the latter—

Tomorrow evening I am to dine at Mrs. Danvers's—in a quiet way, but have no other engagements.

No reviews as yet. I called on the editor of the Athenaeum on Thursday about my Holbein card,[1] and saw he had put Luck or Cunning with three or four other books prominently on his table so that any one who came in must see it; this is doing me a good turn in a quiet way, & I am perfectly sure he will do whatever he can, but I have no idea when the review will appear & was careful not to allude to the book at all. I should not be at all surprised if his review is more or less condemnatory [2]—he may think it advisable not to commit the Athenaeum too decidedly to an anti-Darwinian line in view of the great preponderance of Darwinians among his readers, but however much his reviewer may attack me, I am satisfied that I have few better allies in a quiet way than Maccoll [3] —nor do I doubt that he will time his review whenever it appears in consequence of considerations which if I knew what they were I should see to be no less friendly to myself than reasonable from his own point of view. At the same time I shd not be in the least surprised if the review was a severe one.

As for other papers—I imagine the reviewers hardly know what to say. At any rate it is better for me that people should have had time to read it & form an opinion about [it] before the reviews come out.

I am glad to hear of your being well enough to play, and hope that both you & Harrie are beginning to recover from

Letter 103:

[1] Butler, as he mentioned in Letter 89, had had a card printed with photographs of the drawings to prove his point that they were by Holbein.

[2] The review of *Luck or Cunning?* in the *Athenaeum* (January 22, 1887), pp. 131–132, makes the point that Butler's valuable insistence upon the contribution of earlier theorists to the study of evolution has gained widespread acceptance, though his own theory of evolution has not. The anonymous reviewer is most respectful, but regrets Butler's excessive contentiousness—"a mind of considerable power frittered away in ephemeral conflicts."

[3] Norman Maccoll, editor of the *Athenaeum*. (See Letter 87.)

the inevitable & heavy anxiety of the last fortnight. Believe me

Yr. affte. brother
S. Butler—

104. *May to Butler*

Text: British Museum MS.

[Wilderhope]
Monday morning
Dec. 13. [1886]

Dearest Sam

We did not think my father *quite* so bright yesterday, though he did not seem to feel it himself, and Dr. Burd & Mr. Rope [1] (who came yesterday in Dr. Burd's place) both seem satisfied. He is certainly eating better & with more real appetite, but the greatest trouble just now is his arm, which is all covered with irritable exema rash. The doctors do not seem to mind it—& I have a feeling that it may act as a sort of safety valve, but it is wearing to him, & at present keeps increasing in spite of all the ointments. He is bright this morning—and I have just left him sitting in the work room—fully dressed except that he has dressing gown instead of coat, with his cat on his knee. Yesterday he seemed rather more drowsy & tired, but on the whole he is very much improved in general condition—& helps himself to little biscuits &c between times as if he rather liked them. I have a scrap of a cold & am keeping in. Harrie is well, & people are very kind in coming to see him & inquire.

With our love, I am your very affectionate sister

May

He sleeps well—with, & without, opiate—& does not cough much.

Letter 104:

[1] H. J. Rope, medical officer at Shrewsbury School.

105. May to Butler

Text: British Museum MS.

[Wilderhope]
Dec. 16, 1886.

Dearest Sam

We *have* Maysie! [1]—we telegraphed for her yesterday, as both Harrie & I are nursing colds, & were a little afraid of being too much in my father's room lest we should give them to him. They are tiresome—but not very bad—& neither of us are keeping entirely in bed—tho' not up to breakfast.

Papa himself goes on capitally in the main—though he varies a little from day to day. From Friday to Monday we did not think him quite so strong, but it was chiefly I think the irritation of the arm that fretted him. Dr. Burd expressed himself perfectly contented about that yesterday, and said that his tongue was clean & good—better than for many weeks—& his appetite is now very fair. He asks for pea soup & carrots—very bad for him! but he is to have them.

The difficulty of writing is not at all the *trouble*, & certainly you shall have a daily report at present but it is that the report of a day or two together gives really so much truer an idea whether for better or worse than the little varying report of each day. I am sure you would think him *very* much better than when you were here. Of course we all feel alike about his age & weakness, but though Dr. Burd does not expect him ever to be what he *was*, quite, I think he has no *sort* of immediate anxiety about him now, unless he caught cold, or some quite unexpected turn came. Lizzie wants me to put on a linseed poultice so goodbye, with our love

Your very affect. sister
May.

Letter 105:
[1] May's niece. (See Biographical Sketches.)

106. *May to Butler*

Text: British Museum MS.

[Wilderhope]
Wed. night.
[December 22, 1886]

Dearest Sam

My father is in much the same state, but Dr. Burd says he has "seen him worse" & thinks it *possible* that he may rally for awhile again. He is more conscious today, but sleeping almost all the time. He has had a slight attack of sickness chiefly phlegm from the chest, which nurse thought would relieve him for a time. Dr. Burd said he would go on as long as he could throw off the phlegm; his pulse was steady. We have two nurses, for after telegraphing for one from St. Bartholomew's yesterday to come today we found we must have one last night, so sent for a temporary one from here last night. She does very well, but the London one is simply wonderful. We have put a small bed into his room where the wardrobe was, & he will be much more comfortable so & much more easily moved about. Tho' conscious in a *way*, he takes no notice & tho' he knows me, has not consciously spoken to me since yesterday morning. Rogers is to go quite away from the room tonight. He is very good & kind.

I think my father is quite aware of his condition tho' he does not say much. As to your coming or otherwise please do just what you think yourself best. There is nothing you can *do*. He might not know you—& in no case would recognise I think that it was a fresh return—and we could not at present take you in here—on account of the nurses'—but on the other hand he might know you. I think Dr. Burd is quite uncertain as to the length or shortness of time.

H & I are better but of course not well, but we are well looked after. Our love.

Your very affte. sister
May.

107. Butler to May

Text: British Museum MS.

15. Clifford's Inn
E. C.
Dec. 23, 1886

Dear May

On receipt of Maysie's post card [1] last night I decided to go down to Shrewsbury on this morning, but your letter received this morning made me reconsider the matter and I put off going till tomorrow.

Reggie Worsley & I shall leave Paddington at 10 tomorrow and on reaching Shrewsbury will go to the George ⟨& take bed rooms⟩ and get something to eat. I will then walk down to you & see how my father is. If he is better, we will go on to Church Stretton [2] (either Friday or Saturday). If not I will stay at Shrewsbury for a few days & my cousin can go on to Church Stretton alone—

As long as my father is alive it is impossible not to remember the many wonderful rallies he has made at one time or another—but I confess to thinking this by far the most alarming illness he has ever had. Please thank Maysie for her note received last night & believe me

Yr. affte. brother
S. Butler— [3]

Letter 107:

[1] Maysie's postcard dated December 22, 1886, begins: "Grandpapa has sunk so much since yesterday that Dr. Burd & Mr. Rope say that he cannot last more than two or three days" (British Museum).

[2] A town 13 miles from Shrewsbury.

[3] Butler remained at Shrewsbury until his father died on December 29. His account of his father's death, which he included with these letters, reads in part: "My father [died] on the evening—about half past five—of Wednesday Dec. 29, 1886. I, and Rogers, & the nurse were alone present. I was supporting his head between my hands as he died—which he did without any kind of fight with death—but Rogers told me shortly before I was called into the room, he had fought hard for life. . . ."

108. Butler to May

Text: British Museum MS. *Extracts published: Memoir,* II, 47.

15. Clifford's Inn
E. C
Mar 27. 1887.

Dear May

I am afraid I have allowed too many days to slip by without writing, and owe a letter both to Harrie & yourself. I never knew time to fly so rapidly as at present: the week seems over before it is begun—and yet I do not see that I get on with what I am doing as fast as I wish. I have got the lecture over [1]—I believe it was a great success & Jones & Gogin [2] who were there were very much pleased with its reception—I, of course could not form much of an opinion for I read my lecture & was unable to look the people in the face as I did when speaking. I think I shall speak in future, but was afraid of over looking points & so wrote it out. I am to deliver it again in the Autumn [3] at another similar institution and shall then I think speak it—

Mr. Hay [4] thinks Jones's final chorus too long & I am afraid it won't come off—but my introduction & Jones's march will probably be done; I don't think that this is quite settled, but it will I expect be arranged. We don't get on with Narcissus, but Jones leaves the Paines [5] at the end of this week and then things will move more rapidly. I am very much bothered with one part of one chorus which I am still rewriting, but when I have got this straight I too shall be able to move on faster. Jones & I went to the Philharmonic the other night & sat in

Letter 108:

[1] "The Subdivision of the Organic World into Animal and Vegetable," the lecture postponed from December. (See Letter 85.)

[2] Charles Gogin. (See Biographical Sketches.)

[3] Butler did not deliver this lecture again.

[4] Walter Cecil Hay, music master at Shrewsbury School, where Butler wanted *Narcissus* performed.

[5] The law firm of Thomas Paine (1822–1908), where Jones was employed as managing clerk. Upon receiving his inheritance, Butler paid Jones an allowance of £200 a year so that he could give up this position.

the orchestra just behind the drums to study orchestration. We thought the playing very good & the music most of it very long & dreary.

I am much interested in your changes, and have no doubt you have made your rooms very nice & pretty. I do hope Harrie will be able soon to get out, but she must be very careful not to overdo things at first. When do you think of getting away? The weather really does seem to have taken a turn. No—I have no vote for the hospital for incurables. There is another S. Butler [6] who stands sometimes for Somersetshire or Dorsetshire or somewhere in that direction, & there is another who writes to the Times about coal supply—I am sorry not to be able to be of use. I shall be very glad to hear of your both getting an outing and am

Yr. affte. brother
S— Butler—

109. *Butler to May*

Text: British Museum MS.

15. Clifford's Inn
E. C.
Dec. 13. 1887.

Dear May

Thank you for your letter of this morning and Harrie for hers of a few days ago. I am more sorry than I can say for the worry & trouble you are having,[1] but am very glad to hear you are in Mr. How's hands. As long as you do what he tells you you are all right. Every one makes mistakes but a mistake can be turned into a mere nine days wonder if it is not made

[6] The name S. Butler which May saw in connection with a proposed hospital for incurables was probably that of Spencer Perceval Butler (1828–1915), conveyancing counsel to the Office of Works.

Letter 109:

[1] In a letter to Jones dated October 7, 1893, Butler wrote: "My sisters have been losing about £500 a piece in some labourer's dwellings company in which they invested 6 or 7 years ago."

worse by after mistakes. You have gone to the leading, most respected adviser in Shrewsbury and even if he gives you mistaken advice you can always say you did as Mr. How advised, and this will stop any one's mouth, for he carries much more weight than any one else in Shrewsbury. I won't add any more, but assure you that I am extremely sorry for the anxiety you must [be] suffering & heartily wish you well through it.

I shall be down at Shrewsbury in a few days. I shall very likely have Russell Cooke [2] with me, and any way shall go to the George, as I shall certainly be at Shrewsbury on Sunday, but cannot quite fix what day I shall come. I am very busy. My lecture [3] comes off on Thursday, & I shall be thankful when it is over. I shall start for Varallo on Xmas eve—with Camera & dry plates—It is absolutely impossible for me to finish my book [4] without going there. I have written 200 pp and am purposely leaving the rest till I have been there. They are very much pleased with me for coming.

The Darwins did not answer my Athenaeum letter [5]—I am very glad. Of course they would if they could, and they have *at last* in a new edition of 'Erasmus Darwin' corrected their father's misstatement [6]—so I suppose I must take this, (which appeared since my letter to the Athenaeum) as an ***amends***—sulky & ill conditioned though it is.

I have a lot to do and will add no more.

Yr. affte. brother
S. Butler—

[2] William Russell Cooke, called to the bar in 1879, Butler's solicitor.

[3] "On the Genesis of Feeling," delivered at the City of London College on December 15, 1887, and reprinted in Shrewsbury Edition, XVIII, 186–210.

[4] *Ex Voto,* Butler's book about Varallo.

[5] See note 3 for Letter 76.

[6] "Mr. Darwin accidentally omitted to mention [in the first edition] that Dr. Krause revised, and made certain additions to, his Essay before it was translated. Among these additions is an allusion to Mr. Butler's book, 'Evolution, Old and New'" (Ernst Krause, *The Life of Erasmus Darwin, by Charles Darwin, being an introduction to an Essay on His Scientific Works,* 2nd ed. [1887], p. iv).

110. *Butler to May*

Text: Chapin Library MS.

15. Clifford's Inn E. C.
Nov. 12. 1888

Dear May

I am ashamed of myself for having let such a long time go by without writing but the days slip by so rapidly & I am working so very hard that I have failed to do what I intended in the way of writing—I do hope you are better & both fairly well—I am all right but must really do something to stop the high pressure at which I am going—I think I shall have to steal a pair of boots or a pound of cheese or some such trifling article just to get 14 days imprisonment, but it must be something without hard labour. I have finished my article for the Universal Review.[1] It will appear this week. I have written the overture to Ulysses which Jones says will do very well. I have printed, toned & fixed more than 300 prints since my return & mounted over 100 to send away—which have duly gone. Alfred says it must not occur again—& he is right—the tax on my protoplasm is really too severe, and they must get the local photographer to do them. All very fine, but I don't for a moment suppose that I shall be let off so cheaply—they *will* be taken & there is no refusing them. I have also revised 'Ex Voto' [2] & put in all the new matter—no light work for it has to be scattered all over the book. In fact I have done more than is good for me, & have still a lot to do before I can get straight.

Letter 110:

[1] "A Sculptor and a Shrine," *Universal Review,* 2 (November, 1888), 317–339, a discussion of the artist Tabachetti (Jean de Wespin) and the sanctuary at Montrigone. Partially reprinted in Shrewsbury Edition, XIX, 159–169.

[2] *Ex Voto* was published on May 17, 1888. In preparing his article, "A Sculptor and a Shrine," Butler discovered additional information and some corrections which he wanted to incorporate. He issued a leaflet dated November 30, 1888, to be given to purchasers of the book, and in 1890 prepared, but did not publish, an extensively revised edition from which the Shrewsbury Edition of *Ex Voto* was printed.

Alfred [3] is *very* good & very useful. News I have none—I have dined at the Beales once & at Mrs. Danvers—also I lunched one day at Chester Terrace, but I think I told you this. We are all very much interested with the Parnell commission,[4] of course, & have very little doubt that the judge will make a crushing report. Also I have with Alfred's approval bought an old second hand walnut bureau—I have long wanted something of the kind—like the old study bureau that you have in your morning room, but smaller & not so high & without glass front—I think I shall like it very much [5] —Please excuse more &

Believe me Yr. affte. brother
S— Butler—

111. Butler to May

Text: Chapin Library MS.

15. Clifford's Inn E. C.
Jan 13. 1889—

Dear May

Thank you very much for the library catalogue.[1] I have not yet undone the other papers you sent being occupied with the letters which are a very long business. I have burned a great many to my grandfather, but not one of his own, nor any about which there can be a shadow of doubt. I find some wonderful letters from Mrs. Wynne,[2] Dr. Parr's daughter—

[3] Alfred Emery Cathie (b. 1862) whom Butler hired as his servant on January 18, 1887, after his father's death—three weeks earlier—made it financially possible for him to do so. (See Biographical Sketches.)

[4] Beginning in September, 1888, a special commission of three justices sat to investigate charges by the *Times* that Parnell had criminally conspired with Irish revolutionists. (See note 5 for Letter 113.)

[5] Butler later noted: "November 15 [1888]: Bought my *bureau*, and have grumbled at it ever since" (MS Notebooks, III, 125).

Letter 111:

[1] The sale catalogue of Dr. Butler's library; Butler was working on his biography of his grandfather. (See *The Life and Letters of Dr. Butler*, II, 440.)

[2] Mrs. Sarah Anne Wynne (1772–1810), eldest daughter of Samuel Parr (1747–

what a brilliant woman she was! Do you know any thing about her? If you can find out any thing from the archdeacon [3] pray do. She must have been very troublesome to my grandfather, and I have no doubt her husband had a good deal to say in his own defence, but she was a wonderful woman and I am very glad to have seen her letters—all of which, however, I have not yet read. Dr. Parr's are simply illegible [4]—but I shd think there is not much in them for Dr. J. Johnstone is sure to have had them for his life of Dr. Parr [5] & to have printed any thing important. Of our grandfather himself it is hardly possible to be too enthusiastic & I do not doubt that I shall have abundant material for a very interesting & striking memoir—one which will I hope be if not worthy of his memory, at any rate as worthy as I can make it—but—there goes another £80 or £100! for who will buy it? [6] However, happily that is not a very important consideration, and the thing has got to be done. The thing that especially strikes me about him is his amazing long-suffering & forbearingness under great provocation, & his marvellous placability. This & his tremendous energy & power of work. No wonder he wore out before his time.

I have not been able to get on with your & Harrie's photos —since Xmas we have not had a single fair printing day—

1825), schoolmaster and scholar, lifelong friend of Dr. Butler. Mrs. Wynne visited Dr. Butler frequently, and lived at Shrewsbury School (1807–1810) while instituting a suit for divorce. The *Dictionary of National Biography*, under "Samuel Parr," comments: "Mrs. Wynne had been the cleverest of Parr's daughters, and showed some of her mother's sarcastic temper."

[3] Probably Thomas Bucknall Lloyd (1824–1896), archdeacon of Salop, son of Harriet, Dr. Butler's younger daughter.

[4] "The difficulty of ascertaining some words correctly is inconceivable to those who are unacquainted with Dr. Parr's hand" (John Johnstone, *The Works of Samuel Parr . . . with Memoirs of His Life and a Selection from His Correspondence* [1828], I, 541*n*.).

[5] Johnstone prints ten letters from Parr to Dr. Butler, most of them turgid personal eulogies. The most interesting is Parr's request that Dr. Butler preach at his funeral, which Parr thought—rightly—would be soon (I, 531–532, 838; VII, 359–373).

[6] In 1901 Butler calculated that he had lost £193 18*s*. 0*d*. on *The Life and Letters of Dr. Butler*, almost double what he lost on his next most costly book, *Ex Voto* ("Account Slip" in MS Notebooks, VI; Shrewsbury *Note-Books*, pp. 375–376, 376*n*.).

and after all I am afraid the improved negatives are hardly very satisfactory. They will come as soon as ever I can get to them, but what with Xmas balancing of my books—a long business—what with my grandfather, the correcting of 'Ex Voto' (of which by the way you will have seen the Guardian review [7]—as much, I suppose, as I could expect from that quarter) & with Ulysses which creeps on—I have had my hands exceedingly full. Alfred keeps *very* good, & does his best to keep me straight.

I am very sorry to hear you have had a cold, and hope you are better. By the way I ran down last Thursday week to Kenilworth for a day returning the same evening and spent 3 hours with Mrs. Butler [8] to ask her a few points which I thought she might know. She knew nothing. I photographed her, & got what seems to me a very good & not unpleasant likeness, but she is very distinctly of a different opinion. I see I must never photograph any one over thirty. I thought her a good deal aged. No more news—Love to Harrie

Yr. affte. brother
S. Butler—

112. *Butler to May*

Text: Chapin Library MS.

[15 Clifford's Inn]
July 1, 1889.

Dear May

I am sorry you cannot give a better account of Harrie though you do say that she seems somewhat mending. It is very good of you to wish me to come to Wilderhope but I will, please, definitely, stick this time to the George. I shall be on duty all 3 days—Tuesday with the Camera Club—Wednesday

[7] A one-column review which commended Butler for illuminating an obscure corner of Europe but criticized him for being unsound on art and for writing "over-wrought panegyrics" (*Guardian*, 44 [January 2, 1889], 20).

[8] Mrs. William Henry Butler (d. 1891), widow of Dr. Butler's cousin, living at this time in the Stone House, Kenilworth.

at Harnage—Thursday the speeches,[1] & I mean getting away Thursday evening if I can as I leave home for my Summer outing on Saturday, and want as much time as possible to finish my preparations, but I will pay you sundry visits.

I am writing for the first time in my new spectacles—the lower ½ rather stronger, the upper half the same as before. I dare say I shall come to like them but at present I do ⟨fa⟩ not do so & they put me out—which I suspect means that they will not do.

I hear with regret that no letters from our grandfather have been found among Baron Merian's papers [2]—but the family have a portrait of him which I am to photograph on my way thro' Basle [3]—and I am to see the old lady his niece [4] who remembers him, & will no doubt tell me something about him. I feel sure that J. H. Klaproth [5] took the letters ⟨on that⟩ from our grandfather on the Baron's death.

I have evidence in his own handwriting that he had the run of all Baron Merian's papers on his death, & the family tell me they have not found a single scrap of Klaproth's, though I also find in Kl.'s handwriting that he & the Baron were "in daily correspondence." Klaproth, as you know, corresponded with Dr. B. till his death [in] 1835, & Dr. B. sent him once a present of 1000 francs when he was in difficulties: I find he staid at Shrewsbury in 1825,—at least the Baron thanks Dr. B. for "having taken such excellent care" of him. I find from the Biographie Universelle that Kl., though a man of wonderful attainments, bore a shady character,[6] I gather in respect of

Letter 112:

[1] Shrewsbury School Speech Day, held Thursday, July 11, 1889.

[2] Baron Andreas Merian (1772–1828), a philologist; he met Dr. Butler in Cambridge in 1798 and corresponded with him thereafter. Butler prints twenty-eight of his letters to Dr. Butler.

[3] A reproduction of this portrait appears in *Basler Jahrbuch* (1917), opposite p. 280.

[4] Elizabeth Bischoff-Merian (1823–1894). Butler reports (*The Life and Letters of Dr. Butler*, I, 135–136) that she was able to give him brief biographical notes on the Baron.

[5] Jules-Henri Klaproth (1783–1835), a student of comparative linguistics, friend of Dr. Butler through Baron Merian (with whom he collaborated on many philological studies).

[6] "Klaproth avait le goût et les habitudes de la haute société, ainsi qu'un penchant très-décidé pour ce qui compose une douce et élégante existence; il

integrity; and I think it exceedingly likely that he stuck to the letters of Dr. B. perhaps indeed with the consent of the Merian family & possibly with Dr. B.'s own knowledge. At any rate I am now in search of what became of Kl.'s papers on his death—& if I find they were destroyed shall then give up the search.

Alfred (who has a bad boil on his neck & took it into his head this morning to *faint away*, so I sent him home) has copied out *in type* all Baron M's letters ⟨by⟩ but ½ dozen which he will finish before I go. I take the originals to Basle to show the Merian family who some of them read English & much wished to see them; I am to have them again but wd not let them out of my possession till I had a copy of them. This is why I have not got on with the remaining letters I took from Wilderhope in the spring. These will be next attended to. I met Josephine Sherrington on Saturday at Mlle Vaillant's[7] concert where two songs of Jones's were done with much *éclat*. She sent her love (with some apology) to you & Harrie. I don't suppose I shall see you till tea time on Wednesday as I don't know when the Camera club affair will end. Glad the building progresses to your satisfaction.

Yr. affte. brother
S— Butler

113. *Butler to May*

Text: Chapin Library MS.

15. Clifford's Inn E C
Mar. 6. 1890

Dear May

I owe you a letter badly, but have no particular news to write about. I am much occupied with my lecture on the

---

n'était l'ennemi ni de la gaieté ni des plaisirs. C'est peut-être à ce partage entre l'étude et les dissipations mondaines qu'il dut le déclin rapide de sa santé."

[7] Gabrielle Vaillant (1853–1899), a violinist, introduced to Butler by Miss Savage. "I disliked Mlle V. from the first moment that I saw her, and my dislike and distrust always deepened. . . . S.B., August 27th, 1901" (*Butler-Savage Letters*, p. 121).

relations between thought and language,[1] to be delivered at the working men's college on the 15th inst. It is a rather alarmingly dry subject but I don't believe intelligent working men think that they have had their due unless they are given something pretty stiff. At any rate they are told what they must expect & if they come to a lecture on relations between thought and language they must not expect it to be illustrated by a series of comic magic lantern slides. Jones has just completed a fine quartet & I am muddling on with Ulysses. Jones met Fuller Maitland [2] the other day (he is musical critic to the Times) & told me afterwards that highly as he himself & I thought of Narcissus, Fuller Maitland certainly thought more highly still, & complained bitterly that no one had done it—he said "It would do a lot of good." I get on more slowly than I should like with Dr. B. but he cannot move faster till the lecture is over. Alfred has been type-writing it at my dictation; for some days he said nothing, but the fire was kindling within him & yesterday he said, "Well, Sir, this *is* a dry one." So I flew at him, & he said he was very sorry but it was really so *very* dry that he could not contain himself. So I had to make the best of it. I hope you are satisfied with the Parnell Commission report.[3] I should have pitched it a little stronger myself, but have no doubt they know best; nothing however will make me believe that the original letter of Parnell's that the Times published is not by him.[4] Some of the later ones no

Letter 113:

[1] This lecture was delivered at the Working Men's College on March 15; Butler revised it for delivery four years later; the revised version is printed in Shrewsbury Edition, XIX, 61–90.

[2] John Alexander Fuller-Maitland (1856–1936), at this time music critic of the *Times*, later editor of *Grove's Dictionary of Musicians*. Butler was to meet him for the first time at Mlle Vallant's house on April 27, 1890 (MS Notebooks, III, 127).

[3] The Commission's report (see note 4 for Letter 110), issued in February, 1890, was variously interpreted as vindicating and condemning Parnell. It actually found him not guilty of the *Times'* charges of criminal activity but censured him for inflammatory actions.

[4] The last article in the *Times'* series, "Parnellism and Crime" (April 18, 1887, p. 8), contained an incriminating letter, allegedly written by Parnell but probably forged by Richard Pigott (1828?–1889). Defending itself against a lawsuit, the *Times* produced other "Parnell letters" which Pigott forged—less successfully

doubt are forged but Pigott stuck to it that the earlier ones were not. I won't add anything, for when people take to writing about politics it is a sign that they [have] pretty well exhausted their stock. Oh yes! They are moving on fast with the Italian translation of Ex Voto [5] & keep sending me over chapters to revise. It is in the hands of one who belongs to the clerical party so I said "pray cut out anything you find likely to wound or offend a good Catholic," [6] and he replied that there was really nothing they objected to. We have a great deal to learn from them in the matter of not being too abominably logical. I hope you both continue to escape influenza & am.

Yr affte brother
S. Butler.

114. *Butler to May*

Text: Chapin Library MS.

Carate—Lario [1]
Lago di Como [Italy]
Sett. 18. 1890

Dear May—

A few lines only to say that though I have been incessantly on the look out for the right lady ever since I last wrote I have not yet succeeded in finding the one whom I can trust not to raise difficulties either before marriage or afterwards. I

—for the occasion. Pigott committed suicide after implicating himself before the special commission, but Butler tried to salvage what he could of what had seemed such promising anti-Liberal evidence.

[5] A translation of *Ex Voto* by Angelo Rizzetti was published in Novara in 1894. Butler wrote a preface to this edition in Italian, an English translation of which is printed in the Shrewsbury Edition, IX, xvii–xxi.

[6] The only possibility of offense to a Roman Catholic is in Butler's occasionally flippant treatment of the subject matter of this art—his remarks on the weight of the Virgin (p. 26), or his having himself photographed with one of the statues (p. 160), for example.

Letter 114:

[1] Hotel Lario, Carate (about six miles above Como on the west bank).

am therefore still hesitating & in matters of this sort the man who hesitates is generally saved; but there is no knowing, and with Dick's example before me I am—well—perhaps the most sensible thing will be to wait till Dick has been married a year or two and see whether it kills him or not.

I did a lot at Varallo and again met the Bishop of Chichester & Archdeacon Mount [2] who were very gracious; the editor of the Pall Mall Gazette [3] & his wife (not Mr. Stead the late editor, but his successor) were there. They had my Universal Review articles [4] all cut out of the Review & bound together, & they had 'Ex Voto,' & were doing everything as directed, so of course I was greatly flattered.

We have also had a letter from my friend Gogin who writes of an English friend of his at Paris who likes Jones's & my music very much. He says "She often plays your & Jones's things to people in Paris & they like them very much, but she dares not say they are either modern or English, so it is 'Je vais vous jouer des oeuvres posthumes de Haendel,' & they are happy. One of them who not only listens, but composes went so far as to say 'C'est charmant, c'est ravissant, c'est du Lully tout pur!' " [5]—which is very gratifying, the more so that Gogin does not reveal whether it is Jones's music or mine that is pure Lully—so we can each settle the question in his own favour.

I am very glad you are feeling better. I am all right, thank you, & I think my wrist, which I hurt at Saas, will come right, though it is still not all I shd wish—I fell in the dark with all

[2] Richard Durnford (see Letter 83) and his nephew, Francis John Mount (1831–1903), archdeacon of Chichester.

[3] Edward Tyas Cook (1857–1919), who succeeded William Thomas Stead (1849–1912) as editor in 1889.

[4] Only three of Butler's eight articles which the Cooks could have seen in the *Universal Review* would have been useful in touring: "A Sculptor and a Shrine" (2 [November, 1888], 317–339), on Montrigone; "L'Affaire Holbein-Rippel" (5 [November, 1889], 377–392), on the drawing in Basel; and "A Mediaeval Girl School" (5 [December, 1889], 551–566), on Oropa and Varallo.

[5] In a postcard to Gogin, written the day before this letter, Jones says: "We have been purring and wagging our tails ever since your letter came about the 'oeuvres posthumes de Haendel' & 'Lully tout pur'—we quite agree" (Chapin Library).

my weight on it. Jones desires to be remembered very kindly; with love to Harrie believe me

Your affte. brother
S. Butler

P. S. I intend being back at the end of next week. Today I go to Mendrisio to hear all about the revolution.[6]

115. *Butler to May*

Text: British Museum MS. *Letter published:* Garnett, pp. 215–217; *extracts published: Memoir,* II, 103.

15. Clifford's Inn E. C.
Feb. 14, 1891.[1]

Dear May

Thank you for your's received this morning. I am coming down to Shrewsbury for a day or two. They are going to have an exhibition of lantern slides at the Town Hall on Mond, 23rd inst. & I have sent a few of my summer shots. I have asked Mr. Naunton [2] to send you down a couple of tickets if they have them to spare. I unfortunately returned them the spare tickets they sent me, not intending either to send slides or to be present. I thought the exhibition was limited to Shropshire subjects. I have since learned I was mistaken. If either of you care to go please take an opportunity of calling on Adnitt & Naunton (Mr. Naunton) & seeing whether personal suasion cannot extract a ticket. I shall go to Harnage either Tuesday or Wed. & shall return on Frid, or Thursd. Seriously, this time I will, please, go to the George.

I hope it will prove that a letter from Ada [3] has miscarried.

[6] The liberal leaders of the Swiss canton of Ticino took control of Bellinzona, the capital, as well as smaller towns like Mendrisio in a short-lived rebellion on September 11, 1890.

Letter 115:

[1] Garnett incorrectly reads 1892.

[2] Walter William Naunton, partner in the Shrewsbury publishing firm of Adnitt and Naunton.

[3] Ada Wheeler, who had recently become the wife of Henry Thomas Butler, and thus Etta's daughter-in-law.

I shall, as usual with stupid mankind, lag a little behind, & refuse to be indignant till an extreme case has been made out & counsel heard on both sides. You see it is so easy to preserve a judicial frame of mind when it is not one's own susceptibilities that are wounded. No doubt, however, it is very wrong. A daughter in law should always write to her mother in law by the first post after the ceremony.

Alfred and I were in the dark room making slides. I was afraid of exposing the same plate twice & said "now Alfred, we must be careful. I am afraid I shall get confused." Alfred replied "Yes, sir, *you* will, but *I'm here*," all said quite unconsciously. Yesterday he said "Let me see; yes; perhaps I shall see that you have your hair cut tomorrow." This afternoon I am to call on the Tillbrooks,[4] so this morning he examined my hair and said reproachfully "Oh no, sir, you can't go; it's all ragged—it ⟨would⟩ won't do at all; you can go to Mr. Evans's [5] in the Turnstile as you go to the Museum if you like, or if you haven't done it then I'll have a cup of coffee for you at half past two, & then you can go down to Mr. Hunt's [6] —that's how I'll settle it. Don't forget." And then he looks perfectly satisfied. Of course I went to Mr. Evans's straight away, for I knew if I didn't I must go to Mr. Hunt's & I might as well get it over—from which you will gather that I am doing what I ought not & writing letters at the Museum. I am very sorry about poor Crib.[7] Love to Harrie.

Yr. affecte. brother
S. Butler—

[4] Philip Limborch Tillbrook, Standard Bearer, Corps of Gentlemen-at-Arms. His father was a close friend of Dr. Butler's. (See *The Life and Letters of Dr. Butler*, I, 125–126.)

[5] In the *Memoir*, Jones silently corrects Butler throughout this passage and reads "Mr. Skinner" for "Mr. Evans." Apparently Butler confused Skinner, a hairdresser whose shop was in Great Turnstile, on the way to the Museum, with Evans, whose shop lay in the other direction.

[6] A hairdressing shop in Fetter Lane, just a few doors from Butler's rooms.

[7] The family's black mongrel dog.

116. *Butler to May*

Text: Chapin Library MS.

Address Poste Restante
Bormio, Valtellina, Italy—
[Mid-August, 1891]

Dear May

I write from Chiavenna where I wait Jones who arrives tomorrow. I went straight to Beckenried on the Lake of Lucerne where I staid a few days. Dr. Sieber [1] of Basle was there, who is a cousin of Mrs. Refardt,[2] Baron Merian's great niece. He is librarian of the Museum at Basle—and I knew he was there so went to meet him: he is a very fine old gentleman & completely with me in the Holbein affair. Also there was there Dr. Krantz [3] director of Dresden musical conservatory. He played Narcissus all through & seemed very much pleased with it, only he said he could not see where the comedy lay—for the music seemed to him throughout most serious & classical! That is rather what we hoped it might. He had a fine Queen Arētē wife [4] with him & a lovely Nausicaa daughter, & he was not a bad King Alcinous himself, for as you know my notion of King A. is nothing very regal.[5]

I am going on with the Odyssey & have done 3 books since leaving London. When Jones comes I shall stop—till he goes. I have taken some lovely shots, the King Alcinous group of course & Dr. Sieber—& I have very nearly had my head ⟨my⟩ punched more than once.

By the way Menelaus proposes to Telemachus & Pisistratus

Letter 116:

[1] Ludwig Sieber (1833–1891), director of the Bibliothèque Universitaire at Basel.

[2] Elizabeth Refardt (1853–1923), an adopted daughter of Baron Merian's niece, Elizabeth Bischoff-Merian. (See note 4 for Letter 112.)

[3] Eugen Krantz (1844–1898). He purchased the Dresden Conservatory and became director of it in 1890.

[4] Butler's mind was full of the *Odyssey* at this time. He was translating it, and "it was during the few days that I was at Chiavenna that I hit upon the feminine authorship of the *Odyssey*" (*Memoir*, II, 106).

[5] "[Alcinous] is hardly mentioned at all except to be made more or less ridiculous" (*The Authoress of the Odyssey*, p. 120).

that they should make a little tour through the Peleponese and that he shd personally conduct them.[6]

It will be very cheap, he says, for every one will give *us* something, either a pot or a kettle or a couple of mules, or a gold cup. He seemed to think they might make rather a good thing out of a sponging tour. However Minerva put her foot down & Telemachus was to go back at once. I find Etoneus the butler *lived out of the house*—that is not very regal— & when he came up after having just got out of bed Menelaus told him to light the fire & begin cooking dinner.[7] Fancy what Rogers or Hodgkinson [8] wd have said to this! I am certain that neither P. nor Tel. tipped Etoneus when they went away. We shd have heard they had given £50 if they had given him a shilling. But I am sure they gave him nothing at all. If the sponging tour had come off Menelaus would have stuck to all the gifts. He might have given Tel. a kettle, but certainly not more. Telemachus probably rather felt this, so he said Minerva wd not let him. The more I see of the Odyssey the better I like it—it is wonderful, but nothing can well be more *franchement bourgeois* & unheroic. I am going ahead with it as fast [as] I can for on my return I mean hawking it about to every publisher of any respectability in London [9]—& I cannot go about with half an Odyssey. Looking ahead the most horrid thing I see is that when U. has killed the suitors he finds out from Euryclea which of the maids had misconducted themselves. 12 names are given to him so he sends for them & makes them mop up the blood & clean every thing up, & then he hangs them.[10] Now will you or will you not have one particle of respect or sympathy for U. after that? I think you will say

[6] Book XV, ll. 80–85; Butler's translation, p. 229. He includes this view of the tour in *The Authoress of the Odyssey*, pp. 145–146.

[7] Book XV, ll. 95–98; Butler's translation, p. 229. (See *The Authoress of the Odyssey*, p. 146.)

[8] The family butlers.

[9] The translation was complete by the end of September, 1891. He offered it to publisher after publisher in 1892, but none took it; in 1893 he had sample passages printed to show them—still without result. It was finally published by Longmans, Green in 1900, at his expense.

[10] Telemachus hangs the maids.

that he cannot get more at my hands than he deserves. To me from first to last he seems a servant's hall hero. However—

I shall probably start for the Valtellina on Friday, & be at Varallo at the end of the month. I am quite well and hope you are both the same.

Yr. affte. brother
S— Butler

117. *Butler to May*

Text: Chapin Library MS.

15. Clifford's Inn
E. C.
Sep. 30. 1891

Dear May

Thank you for your's received this morning. I got back on Monday night, & am as you may imagine very busy—and Alfred keeps me fully employed with never less than ½ dozen things at a time. I have Jones really very ill with ulcerated sore throat, & tonsils. There is no danger, but he is very bad and requires a good deal of attention. I shall be very glad when I have seen him take a turn. Mlle Vaillant is very kind and is helping to nurse him.

Did I tell you that I was reduced to a state of pulp by the people I met at Pesio? It was a singularly agreeable company and I was very sorry when it all broke up.

I have finished my Homer having got the 12 books done as I intended. I then rushed back to Varallo & went through the whole of the Italian translation of Ex Voto, putting in the discoveries of the summer. Then I came back straight & got here on Monday night.

I will, please, come down next week for a couple of days if Jones is all right again. I want to arrange about sticking a few more trees into the woods at Harnage—and October is the right time.

By the ⟨twice⟩ way twice this Summer, Italians, one an

elderly married lady, & one an elderly married gentleman, have come up to me affectionately & caught me by the beard, as a way of testifying their pleasure at seeing me. I do not remember this before, but was struck by it because I had just translated the meeting between Ulysses & Euryclea, where Eury. does this very same thing.[1]

Please excuse more—I will come on Tuesday leaving Paddington at 10. A. M. unless I hear to the contrary. Love to Harrie

Yr. affte. brother
S— Butler.

118. *Butler to May*

Text: Chapin Library MS.
Stationery imprinted: SAMUEL BUTLER. 15, CLIFFORDS INN, LONDON. E. C. ________189

Jan 18 1892

Dear May

I am exceedingly sorry to hear that ⟨y⟩ Harrie has the influenza—and hope she will be very careful. Eucalyptus oil is all the rage now so we have got some. I am all right again now—and today's really milder weather makes a very agreeable change.

I do not mean Dr. B.'s life to be a page shorter than 300 pp.[1]—but Mr. Moss[2] and [I] both feel that Dr. B.'s memory is best served and best preserved by that which shall be most widely read, and that the long book already three parts done would be confined to a few while the smaller one would probably have a far wider circulation. The large book will be completed as though it were going to be published, and then given

Letter 117:

[1] Book XIX, l. 473; Butler's translation, p. 303.

Letter 118:

[1] The two volumes of *The Life and Letters of Dr. Butler* amounted to almost 800 pages when published at Butler's expense in 1896—and Butler had reduced his manuscript by a third in 1895.

[2] Headmaster of Shrewsbury School. (See note 4 for Letter 84.)

to the British Museum.[3] I had a small interview with Murray the publisher the other day and told him what I proposed. He said "depend on it you will do much more wisely if you stick to this." So I have finally settled the size of my canvas, i. e., 300 pp., Life & Habit size. The moment I have finished my lecture for the Working Mens College (30th Inst.) [4] I return to Dr. B. & shall not leave him till he is completed.

I had a great triumph this morning. I settled that if the City of the Phaeacians could be identified [5] it should (1) be at no great distance from Marsala. (2) There should be a town & a harbour—not very big but with a good long extension *but no river.* (3) There should be no river for 3 or 4 miles. (4) There should be a good big mountain near the town—pretty close over it. (5) There should be a sunken rock just about level with the sea—or what is called by sailors "awash" within easy sight of the ⟨river⟩ harbour. (6) There should be no range of hills between the river & the town, & the river should be quite a little one, with flat ground between it & the town.

Armed with these requirements I went down to the map-room of the British Museum and demanded to see the admiralty charts of the coast near Marsala: I explained what I wanted and the keeper of the maps had no sooner unrolled the chart than he said "Why here it is—the very first thing"—just 9 or ten miles north of Marsala—every condition absolutely fulfilled, and nothing like it anywhere else. So I have no longer any shadow of doubt about my view being correct. Love to Harrie and condolences

Yr. affte. brother
S. Butler—

[3] Butler gave the Museum a copy with two additional volumes of letters.

[4] "A Lecture on the Humour of Homer," printed in Shrewsbury Edition, XIX, 239–271.

[5] Butler was trying to identify the topography of the *Odyssey.* He outlined his case for Sicily as the location of the city of the Phaeacians (essentially as he gives it to May in this letter) in a letter to the *Athenaeum* (January 30, 1892, pp. 149–150). The fullest statement of his theory is in chap. 8 of *The Authoress of the Odyssey.*

119. Butler to May

Text: Chapin Library MS.

15. Clifford's Inn
E. C.
Feb. 27. 1892

Dear May

I beg your pardon—I thought I had long told you that Nausicaa *did* write the Odyssey.[1] I only wish some one wd venture to tell me she didn't in a place where I could lay my hands about him. Of course I don't say this in the Athenaeum because I think it wd frighten people, but I have no doubt about it myself.

I send my second Athenaeum letter, [2] but please return it when read.

Another singularly unexpected and very pretty confirmation turned up yesterday.[3] I expect I shall have to write to the Athenaeum about it again.[4]

I don't mind Alfred's buzzing the least bit. I did *not* go to Peele's nor Wilkinson's nor Drury Lane. It is perfectly understood between us that he is to say what he likes & I am to do what I like; [5] but to muzzle Alfred's mouth considering what

Letter 119:

[1] Butler first presented his theory of Nausicaa as the authoress of the *Odyssey* in his lecture on the humor of Homer in January, 1892.

[2] His second letter about the topography of the *Odyssey* appeared on February 20, 1892 (pp. 245–246).

[3] "[After my first letter to the *Athenaeum*] I had written to Trapani for information about the rock *Malconsiglio*, and was told of two legends in connexion with it—one palpably absurd, and the other that it was a ship of Turkish pirates who were coming to attack Trapani, but the Virgin turned it into stone just as it was entering the harbour, *i.e.*, the Odyssean version, Christianized, was still current, while the name of the rock clinched its connexion with the poem" (*On the Trapanese Origin of the Odyssey* [1893], Part II, 6–7).

[4] No further letters appeared.

[5] Alfred always left detailed instructions for his employer. A note which particularly amused Butler and which he might have quoted to May, reads: "Feb 8. 1892. You are to work here tomorrow (Tuesday) until 12 o'clock, then you are to go to Peele's or Wilkinson's & get your dinner. Then reach Drury Lane by 5 to 1 (not later). Pit early door 2/6. When you are inside & cannot get a seat in the middle go to the left hand side & you will see better—" (MS Notebooks, VI, 64–65; *Butleriana*, p. 130).

a lot of corn he treads for me & how devotedly—it would be like keeping a tame snail and insisting that it shd never put its horns out. Every now & then I brush him away, but never so as to prevent him from coming back & buzzing again almost immediately.

By the way I am strictly enjoined to send you the photo enclosed herewith & to register them, as a number of letters have been going wrong lately.

I see I have not said that there has been no reply to my Athenaeum letter [6] which I & my friends take to mean that no one sees how to attack my position successfully. Love to Harrie

Yr. affte. brother
S. Butler—

120. *May to Butler*

Text: British Museum MS.

Wilderhope
Ap. 25, 1892.

Dearest Sam

I have just been looking at the yellow auriculas—through the window—for I am kept in a bit with a cold. They are coming out, but will be the better for a few days more, I think. Then you & Alfred shall have your spoils but they won't be as fine this year as last, for want of rain.

Harrie is away at Ventnor, Washington Villa, and May comes here some day this week, I think; Etta & Elsie, who are now at Clifton joining Harrie at Ventnor by & bye. I hope you were the better for your change. It was breaking quite fresh ground wasn't it? And I fancy that queer Holland country has a very special charm of its own, in its white skies & water lilies.

Have you seen how you have been slashed in the Spec-

[6] There was no answer to Butler's letters about the topography of the *Odyssey*.

tator? [1] I have been wondering whether it hurts—it hurts one for you a little—I am afraid I too felt—I told you so—as if you had been treating Homer very irreverently! When you read things you made me laugh because you *put* the fun in them, but I didn't find I laughed when you didn't read them. One felt somehow as if the scholars would be very angry, and I feel as if the ghost of our grandfather would haunt you! But perhaps you will say it is all right, & that the notice at all shows it was considered worthy of notice. I hope it *didn't* hurt much. I send you a special bit of love.

I have been writing nearly all the morning, so won't go on now, but I am always

Yr. very affectionate sister
May.[2]

121. Butler to May

Text: British Museum MS. *Extracts published: Memoir,* II, 132.

[15 Clifford's Inn]
Ap. 26 1892

Dear May

I have to thank you for the ancient atlas received some few days ago which will be very useful to me, and also for your promise of auriculas which will be highly valued both by Alfred & myself. I got a good lot of cowslips on Sunday which will last me some days.

The review in the Spectator was intended no doubt to do me as much harm as the writer could do, but I do not think my friends consider that much of a case has been made out

Letter 120:

[1] A most unfavorable review of Butler's pamphlet, *A Lecture on the Humour of Homer* (Cambridge, 1892), appeared in the *Spectator,* 68 (April 23, 1892), 555–556. It was entitled, "How to Vulgarize Homer."

[2] In a note on this letter dated March 10, 1902, Butler says that he kept it because it was so characteristic of May; he also attacks the *Spectator* review for treating so seriously a popular lecture intended for working men.

against me, & the few capable people whom I have yet spoken to on the subject consider that by putting my translation & Church's [1] so fully side by side the writer has done me good service. I certainly prefer my own myself & find most people tell me (to my face at any rate) that they do so also. As for "Lazy," & "traitorous scoundrel," & the few small holes the writer picks with the translation—I believe myself to be in each case perfectly right and in wanting to make out that I have attempted "to fix attention on the ideas which we connect with the adjective 'dirty,' " the animus of the writer is so clearly shown that I should think none but those who are so weak kneed that I need not trouble about them will fail to see through it. We believe the article to be by a Miss Jane Harrison,[2] who wrote a book about Homer a dozen years ago or so in the affected Church style which so many people unfortunately mistake for culture. She was at my lecture [3] with the two Miss Butcher's [4] (Butcher and Lang's sisters). She told me she had disliked it very much, & the Miss Butchers glared at me, so I went off to those who were more sympathetic. I am told she was scowling the whole lecture through—of course I may be wrong—the review may be by Mr. Gladstone, but we think Miss Harrison more likely. I think most people will see that it is by an angry woman who is determined to see nothing but bad and she will not even deign to notice the topographi-

Letter 121:

[1] The reviewer set passages from Butler's translation next to some from Alfred J. Church's (1829–1912) adaptation, *The Story of the Odyssey,* also published in 1892. One's confidence in the reviewer's judgment is strained by his preference for the passages from Church.

[2] Jane Ellen Harrison (1850–1928), whose *Myths of the Odyssey in Art and Literature* appeared in 1881. Butler later noted on his copy of this letter that Miss Harrison assured him that she had not written the review. Butler came to believe that the author was Gladstone.

[3] The lecture on the humor of Homer which was later printed and reviewed in the *Spectator.*

[4] Augusta (d. 1899) and Eleanor (d. 1894) Butcher, sisters of Samuel Henry Butcher, whose famous translation of the *Odyssey* in collaboration with Andrew Lang was frequently attacked by Butler. Three years later, Augusta Butcher married Charles Crawley, vice-principal of the Working Men's College and a personal friend of Butler's.

cal suggestions which she cannot contradict. In fact we believe it to be just on a small scale Blomfield and Dr. B[5] over again. If my way of doing the thing is right Miss Harrison's is wrong and so is Mr. Butchers; so naturally Miss Harrison and the Miss Butchers abuse me as much as they can. As for Dr. Butler, I should think he would be delighted with the whole thing—at least you may be sure I should not take so much pains with his life & memory and then go & do anything which I believe he would consider in bad taste. However, it is hopeless my trying to please the Spectator or those who take in the Spectator, and I may as well irritate them as I know I cannot please them.

Yr. affte. brother
S. Butler—

122. *Butler to May*

Text: Chapin Library MS.

15. Clifford's Inn
E. C.
May 22, 1892

Dear May

I am extremely sorry to hear you have been unwell and hope you will soon be all right again. I am very well, but dreadfully busy. I have really got rid of everything down to the end of 1831 now,[1] and trust to have every letter out of my hands & in the museum before I go for my holiday. Then the writing of the book will be very rapid work, but I can do

[5] Two unfavorable reviews of Dr. Butler's *Aeschylus* by Charles James Blomfield (1786–1857) precipitated a long quarrel. (See *The Life and Letters of Dr. Butler,* I, 61–63.)

Letter 122:

[1] Butler was working on *The Life and Letters of Dr. Butler.* The "Literary Gossip" column in the *Athenaeum* for May 21, 1892 (p. 668) reported that Butler was making slow progress but that when he mastered the great volume of correspondence he would proceed rapidly to writing the memoir.

nothing till all the interesting letters are copied & the rest either burnt or in the Museum—but I burn very few. The Museum are omnivorous & set great value on the collection. Alfred & I are continuously at work upon them.

No more reviews of my Homer, but the publishers [2] write me from Cambridge that their "classical customers" generally agree with the pamphlet, tho' whether this means topography only, or female authorship as well, I know not. The row however is not yet fairly begun—it is sure to come—in Italy as well as here. I have many additional facts in support of my view and not a word against it—I mean not a word of serious argument has reached me. It is a delightful fighting ground, for it touches no burning question, can wound no one's feelings—is eminently respectable, appeals to the whole literary world, & touches a question of permanent interest. I shall never get another on which to crow & clap my wings more comfortably to myself and with less serious offense to other people—though I admit that some people have seemed to be somewhat seriously offended. Indeed my friend Mr. Garnett [3] will hardly speak to me. I am learning the poems [4] in the Greek off by heart—before breakfast—as I dress, & saying it to myself as I go along the street. Alfred says I shall be run over, but I do not think so. Alfred is very well, & always funny, but he has not out-Alfreded himself particularly very lately. I don't very well see how he can.

The rooks in Gray's Inn had a parliament on the grass some ten days ago, and have left Gray's Inn in a body leaving their young to die in the nests. This is because the Benchers have put up a corrugated iron shed in the gardens. So good bye Gray's Inn rooks. I hope they may be happy, but it is rather a shame of them considering that they have been there from time immemorial.

I shall be at the Speeches,[5] but I do not quite know what is

[2] Metcalfe & Co., Cambridge.

[3] For a fuller discussion of the reaction of Richard Garnett (see note 4 for Letter 31), see *Memoir*, II, 123–124, 131.

[4] The *Odyssey* and the *Iliad*.

[5] Shrewsbury School Speech Day, June 29, 1892.

to happen if Dr. Butler of Trinity[6] & I come across one another. I shall keep out of his way as much as I can, for he has treated me with great rudeness. Love to May & to Harrie if she is returned.

Yr. affte. brother
S. Butler—

123. *Butler to May*

Text: Chapin Library MS.

[15 Clifford's Inn]
June 18. 1892

Dear May

One line to ask how you both are—I trust fairly well. I am very busy—chiefly with Dr. B. who is now in 1834. I hope to finish 1836 before I go for my holiday but it is hopeless I fear to think of getting all the letters done before I go. I snatch time for Homer, or rather for Nausicaa. No more reviews, and if they are to be like those that I have had,[1] they will not tell me anything I did not know, & this is the only thing that can be of service to me. Do you see why Laertes was made so poor, and sent to live away in the country with an old woman to look after him? He wasn't poor at all really. How could his son (who left for Troy when he was about 20) be so enormously rich in his father's lifetime while Laertes was going about almost in rags? He is disposed of in this way to account for his not interfering with Penelope & the suitors. Of course the question wd arise what was he about & why did not he

[6] Henry Montagu Butler (1833–1918), master of Trinity College, Cambridge; he spoke at the Speech Day. Butler's hostility arose in 1889 when Henry Butler wrote asking for information about his father, former headmaster of Harrow and correspondent of Butler's grandfather. Butler sent what information he had, but Henry Butler "never took any notice of this reply to his own request and stuck to the two letters I had imprudently sent him" (Butler's note on a copy of his letter to Henry Butler, dated April 14, 1889, British Museum).

Letter 123:

[1] In addition to the *Spectator* review of *A Lecture on the Humour of Homer*, a long, unfavorable review by Andrew Lang appeared in *Longman's Magazine*, 20 (June, 1892), 215–218. Lang thought Butler's theory and translation irresponsible.

protect his daughter in law—so it is met by saying he was poor & powerless. The fact really being that he was so scandalized with Penelope that he washed his hands of the whole business. And as for the web—you may be sure that the original story, out of which Nausicaa was trying to hobble as best she could, was that Penelope unpicked the web not so much to delay the marriage as to prolong the courtship. As soon as one sees that Penelope is being whitewashed the whole thing becomes intelligible whereas at present it is all in such a mess that no coherent definite idea as to Penelope is fashionable at all.[2] They are translating my pamphlet at Trapani [3] & are very keen about it.

I shall come down next week to the speeches. No more, please, for I have a lot of letters to write. Love to Harrie

Yr. affte. brother
S— Butler—

124. *Butler to May*

Text: Chapin Library MS.
Postcard.
Postmark: Trapani, 10 8 94; *address:* Miss Butler / Wilderhope House / Shrewsbury / England.

Trapani [Italy]
Frid. Augt. 10. 1894.

Dear May

I send one line lest you may be alarmed about me, when you see what a very severe earthquake or rather succession of earthquakes have occurred at Acireale, Catania, & the neighbourhood.[1] There was a slight shock when I was there: my

[2] Butler rests much of his theory of the authoress on the points he makes here. (See chap. 5, "On the Question Whether or No Penelope is Being Whitewashed," pp. 130–139, and chap. 6, pp. 140–142.)

[3] The pamphlet on the humor of Homer was translated privately (letter from Biaggini, May 10, 1892, British Museum), but not published.

Letter 124:

[1] The *Times* (August 9, 1884, p. 56) reports that an earthquake on August 8 caused only minor damage at Acireale and Catania, more serious damage in neighboring towns.

friends all felt it and exclaimed. I noticed nothing, & was vexed not to have perceived it—I said so, but added that I dare not wish there might come a second shock for fear it might be more serious. I left at 2 o'clock on Tuesd. & on the following morning abt. 6 a.m. the first shock occurred—since which there have been several, & an eruption of Etna is expected hourly. I shall not go this time.[2] I am quite well. They have made a most interesting confirmatory discovery here—a part under Mt. Eryx actually now is called Iazzino—no doubt a corruption of Iacino—doubtless my coin came thence.[3] Here they treat one like a prince—a dozen came to the station to meet me. I shall be here another three weeks. No news re Dr. B.[4] Love to Harrie. It is all I can do to get 5 minutes to myself—Yr. affte. brother

S— Butler

125. *May to Butler*

Text: British Museum MS.

[Wilderhope]
Jany. 25. 1895

Dearest Sam

As far as I am concerned, I don't think it would seem to me desirable to give up any share of the capital which may come thro' Aunt Bessie's death.[1] Etta would have no claim at all, I think, & if I should wish—& I think one would wish—, to let the children get some good out of it, I would rather give them extra presents, as seemed useful, out of the income which

[2] Butler went to watch Etna erupt in 1892 (*Memoir*, II, 145).

[3] Butler found a fifth-century Greek coin in the British Museum with a representation of Ulysses' brooch. He tried to identify the coin as Sicilian to prove that Sicily was known in classical times as the locale of the *Odyssey*. (See *The Authoress of the Odyssey*, chap. 13, pp. 236–242; plate opposite p. 294 in Butler's translation of the *Odyssey*.)

[4] Butler was again offering *The Life and Letters of Dr. Butler* to publishers.

Letter 125:

[1] Bessie Worsley died on August 29, 1894, leaving equal inheritances of about £700 each to Butler and his sisters. There was some question of May and Harrie refusing their shares in favor of their nephews; Butler advised them against doing so.

might possibly have fallen under the circumstances to their share. One at least wd. know that the capital was safe & the money made useful. But I should not hold myself *pledged* even to this, tho' I think it would seem nice. It would not seem even necessary to give any *reason* for such presents if they came. I have a strong idea of the "responsibilities of property" & would rather hold on to the capital in their case, unless one saw much stronger cause for acting otherwise than I do.

All *Etta's* money from our father is absolutely tied down & in trustee's hands.

Elsie & Cara are both with us, Cara still uncertain about the matronship of the new Schools Sanatorium here, for which she sent in testimonials. I think they want to have her, but we doubt if it is good enough. Elsie goes today to Edgmond for a night. I never admired her character so much. She is *strong* as well as sweet, & has such thoroughly nice ideas. I think they are all well aware that Charlie [2] may fail in the new venture. He probably will, but I think they were right [to] try. We have just had a heavy snow & are quite white again. Bessie Bather has had a sharp attack of influenza, & it has left her more weak & ill than one likes; it touched her heart rather.

With my love, dear Sam, I am

Yr very affectionate sister
May—

126. *Butler to May*

Text: Chapin Library MS.
Stationery imprinted: SAMUEL BUTLER. 15, CLIFFORDS INN, LONDON. E. C. ___________189

Mar. 15 1895

Dear May

I have no news but send a line to say so. I do not know whether I shall get the land near Harnage or not.[1] I shall not

[2] Butler's nephew. (See note 4 for Letter 128.)

Letter 126:
[1] Butler was attempting to buy property adjoining his land at Harnage.

buy it unless I can do so well. Bather [2] has the negociations in hand & if they will not take my figure I shall let it alone.

I believe myself to be better, but it will be some months before I get rid of mischief which has been gathering long, and was neglected through ignorance of its real nature for many months ⟨to⟩ after it had gathered. I am told however that if I persevere in doing very little (even a letter sometimes bringing on the symptoms in full force) I shall get right & be none the worse.

I am sorry for the trouble you have with your committee. The more I see, the more firmly I believe that there is very little good to be done except⟨ing⟩ by individual attention to cases which come within the continual near influence and observation of the person who is trying to do the good. Those who hold the purse strings will always insist on controlling the management, and often with great want of judgement.

I shall leave home about the 31st of March, but will let you know if I come down to Shrewsbury first. Believe me

Yr. affte. brother
S— Butler—

127. *May to Butler*

Text: **British Museum MS.**
Stationery imprinted: **WILDERHOPE HOUSE, SHREWSBURY.**

Nov. 26. 1895.

Dearest Sam

Mrs. Draper [1] is a nice little woman, but very *young* and rather 'casual.' He is a nice person. We know them very slightly, owing partly to their being very busy, & partly to

[2] John T. Bather, manager of Butler's properties near Shrewsbury.

Letter 127:

[1] Wife of William Henry Draper (matriculated Keble College, Oxford, 1875, age 19), pastor of the Church of the Holy Cross in Shrewsbury. He wrote to Butler asking if he would donate some of his land for a church social center. Instead, Butler agreed to give 100 guineas toward the purchase of any site, including one he owned, at market value; but the plans were not carried out.

their being so 'casual' but she was a ⟨Beres⟩ Fitzherbert Wright —(or Beresford Wright—I forget which) neighbours of Edith Turbutt, so I asked her to lunch when Edith was here.

She told us they wanted a sight [*i.e.*, site], & asked for your address, which I of course gave. She would have *liked* me to write to you on the subject, but I felt that I knew nothing at all about it—or the merits of the case on either side, and that you and Mr. Draper were quite capable of managing your own business—and declined to be mixed up in it at all—I would not even *hear* much about it on purpose. I had rather gathered that they would—like most people, *like* it as a gift, but nothing very definite was said about that—and if it could be a *parish* council matter no—there are no parish councils in *towns,* and I doubt whether a county council would concern itself about the matter. But if there is any parochial body which could authorise payment I should if I were you ⟨ask⟩ try for it. I think however that there is none which could be consulted about any building or site for Church purposes—except by voluntary subscription—

Even a parish council could only take cognisance of such a thing as a perfectly secular & "undenominational" school or clubroom, I believe. And I fancy the room in question was meant for club &c, & possibly occasional mission services, but *I don't know*—at all events, to be in the hands of the parish clergy. Now I have told you all I know.

I purposely did not mention it when I wrote because I had said I would have nothing to do with it—and felt that I knew nothing about it. I thought it was *he* who would write. He did not speak to me about it at all. The only thing I did tell her was that I was sure they would find you courteous whatever your answer was.

Poor Dr. Burd! I don't suppose he even knows—& it was not anything but simple family friendship that he wished to see you ⟨before⟩ for. He always speaks warmly & kindly of you, & when I asked him to come in to meet you at tea—which he did—he spoke very heartily—

The photographer shall photograph anything he likes. I

hardly expect Harrie quite so soon as tomorrow because of the change to cold, but she *may* come.

I hear Reginald's death was due to apoplexy.

Mrs. Burbury died very suddenly, from some quite unsuspected internal mischief. With my love, dear Sam

Yr very affectionate sister
May.

128. *May to Butler*

Text: British Museum MS.
Postcard.
Postmark: Shrewsbury / AP 28 97; *address:* S. Butler Esq. / Hotel Centrale / Reggio / Calabria / *Italy.*

April. 28. 1897.

I think this will catch you at Reggio, and I hope to find you both in better case. *I* shouldn't like to walk with a book & a slipper! I should expect to get rheumatism in the slipper foot. Good accounts of Harrie. I am much too busy to be lonely, & Lucy J.[1] comes next week. Elsie is looking at a promising little house [2] near Hereford, in which case Hereford would do well for E. & M.[3] & afford the latter plenty of scope for her energies & they would be a nice distance from us. Charlie is—half way between Athens & Larissa!! [4]—He volunteered & went out in a hurry, having volunteered before war broke out but then M. Metasas w. not promise his passage. When war was declared, M. Metasas telegraphed offering passage &c. in charge of a small troop of volunteers going out—& letters of recommendation for a Gr commission. He wrote rather nicely. Don't imagine we stirred a finger to help! but tho' I have no sympathies with the Greeks, I think it was plucky of him. Dr. Burd & the Lloyds think so too—& better

Letter 128:

[1] Lucy Jackson, daughter of the former Bishop of London, John Jackson (1811–1885).

[2] Elsie Butler was about to marry Richard Burton Phillipson.

[3] Etta and Maysie.

[4] Charles Butler accepted a commission in the Greek army during the war with Turkey. Though he had failed in many activities before going and was being supported by Etta, he stayed in the Greek army until his retirement.

than living idly on his mother. Mr. Fletcher has been trying hard to find him brewery work but every one says the same, the supply is greater than the demand. I think the fighting is very hopeless & will soon stop, but he will have a real taste of war first. With my love I am

Yr very affectionate sister
M B.[5]

Nothing in Guardian.

129. *May to Butler*

Text: British Museum MS.
Postcard.
Postmark: Shrewsbury / My 24 97; *address:* S. Butler Esq. / Poste Restante / Rome / *Italy.*

I don't feel as if I had anything to tell you, but you must not miss a line of some sort. House cleaning & hammers resound inside the house, & intervals of Queen's birthday bells [1] outside. I'm convinced we shall have a wet day for the wedding! Charlie has been to the front & in some of the fighting; he writes nicely to Newbury, & I think it may make a man of him.

Ada is going to follow Elsie's example the last week in July, but leaves us a little sooner. I go to Portsmouth for a night after the wedding to see Dora & Matron, & then to Shere, where I shall find Alice & Molly with Gertrude & we shall enjoy being all together. I think I may be back here for the Jubilee time.[2] How nice it will be when all the excitements are over. I hope you are catching no more colds & having no more earthquakes. I hear charming accounts of Elsie's new home from some one who knows it well, as *very* lovely & very healthy & very economical. What can be more to be

[5] May wrote at the top of this postcard: "Elsie wrote with much pleasure & satisfaction of your present."

Letter 129:
[1] Queen Victoria was 79 on May 24, 1897.
[2] The Queen's Diamond Jubilee on June 22, 1897.

desired. She is one of the "lucky ones" of life, so I think it is sure to turn out right! Yr very affectionate sister

May Butler

130. *May to Butler*

Text: British Museum MS.
Postcard.
Postmark: Shrewsbury / JU 17 97; *address:* S. Butler Esq. / Hotel des Alpes / Wasen / Canton Uri / *Switzerland.*

Wilderhope.
June 17. 1897.

The days pass by most uneventfully, but a line to tell of our well-being shall not fail you at Wasen. H. & I have just returned from tea at Portland House,[1] where we met Nelly Adam, pretty but far from strong & May Hall (Bather)— It is so cold that we thought about a fire, & it was almost a disappointment to find the *in*door temperature will hardly authorise it. On Sunday the therm. was 80° & we were all baking. Elsie writes *very* happily. We are expecting a little visit from Guy Bridges [2] in a week or two, we always like him to come. I think I am stationary here till about the middle of July when I may find courage to begin my career of outing again. Ernest is hoping to get an Irish magistracy, a better thing than his post at York, though not one that I should covet. He & George have had a fortnight in Ireland together. The Bathers are back at Meole for the last time, & Bessie fairly well again. He has a place on the steps of St. Paul's as representative of the Hereford chapter. We send you our love, & shall probably not write again till you return. Your very affecte. sister

M Butler.

Charlie is still at Athens, waiting orders, but will probably return if peace is signed.

Letter 130:
[1] Home of George Arthur Bell, Belvidere Road, Shrewsbury.
[2] Guy Bridges (b. 1863), Harrie's nephew, first son of Thomas Walker Bridges.

131. *Butler to May*

Text: Garnett, pp. 218–219.

15 Clifford's Inn
London, E. C.
Oct. 26 [1898].[1]

Dear May,

One line to return enclosed. I will come to afternoon tea soon after four on Tuesday—but will stay at the George.

Of course we all know what Anne [Wade] would be in sickness. One only grieves that such people should ever have any illness at all. Pray keep me informed as to what money may be welcome to her in every comfort that may become necessary. I do not care two straws how much it may be, and am only thankful to have it in case it may be wanted.

Your affectionate brother,
S. Butler.

132. *Butler to May*

Text: British Museum MS. *Extracts published: Memoir,* II, 299.

[15 Clifford's Inn]
Jany 4 [1899]

My dear May

I did not return from Boulogne till Friday, the sea was so rough that one day the boat went over to Folkestone, could not land, & had to come back, and another day it did not go at all, so I waited till the sea was only moderately rough, & left Jones behind me for a couple of days more. He is better, but still far from what he should be. I am all right, but my feet which gave me no trouble at Boulogne became troublesome again, as they always do on my return—I am getting more & more convinced that nervous exhaustion is three parts of the battle.

Letter 131:

[1] Garnett reads 1808, an obvious misprint.

Your's of Dec. 26 was forwarded to me—thank you, and many happy New Years to you both—I have been deluged with Italian letters—two of them requiring long troublesome answers. An old Italian member of parliament keeps wanting all sorts of details about the London School board—all of which I have to find out, and it worries me for it is out of my beat. Then another wants all sorts of questions answered about the Odyssey let alone the numerous New Years letters that I have to answer. On Friday evening, too, I went to the Messiah —done at last without Mozart's accompaniments, as I trust henceforward it always will be, but I am free to confess that in only one place "The people that walked," should I have known whether they were there or not.

I have had a note from Ada, all very nice, & will answer it.

And now for a piece of news. Alfred saw Alice Leamar's [1] name announced to appear at the Metropolitan Music Hall, so I sent him to see if it was the old Alice Leamar whom we suppose, I cannot doubt correctly, to be our niece by marriage. Alfred ⟨He⟩ was there last night, and knew her perfectly well; she seemed in excellent health. Now what are we to think of the story of her death which reached us from our precious Nephew? It looks very much as if he had been contemplating bigamy with the other young lady to whom you informed me that he had been making up, and whose father stopped the match. One must not jump to conclusions, but I believe that man to be such an utter scoundrel that I do not think I am doing him much wrong if I suspect that the story of his wife's death was a pure fabrication of his own. It is too disgusting altogether to have any sort of connection ⟨f⟩ with a nephew of whom you have no sort of confidence that he will not attempt bigamy at any moment. All, however that I know for certain is that Alice Leamar is alive and well; that he declared himself married to her; declared her to be dead; & was carrying on with a young lady to whom I understood you to say he was engaging himself.

Letter 132:

[1] Charles Butler was married to Alice Leamar, from whom he had long ago separated.

I don't think I have any more news, but that is surely enough. With love to Harrie believe me Yr affte. brother

S. Butler—

133. *May to Butler*

Text: British Museum MS.

[Wilderhope]
Jan. 5. 1899.

Dearest Sam

Your news is—hardly suprising [*sic*]—but important, and I am afraid now the information *must* have originated with C [harles] for she would hardly dare to come to life again in her own name! I suppose there is no doubt that it is *Alice*. There was a sister, also *A*, but I think she married & left the staff. Of course one never had much faith in the report, but I had rather it had been circulated by her. I am afraid he will never come to any good. Since the episode of the cheque we have had no intercourse.

You clearly had bigger storms than we, but the Severn has been in higher flood than for some years. Today we have had Jack & Maud to lunch, & Connie, & the Mackays. George & Tommy were hunting. He is growing such a handsome boy, and I've been since at a Dogpole Home [1] "tea," & had a class—so am tired.

We have told Maysie of your news. They ought to know it. I heard of Anne today, her leg often very painful, partly rheumatism in it, & being galvanised which does it good, but she is up in the kitchen a good deal, tho' she cannot walk without help. She sent us sausages today.

Our love. I am always

Your very affectionate sister
May.

Letter 133:

[1] *Wilding's Directory of Shrewsbury*, 1893, lists a "training home" at 8 Dogpole.

134. *Butler to May*

Text: **Chapin Library MS.**
Postcard.
Postmark: **Bologna, 15 MAG '99;** ***address:*** **Miss Butler / Wilderhope House / Shrewsbury / Inghilterra.**

Hotel S. Lorenzo, Verona, [Italy]
Mond. May 15 [1899]

My dear May

Your's of May 10 reached me at Venice which we left this morning. Thank you very much. I am glad to hear that there has been a pretty steady warm rain for my trees— May is I believe the month in which they want it most. I had a sharp attack of lumbago for 3 days in Venice which is now quite gone, but which almost crippled me while it lasted. My feet are hardly troubling me at all. We go on to Bergamo tomorrow and spend one day there, reach Turin (Hotel Suisse) on Thursd. May 18. Sat. May 20—Frid. May 26 we shall be at Hotel Giacosa, S. Pietro, S. Ambrogio, Turin, but shall leave on the last named day for Chambery. Sat. May 27 we reach Paris—stay there two days & return to London Tuesd., May 30. Unless you write to S. Pietro, you had better not write till my return.

Most ⟨some⟩ men can do a great many things better than most women. Most women can do a great many things better than most men; but some men can do the woman things as well as but not better than most women, & some women can do the man things as well as but not better than most men—that is the long & short of the whole matter.

Jones unites in k. regards. Yr. affte. brother

S. Butler

135. *May to Butler*

Text: British Museum MS.

Hound House.
Shere.[1]
Ju. 26. 1899.

Dearest Sam

It is not easy to write letters more than one can help once one is out visiting, but I want to send you a little line from this pretty place. You know the beautiful lie of the country. It is blazing hot, looks like thunder. If *not* we are going up to the woods in the cool by & bye—I had a nice time at Westminster, didn't try to do much sight seeing, contented myself with a Richter concert,[2] where I am sorry to say Beethoven's Pastoral Symphony didn't please me after a 'first part' of Wagner & Tch. . . . . which would probably not have pleased *you*. But it's no good. I do like Wagner. I went to the Tate Gallery, & to a Lambeth Garden party, not so pretty as a Fulham one,[3] & now I am here. Alice is here, hoping to get into her own pretty house next month. It will be *very* pretty, but at present has the garden all to make. Fred is expected this evening. Herbert & Gertrude hospitable & kind as usual, & their garden charming—On Thursday I go to Mr. Robinson [4] who was curate of Meole, & married a Miss Sidebotham, for a night at Busbridge near Godalming, & then on to Cathedral Hotel Salisbury for two or three days. I want to see Guy's new home, & something of Mr. Sidebotham & Gabrielle who are not yet settled enough to take me in. Then back by Clifton, Aunt Sarah & the Bathers at Hereford.

My love to you dear Sam. I have been a bit rheumatic & hope your feet have not been worse for the heat. Oh—I saw

Letter 135:

[1] Near London.

[2] A popular concert series, directed by Hans Richter (1843–1916).

[3] May compares the garden party of the Archbishop of Canterbury unfavorably with that of the Bishop of London.

[4] Albert Gossage Robinson (1863–1948), rector of Busbridge, Surrey, at this time; he married Edith Sidebotham in 1896.

your Mr. Fuller Maitland[5] at the concert, not to speak to; he looks nice. Bee stays there, & says he gives such pleasant parties.

Your very affectionate sister
M Butler

Alice & Gertrude send you their love.

136. *Butler to May*

Text: Chapin Library MS.
Stationery imprinted: SAMUEL BUTLER. 15, CLIFFORDS INN, LONDON. E. C. ________189

July 24 1899

My dear May

I am afraid I owe both Harrie & you a letter, and must ask Harrie's forgiveness if it is to her that I ought to pay my debt more especially.

I am sorry your feet have been troubling you—mine, I am happy to say, have hardly put themselves in evidence at all since my return, & if they would stay like this I should not think about them. Curiously enough poor Alfred has at times complained of his a good deal—but he too is better, and today he and his wife & children have started to Boscombe for a three week's holiday, and I have little doubt will return greatly the better. If the wife and children can be prevailed upon to stay a week on by themselves, after his return, they are to do so, but Mrs. Cathie wd not do so last year & we are afraid she will again be recalcitrant.

I did not go to the Bishop's first garden party[1] being particularly pressed to go to Miss Sichel's[2] on that day—so I went

[5] See note 2 for Letter 113.

Letter 136:

[1] The Bishop of London, Mandell Creighton (1843–1901), gave a garden party on Saturday, July 1, 1899. The bishop admired Butler's work. (See *Memoir*, II, 175–177.)

[2] Edith Sichel (1862–1914), a writer to whom Butler's sonnet "Not on Sad Stygian Shore" is addressed.

to the second garden party instead, on Saturday last—all very gay and pretty, but fearfully hot, and a tremendous thunder storm later on in the night. Yesterday & this morning it was delightfully cooler, but this afternoon it has come on to blaze again.

I go to Cambridge on Thursday for the inside of a day to take my book to the press[3]—it will be printed in Cambridge. It seems to me that I have done for the Sonnets much what I have done for the Odyssey, i.e., upset every one's apple-cart all round, & I do not anticipate being faced or refuted, and shall be disagreeably surprised if I find myself convinced of serious error.

Poor Aunt Sarah![4] I am extremely sorry for her—but if she lives till the time comes for her to move, no doubt the same people whom she has been living with will take her with them, and I should hope that the shock will not be so great as one might fear—but I am very sorry to hear of her having any shock at all.

The last child story—perfectly true.

"And you know, Daisy, when the cake is handed round for the first time, you may take any piece—a large piece if you like. When it comes round a second time you may take a small piece, but when it comes round a third time you must say 'no thank you.' "

The party being over, Mamma said "Well now, Daisy, did you do as I said about the cake?"

"Yes Mamma,—at first: when the cake came round for the first time there was a nice big piece quite near me, so I took it: and the second time I took a little piece & the third time I said 'no thank you'; but it came round a fourth time & you did not tell me what I was to say then."

"And my dear what did you say?"

"Oh—I said what papa says—'*Take the d——d* thing away!' " Tableau.

[3] *Shakespeare's Sonnets Reconsidered*, published by Longmans, Green; the printing was done in Cambridge by Metcalfe & Co., at Butler's expense.

[4] Sarah Worsley. (See Biographical Sketches.)

With love to Harrie believe me

Your affte. brother
S. Butler—

137. *May to Butler*

Text: British Museum MS.

Wilderhope.
Oct. 10. 1899.

My dearest Sam

You will like to hear that I am at home again—and I hope, decidedly the better for all the Bath experiences. It is difficult to tell yet *how* much good it has done, but I feel hopeful, and if it does seem to have improved matters much, shall try to do it again in the spring.

Dr. King Martyn [1] was very kind. Did I tell you that he brought me in his sister's lovely etchings to see, and the last evening he asked me into tea, and showed me many pictures, and we had a little music. I copied for him a few of the notes which he liked.

I saw Mrs. Inman [2] two or three times, and played to her, & I think we liked each other! I liked her *very* much. She gives such an impression of truth and strength.

Harrie thinks to go south next week. When are you and Alfred going to come to Shrewsbury? I will make you very welcome. And you shall read my essay on how to read!—which has just come out in a little book for girls called Life's Possibilities edited by Mrs. Draper.[3]

We had a very good & cheery account of Anne today from Annie James, tho' I think she has now got to her high water

Letter 137:

[1] Gilbert John King Martyn (1869–1950), a physician who practiced at Bath.

[2] Mrs. Thomas Frederick Inman, daughter of Samuel Tillbrook, a correspondent of Dr. Butler's, sister of Philip Tillbrook. (See note 4 for Letter 115.) Her husband was a solicitor at Bath.

[3] May contributed "Our Silent Companions," an essay on the virtues of reading books—especially religious books—to *Life's Possibilities: A Book for Girls*, ed. by E. A. Draper (1899). Mrs. Draper was the wife of the pastor of the Church of the Holy Cross, Shrewsbury. (See note for Letter 127.)

mark. She told us also that *Mrs.* Wood has been taken to the Asylum, since which the house is much more comfortable. One would not have wondered had it been he. We have made a delightful new acquaintance in a young Mr. Coates who lives in the parish, he is a clerk at Lloyd's bank, but *quite* a gentleman, & 6 ft 6½! He is very tame & sociable & "thinks it is kind of us to notice him."

Our parlour maid's young man is just ordered out with the Reserve to Africa, & she has gone to bid him farewell. I wonder whether we shall fight after all! or whether our great preparations will scare the Boers. The papers are very interesting. While at Bath I took the Times for a treat. We heard from Harry & Ada yesterday. The orange-trees were prospering greatly under unusual heat, 104 in the shade, & they hoped to make about £30 this year, but they both feel the great heat, & the constant uncertainty a great strain of nerves.

I don't know whether Charlie has gone back to Greece yet. It was to be soon. He seems to have behaved quite well while at home.

I think this is all, dear Sam. Much love to you, & kind messages to Mr. Jones of whom Dr. King Martyn speaks very warmly. Harrie sends her love to you too

Your very affectionate sister
May Butler

138. Butler to May

Text: Chapin Library MS.
Postcard.
Postmark: Siracusa Reggio Calabria, AP 26 00; ***address:*** Miss Butler / 25. Gay Street / Bath / England; ***picture:*** Taormina.

Taormina, Sicily, Italy
Hotel Timeo
Ap. 26 (Thursd.) 1900

My dear May—Yrs. of Ap 20 reached me yesterday afternoon. I hope the baths may do you as much good as our outing is doing to Jones & me. Weather lovely. I have decided to run over to Malta, to see some prehistoric remains in the island of Gozo. So I may meet Henry Bather. My address will be Hotel Centrale, Palermo, Sicily, Italy at which place we expect to arrive on or about May 6. This is the best post-card the place affords. They were *much* better at Genoa. Pray give our kindest regards to Dr. King Marytyn [i.e., Martyn] and Jones desires to be very kindly remembered to yourself. Believe me Yr. affte. brother S. Butler.

139. *Butler to May*

Text: Chapin Library MS.
Postcard.
Postmark: Malta, MY 7; *address:* Miss Butler / 25. Gay Street / Bath / England; *vignetted photograph:* Strada St. Lucia; *Butler has written near the picture:* "Our hotel is in this street."

Sund. May 6. 1900.
Hotel Imperial, Malta

—Yours of Ap. 27 reached me a day or two before we left for Malta—and I hope this will catch you before you return, or at any rate be duly forwarded. We left Taormina last Wed. and reached Malta soon after midnight; Jones was very ill—crawling to the Custom house with support. They said "Are you a British subject?" He replied most piteously "You would not think it to look at me, but I am." He is now better. I have seen the prehistoric remains in this island, & also those in Gozo—very imposing and interesting. The picture cards are not coloured, with few and unattractive exceptions. We have not run across Henry Bather and his party, and fear we shall hardly do so, for we shall return to Syracuse tomorrow if the weather holds fair. Malta is not picturesque—too glaring and oriental and dusty, but I am very glad to have seen it. Pray give Jones's & my love to Dr. K.M.[1] & my profoundest respects to Mrs. Inman.

Yr. affte. brother
S—B.

Letter 139:
[1] Dr. King Martyn.

140. *Butler to May*

Text: Chapin Library MS.
Postcard.
Postmark: illegible except the figures 00; *address:* Miss Butler / Wilderhope House / Shrewsbury / Inghilterra; *picture:* Napoli, Palazzo Donn Anna.

Hotel Giacosa, S. Pietro, S. Ambrogio.
Valle di Susa— Italy—
Sund. June 3. [1900]

My dear May—Yours of May 29 reached me this morning. Thank you. Yes—pray take as much potting soil as you want, and *of course* don't let Bather [1] charge you! The word "negociating" alarms me. We are weather bound here—pouring steady rain yesterday & today so that we cannot paint. We expect to be back on Mond. 11, so I give no address. Yr. affte. Brother S. Butler—

141. *May to Butler*

Text: British Museum MS.

[Wilderhope]
Monday, July 2. [1900]

Dearest Sam

We are wondering how & when we shall see you? Tomorrow there is a garden party & sale of work at the Council House in the afternoon at which it beseems us both to be present if we can. On Wednesday *I* do not think to go to the speeches.[1] The rheumatism is giving way now, but it has been so bad that I will not sit in tents. Harrie hopes to be there if fine. You will probably be dining at the School, & will want to go back to Shelton & dress.

But do you think that you could come to us for either luncheon or tea which ever suits you best, on Thursday?—

Letter 140:
[1] John T. Bather, Butler's property manager.

Letter 141:
[1] Shrewsbury School Speech Day, Wednesday, July 4, 1900.

Yesterday Mrs. Moss brought in a rather taking Mr. & Mrs. Bolleston, from N. Z, who hoped they might have found you here—he said he was the man who told you there was "the lake" to wash in. He left the enclosed card for you—was leaving today—we decidedly liked them. He seemed really sorry to miss you, and hoped to look you up before leaving England in September.

One of his sons is in the N. Z. contingent at the Cape. Our love, dearest Sam. I hope I shall see you somehow.

Your very affectionate sister
May.

142. *May to Butler*

Text: British Museum MS.

Shrewsbury
Oct. 24, 1900.

Dearest Sam

Thank you very much. I shall enjoy reading it [1] in my solitary evenings, and Harrie will thank you too—it looks enticing.

I have done very little more Greek since you left—days have been busy.

Dick & Elsie were very nice and they also spoke with pleasure of your visit to them. I thought Elsie looking much older, & not well. I don't think she is at all strong. They have gone on to Peniarth—uchaf [2]—another Wynne household—& then to Peniarth proper.

Good accounts of Harrie who had Georgie with her.

I have actually stopped the Evening paper. Things are so little exciting just now!

They got the Colchester fire under in about an hour, but

Letter 142:

[1] Probably Butler's translation of the *Odyssey*, the first copy of which he received on October 18, 1900.

[2] Richard and Elsie (Butler) Phillipson were visiting at Peniarth-uchaf and Peniarth, both towns near Towyn, Merioneth, in Wales.

it was a lively time for the prisoners—as the prison was next door to the fire & the ammunition! I was reading a day or two ago of the falling at 5 o'clk one morning (1545) of the great tower & gate which once stood on the English bridge,[3] I gather in consequence of a very heavy flood. It fell quite unexpectedly, & in it was a locked up prisoner fettered & chained, whose escape was considered so marvellous that they promptly let him go free.

I meant to have taken great pains with my calligraphy in my next letter to you, & forgot! You deserve it, for your writing is so lovely when *you* take pains, & I *can* write nicely. Much love, dear Sam, you were very good to me.

Your very affectionate sister
May.

143. *May to Butler*

Text: British Museum MS.
Postcard.
Postmark: Shrewsbury FE 5 01; *address:* S. Butler Esq. / 15. Clifford's Inn / London / E. C.

Feb. 5.

It seems some time since you heard, but there has been only one thought in all English heads & hearts.[1] Harrie too has been in bed for ten days with an odd cold which neither got better nor worse. Yesterday it began to get distinctly worse, & she is in a state of kettle, poultice &c, not seriously bad so far, but one never likes her to begin. The doctor suspects influenza, but I have not breathed that to her. If you do not hear for a day or two take for granted all is going on right, but she won't be well just yet—I hope you keep better. My love, yr. very affte. sister

M Butler.

[3] The English Bridge over the Severn at Shrewsbury replaced an earlier bridge. The incident to which May refers is related by Thomas Phillips, *The History and Antiquities of Shrewsbury* (Shrewsbury, 1779), p. 149.

Letter 143:
[1] Queen Victoria died on January 22, 1901.

144. *Butler to May*

Text: Chapin Library MS.
Postcard.
Postmark: London 21 OC 01; *address:* Miss Butler / Wilderhope House / Shrewsbury; *imprinted:* MR. SAMUEL BUTLER. 15, CLIFFORD'S INN, LONDON. E. C.

Oct. 21. 1901

My dear May One line to say how *very* glad I am to have so much better an account of Harrie & yourself. I hope now that with this mild weather you will both come round comfortably.

I have had a very gratifying review of Er: Rev: in the last Friday's Athenaeum.[1] If the Spectator & Guardian [2] are very angry with me, as I fear they will be, I must shelter myself behind the Times [3] & Athenaeum—I should *like* to please every one, but that Alas! I cannot do—With love to you both believe me Yr. affte. brother

S. Butler—

145. *Butler to May*

Text: Chapin Library MS.
Stationery imprinted: SAMUEL BUTLER. 15, CLIFFORDS INN, LONDON. E. C. __________190

Jan 6 1901 [i.e., 1902]

My dear May,

Your's of Dec. 30 greeted me on my return from Boulogne where Jones & I spent a quiet but comfortable Christmas. I returned last Monday, & Jones on Wednesday. Feeling ill next day he got up to his sister's—where he was expected—but no sooner had he arrived than it was plain that he had better go to bed. Next morning instead of being better as was ex-

Letter 144:

[1] A long, highly favorable review in which Butler ("one of the striking writers of our time") is compared to Swift and Defoe appeared in the *Athenaeum*, October 19, 1901, pp. 517–518.

[2] The *Spectator*, 88 (February 8, 1902), 223, found *Erewhon Revisited* a poor fulfillment of the promise of *Erewhon*. The *Guardian* did not review it.

[3] A favorable review, which calls *Erewhon Revisited* "a worthy sequel to 'Erewhon'" in most respects, appeared in the *Times*, October 9, 1901, p. 5.

pected he was much worse & the doctor on being sent for declared him to have got pneumonia, the effects of a chill. Next day Sir Douglas Powell [1] was also called in, and, though happily he takes a favourable view of the case, he says it will be four days yet before the crisis arrives. Today I have had fairly satisfactory accounts from his sister. I have been up to Hampstead where she lives, twice, but we both thought I had better not see him as the least thing agitates him. Of course he has a day & night nurse. I thought a good deal better of his head when he was at Boulogne, until the last day when I was again made somewhat uneasy. The doctors say his heart is strong & this it is that makes them take so decidedly hopeful a view as they do.

My troubles are somewhat added to by the visit to London of an excellent Italian whom I have to attend to, and do attend to. Had Jones been well, he would have helped me with him, for he is as much a friend to Jones as to me. Fortunately he speaks a little English & Alfred can help me to take him about to some extent.

I am extremely sorry to hear about poor little Patrick's [2] elbow, & should be glad to hear how Tom Bridges' [3] arm is. Please excuse more & believe me with love to Harrie

Yr. affte. brother
S— Butler—

146. May to Butler

Text: **British Museum MS.**

Wilderhope.
Feb. 17. 1902

Dearest Sam

I do not quite remember when either of us wrote last, but we think you should hear, though you may have seen it in the

Letter 145:

[1] Richard Douglas Powell (1842–1925), a physician who attended Queen Victoria in her last illness.

[2] Patrick Butler, son of Harry and Ada, in Florida at this time.

[3] Tom Bridges (1871–1934), at this time a captain in the Royal Army; he was wounded in the arm in South Africa.

paper of Mrs. How's death at Nearwell. It all came very suddenly. She was out & well a fortnight ago. It was some stoppage. They tried operation, but she could not stand the chloroform, & they had to give it up. Nothing else could be done, and she died on Saturday morning—and is buried this afternoon.—

It is still very cold, and I hear that the river is about frozen over. We are both well, though neither of us get out much. Harrie not at all. A *much* better account of little Patrick came a few days ago, with nicely written & spelt notes from them both to their grandmother. They had had a freeze though—which had hurt badly some of the younger trees—& *damaged* some of the older—but the older trees seem able to stand a good deal. I only hope they have not had a return of it. Tom Bridges is a little better too. Poor Dick & Elsie are much troubled by Mrs. Phillipson,[1] who announced that she was going to remain over the event, & has now in a huff moved herself into one bedroom somewhere in Colchester & won't give the address. Dick thinks she is off her head. I am afraid it will be very worrying for them both, but Elsie seems well so far. It does not happen till the middle of March.—

We saw the Spectator & your answer.[2] Probably you *know* who wrote the review (we don't) but we were a little sorry you said about the *he* & *she*, however true the she—as your letter seemed to lose a little dignity by it.

Jane Lloyd holds her own through this cold weather, but of course cannot make much progress. She has been in the drawing room. We are glad Mr. Jones is better. Did those sea gulls attack a stray passer's fish, or the man who feeds them? I read something about them the other day. Here we have a cocoanut

Letter 146:

[1] Dick's mother.

[2] The reviewer of *Erewhon Revisited* in the *Spectator* (February 8, 1902, p. 223) questions Butler's assertion in his Preface that the *Spectator* received *Erewhon* favorably in 1872. Quoting a statement from that review, the reviewer applies it to *Erewhon Revisited:* if one were to follow the moral of either book he would be nowhere. In a letter which appeared on February 15, 1902 (p. 253), Butler insisted that the review of *Erewhon* had been favorable, except for a final "reviewer's kick" which he, or she, gave the book, and he expresses great indignation at the reviewer's suggestion that he *intended* his moral to lead nowhere.

for the tits, filled with fat & quickly eaten since the cocoanut got frozen. It is very pretty to see them & they are insatiable. Harold Fisher, Lucy Jackson's [3] nephew who was besieged in Ladysmith [4] has just come home, & arrived in his Essex village after dark. He had to submit to having the carriage dragged by the villagers along the slippery road, first to the church for a short thanksgiving service, and then all round the village, the carriage decorated with chinese lanterns & and [*sic*] rockets going off at intervals. He was allowed to go home & supper at 10.

Talking of Africa, we heard a nice account of a visit of one of the Allens' relations to the little King of Uganda who received her in great state (then 4 years old) & "reviewed his warriors" in her honour, but seeing her with a little picture book got on her lap to look at the pictures. Goodbye, dear Sam, don't catch cold, *or* rheumatism. I tried rheumatism inside, lately, & it isn't nice, but I'm quite well now. Love from us both

Your very affectionate sister
May Butler

I hope Alfred will soon get his little son back.

147. *Butler to May*

Text: Chapin Library MS.
Postcard.
Postmark: Palermo 4–02; ***address:*** Miss Butler / Wilderhope House / Shrewsbury / Inghilterra.

Hotel de France,
Palermo
Thursd. Ap. 17 [1902]

Dear May

Your's of Ap. 9. has only reached me after much blundering this morning. I got here last Saturday, & broke down

[3] See note 1 for Letter 128.
[4] The garrison at Ladysmith, South Africa, was praised for its gallant stand against the Boers in 1899–1900.

again at once—sent for doctor,—gastric fever—temp. 41 Celsius [1] (whatever that may mean): bed ever since: milk diet: aconite; [2] and this morning am pronounced to be quite normal both as regards temperature & pulse. Am still very weak: shall stay here a few days & come home at once. Now we know why I have been losing strength & flesh for months past. It is certain I have had this fever latent in me all the time. There is no reason why it should not be got ⟨right⟩ rid of. The F. Maitlands [3] visit me & are very kind, but our joint journey is at an end. The first strength I can regain will be spent in travelling homeward. Love to Harrie

Yrs.
S— Butler

148. *Butler to May*

Text: Chapin Library MS.
Postcard.
Postmark: Palermo Ferrovia 18 4–02; *address:* Miss Butler / Wilderhope House / Shrewsbury / Inghilterra.

Hotel de France,
Palermo,
Frid. Ap. 18. 1902

My dear May

There is not the slightest trace of fever left—temperature & pulse quite normal, but digestive organs much insulted, & until they are pacified I cannot move—for the diarrhaea will not leave me till what food I take is properly digested. Please address to Hotel Vettoria, Rome. I have not smoked for close on a week! Pray believe me that there is no cause for anxiety now that the fever has behaved so excellently—on Saturday the doctor was not sure that I was not on the point of serious illness. Love to Harrie—

Yr. affte. brother S. Butler

Letter 147:
[1] 105.8° Fahrenheit.
[2] A sedative.
[3] The Fuller-Maitlands. (See note 2 for Letter 113.)

149. *Butler to May*

Text: Chapin Library MS.
Postcard.
Postmark: Palermo 19 4–02; ***address:*** Miss Butler / Wilderhope House / Shrewsbury / Inghilterra.

Hotel de France,
Palermo,
Sat. Ap. 19. [1902]

My dear May

Pray believe that I am in good hands & going on quite nicely, but it will be some few days before I can turn my face homeward. The F. Maitlands visit me daily & she is to make me arrowroot this afternoon. I have *no* fever—and the stomach is gradually regaining tone. When the F. Maitland's go, the Consul is to take me in tow & see to my embarking comfortably &c. When I get to Rome I shall probably send for Alfred, but I will not have him here. The doctor says it will take many months of care & quiet before I shake this off. Love to Harrie

Yr. affte brother
S. Butler—

150. *Butler to May*

Text: Chapin Library MS.
Postcard.
Postmark: Palermo Ferrovia 21 4–02; ***address:*** Miss Butler / Wilderhope House / Shrewsbury / Inghilterra.

Mond. Ap. 21. [1902]
Hotel Trinacria
Palermo

My dear May

I am not the worse today for yesterday's move—on the contrary I am sitting up in my clothes to write letters and shall go down stairs shortly. The F. Maitland's are on the same floor—& very good. It will be another three or four days before I can go back to Naples—but I am going on quite nicely—tongue getting clean, & temperature rather below normal. Please excuse more and if you do not hear tomorrow assume that everything is going on normally. Love to Harrie

Yr. affte. brother
S— Butler—

151. *Butler to May*

Text: Chapin Library MS.
Postcard.
Postmark: Palermo 22 4–02; *address:* Miss Butler / Wilderhope House / Shrewsbury / Inghilterra.

Hotel Trinacria,
Palermo
Tuesd. Ap. 22 [1902]

One line to say that I am dressed, down stairs, & writing in the sala di lettura, but still very weak. I shall make a push to start for Rome on Thursd., but I expect it will be Friday. *No more* Sicily for me if you please. It is a *horrid* place to be ill in. Love to Harrie. Yr. affte. brother

S— Butler

Address: Hotel Vettoria Rome.

152. *Butler to May*

Text: Chapin Library MS.
Postcard.
Postmark: Napoli Ferrovia 15 5–02; *address:* Miss Butler / Wilderhope House / Shrewsbury / Inghilterra.

Bertolini's Palace Hotel
Naples.
Wed. May 14 [1902]

My dear May

Alfred starts today & we hope that I & he & the nurse will do so on Saturday. She will probably leave me at Basle. The doctor evidently expects that I shall reach London alive—but

I do not think he thinks that I have many months—if weeks to live after I get there—*no more do I.* Love to Harrie. Yr. affte. brother

S. Butler—

153. *Butler to May*

Text: Chapin Library MS.
Postcard.
Postmark: illegible; *address:* Miss Butler / Wilderhope House / Shrewsbury / Inghilterra.

Bertolini's Palace Hotel,
Naples,
Frid.—May 16 1902

My dear May

Alfred is expected hourly but is not yet come. The Doctor is to see him, nurse, & me off and give us a start—tomorrow by the quick train. I cannot say what our route will be till I know by what route Cook's recommended Alfred to take his return ticket. I must send this off before he can come—

The doctor vows I shall get home alive, & I think he takes rather less gloomy view of what will then happen in the immediate future, but we must wait & see Dudgeon [1] to whom Dr. Gairdner [2] is writing today. But I confess I dread the journey. No more please love to Harrie your affte. brother

S— Butler— [3]

Letter 153:

[1] Butler's physician in London. (See note 4 for Letter 89.)

[2] William Tennant Gairdner (1824–1907), an English physician who retired to Italy in 1900 and practiced there.

[3] Butler returned to a nursing home in London; he died on June 18, 1902.

INDEX

www.ingramcontent.com/pod-product-compliance
Lightning Source LLC
Chambersburg PA
CBHW021645110726
47902CB00007B/1839

* 9 7 8 0 5 2 0 3 3 1 1 9 8 *